The Enclosures of Free Verse

The Enclosures of Free Verse

Racializing Poetic Form in the Modernist Era

Erin Joyce Kappeler

The University of North Carolina Press CHAPEL HILL

Set in Merope Basic by Westchester Publishing Services
Manufactured in the United States of America

Library of Congress Cataloging-in-Publication Data
Names: Kappeler, Erin (Erin J.) author
Title: The enclosures of free verse : racializing poetic form in the
    modernist era / Erin Joyce Kappeler.
Description: Chapel Hill : The University of North Carolina Press, 2026. |
    Includes bibliographical references and index.
Identifiers: LCCN 2025045067 | ISBN 9781469693057 cloth | ISBN 9781469693064
    paperback | ISBN 9781469684208 epub | ISBN 9781469693071 pdf
Subjects: LCSH: American poetry—20th century—History and criticism |
    Free verse—History and criticism | Poetry—Political aspects—United States |
    Modernism (Literature)—United States—20th century | White people—
    Race identity—United States | United States—Race relations | BISAC:
    LITERARY CRITICISM / Poetry | SOCIAL SCIENCE / Ethnic Studies /
    American / Native American Studies
Classification: LCC PS309.F7 .K53 2026
LC record available at https://lccn.loc.gov/2025045067

Cover art: Variant of *Abstraction, Porch Shadows*, Connecticut, by Paul Strand. 1916.
Library of Congress Prints and Photographs Division, Washington, DC.

This book will be made open access within three years of publication thanks to Path to Open,
a program developed in partnership between JSTOR, the American Council of Learned
Societies (ACLS), the University of Michigan Press, and the University of North Carolina Press
to bring about equitable access and impact for the entire scholarly community, including
authors, researchers, libraries, and university presses around the world. Learn more at
https://about.jstor.org/path-to-open/.

For product safety concerns under the European Union's General Product Safety
Regulation (EU GPSR), please contact gpsr@mare-nostrum.co.uk or write to
the University of North Carolina Press and Mare Nostrum Group B.V.,
Mauritskade 21D, 1091 GC Amsterdam, The Netherlands.

What poetics has to do is not "forget" its past (or present) errors but, naturally, understand them better to avoid falling into them all over again.

—GÉRARD GENETTE

There is nothing to cut loose from. Remember that this is do not remember but know this when there is no more to tell about what prose and poetry has been.

—GERTRUDE STEIN

I be into memory, more than the avant-garde.

—DAVID HAMMONS

Contents

Acknowledgments

I will not be able to properly thank all the people who contributed to this project in all kinds of ways in this short space, but it is a pleasure to try. I am grateful to many institutions for supporting my work, including the National Endowment for the Humanities and the Massachusetts Historical Society, which jointly provided a crucial year of funding when I was contingently employed, and the American Council of Learned Societies, which funded both my dissertation (2011–2012) and the book it eventually became (2021–2022). Missouri State University offered generous research support from 2016 to 2019, and Tulane University offered research support from 2019 to 2024. Margo Lukens, Ben Friedlander, and the Clement and Linda McGillicuddy Humanities Center at the University of Maine welcomed me into an interdisciplinary conversation about decolonization that helped me to hone my claims in chapter 4. I am grateful to the organizers of and engaged interlocuters at the annual conferences of the Modernist Studies Association, the American Comparative Literature Association, C19: The Society of Nineteenth-Century Americanists, The Space Between Society, and the Modern Language Association, where I worked through many of the ideas in this book. Lucas Church has been a patient and encouraging guide to the publication process, and I am thankful for his editorial guidance and for the work of everyone at UNC Press who has helped to make this book a physical object. The press's anonymous readers pushed me to clarify the stakes of my argument throughout the manuscript, and I appreciate their attention and their generative suggestions.

I have lived many lives during the writing of this book and have been lucky to have kind and supportive colleagues at each institution where I have worked along the way. At the University of Maine at Farmington, Kristen Case, Jonathan Cohen, Christine Darrohn, Daniel Gunn, Michael Johnson, Sabine Klein, Misty Krueger, and Shana Youngdahl helped to make a precarious position tenable. The English Department at Missouri State University continues to create opportunities and open worlds to students in spite of hostility to public education from local and national legislators. Everyone there, but especially W. D. Blackmon, Sara Burge, Lanette Cadle, Marcus Cafagna, Matt Calihman, Cathie English, Lanya Lamouria, Etta Madden,

Linda Moser, Jen Murvin, Jonathan Newman, Lori Rogers, Leslie Seawright, and Shannon Wooden, was and is an incredible collaborator, thinker, and scholar. Angie Anderson and James Chang made daily life in the department easy. The students I taught deserve a better world than the one they inherited. My time at Missouri State was indelibly shaped by the 2016 presidential election; I was and am inspired by everyone who threw their shoulders to the wheel right away and who continued to do the work they had already been doing, especially Hannah, Gene, Kathy, Federica, Rachel, Estevan, Crystal, Alex, Artemis, Andy, Rylea, Joy, Bethany, Jonathan, Angie, Holly, Stacy, and Lyndsey, among many, many others. At Tulane, I was grateful for the collegiality and integrity of Kate Adams, Tom Beller, Patty Burns, Patrick Butler, Ruth Carlitz, Steven Gin, Matthew Griffin, Z'étoile Imma, Brittany Kennedy, Michelle Kohler, David Kumler, Jana Lipman, Rebecca Mark, Jane Mathieu, Analene McCullough, Isa Murdock-Hinrichs, Cheryl Naruse, Scott Oldenburg, Ebony Perro, Karisma Price, Selamawit Terrefe, Molly Travis, Carola Wenk, Ed White, and Justin Wolfe. (I would like to extend no thanks at all to the tenured faculty and administrators who thought the best use of their time in the post-COVID corporate university was to organize against the rights of their non-tenure-track colleagues.) I still cannot believe the good fortune I have had in joining the Academic Innovation and Distance Education team at Bunker Hill Community College. Thank you to John Brittingham, Janelle Heideman, Grace Mah, and the AIDE team for making BHCC a genuinely fun place to work. I would not have had the courage to change professional course without Rebecca Smith's guidance. Thank you, Rebecca, for giving me just the right metaphors at just the right time.

The Historical Poetics working group is a source of constant intellectual provocation and camaraderie. Max Cavitch, Michael Cohen, Ben Friedlander, Mary Ellis Gibson, Charles LaPorte, Naomi Levine, Tricia Lootens, Meredith McGill, Yopie Prins, Jason Rudy, Alexandra Socarides, and Carolyn Williams have taught me so much about poetry, poetics, and institutional life. I owe extra, unending thanks to Virginia Jackson and Meredith Martin, who have been champions of this book since it was just a vague idea. I am also indebted to Melissa Bradshaw, Emily Bloom, Natalia Cecire, Mike Chasar, Amy Clukey, Sarah Ehlers, William Fogarty, Melissa Gerard, Ben Glaser, Martin Harries, Zoë Henry, Louise Hornby, Sharon Kunde, Lizzy LeRud, Jonathan Radocay, Sean Scanlan, Kate Schnur, Jennifer Sorensen, Eve Sorum, Adam Spry, Erin Templeton, Ryan Tracy, and Karen Weingarten, among others, for wide-ranging conversations about poetics, modernism, and disciplinary formations at a variety of conferences and symposia.

I am certain that this book would not exist if Claire Buck had not convened a small writing group years ago at an MSA conference. Claire and Janine Utell have been remarkably sharp, attentive readers, and this book is better for having incorporated their feedback.

In very different ways, Elizabeth Ammons, Lee Edelman, Judith Haber, Joe Litvak, Lecia Rosenthal, Modhumita Roy, and Christina Sharpe shaped the way I think about literary scholarship, as did Jacob Crane, Leif Eckstrom, Nicole Flynn, Caroline Gelmi, Laurel Hankins, Matthew Nelson, Jackie O'Dell, Maik Stanitzke, Seth Studer, and Nino Testa, who helped me figure out where to go when I was lost in the details of Francis Barton Gummere's dissertation. I would not have gone to graduate school if not for Diana Fuss and Craig Dworkin, and I am so glad to be able to thank them in print for believing that my ideas mattered at a time when it was difficult for me to believe that they did.

The Idea Gazebo (Bryn Gravitt, William Zachary Hodges, Marcus Hoige, James Mulder, Jackie O'Dell, Judy Rubio, Spice, Buttertub, and Serenity) helped to ensure that years of precarity were also years of joy and collectivity. The dance parties and the exquisite corpses are part of this book too. I do not have adequate words to describe my love and my gratitude for my parents, Glenda and Doug, and for my brothers, Connery and McKennan. Connery, thank you for bringing Rocío and Julian into our family! Duncan, Charley, Lana, and Norm make every day brighter.

And finally, there is Ray.

Sweet Ray!
So knowing.
So trusting.
So love . . . éd.

The Enclosures of Free Verse

Introduction

The Poetics of White Supremacy

Free verse is poetry by and for white people.

Or at least, that is how white editors and critics in the United States pitched free verse to various reading publics when it started to come into vogue in the 1910s. *The Enclosures of Free Verse* tells the story of how free verse became an exclusionary category wielded by white critics against Black and Indigenous poets and critics in the early decades of the twentieth century. These critics defined free verse in textbooks, handbooks, and magazines as the formal expression of an emerging white American race, believed to have roots in an imagined Anglo-Saxon past. For Black and Indigenous authors in the modernist era, free verse did not consistently function as a break or an opening, as it seemed to for white poets; it was instead a form of enclosure, used to shore up racial hierarchies within and beyond the world of poetry and poetics. We have many stories about how and why free verse developed in the early twentieth century, but this story of the racialization of free verse in the United States has consistently been overlooked and edited out of our literary historical accounts of modernism—especially those accounts that focus on how free verse was promoted in modernist little magazines like *Poetry* and *Others*. This book returns to those little magazines and to their associated anthologies to show that free verse in the modernist era was a racial formation of whiteness and to explore how Black and Indigenous poets navigated this racialization of poetic form.

Why has the explicit racialization of free verse as a white form gone overlooked in prosodic scholarship for so long? Part of the answer is that studies of free verse prosody and of modernist poetry tend not to question which terms we hold stable to narrate the literary histories that structure our scholarly inquiries—especially the terms "traditional" and "experimental" as they are applied to poetic forms. The prevailing consensus in classic studies of free verse is that free verse is antimetrical and was formed in reaction to a coherent, singular tradition of English meter that seemed to be out of step with modernity.[1] This premise leads to a fairly tidy story in which the political and conceptual upheavals of the 1910s helped to foment an explosion of interest in free verse, which was published and intensely debated in modernist little magazines (*Poetry*, *The Little Review*, *The Egoist*, *Others*, *The Dial*) and in more widely read publications like *The New York Times*. Scholars read the politics of free verse in divergent ways (Timothy Steele laments what he sees as the loss of meter as a cultural resource; Walter Sutton celebrates what he sees as the liberation of poetry from metrical constraints),[2] but they tend to agree that, sometime in the 1910s, there was a real break with the prosodic past, and an outdated metrical tradition was left behind in favor of the pursuit of looser, nonmetrical poetic rhythms. To be sure, since the advent of the "new modernist studies" in the 1990s, this narrative has been nuanced, and the most polemical claims of modernist free versifiers are treated with much more skepticism now than they were earlier in the century. In the revised twenty-first-century version of the tale, we tend to acknowledge that free verse opened new formal possibilities for poets but that many poets still wrote in other forms and that a sonnet could be as radical and revolutionary as a poem in an "experimental" form. Even in this revised version, however, it is taken for granted that we understand what "traditional" meters and forms are. This book aims to convince you that we do not and that modernist studies is impoverished by the ongoing assumption that we do.

Scholars of nineteenth-century poetry have been telling scholars of modernism for decades that "traditional" meter is a canard that distracts us from a much more complex and contentious history of debate about poetic form, but modernist studies has been slow to incorporate this understanding of the complexity of nineteenth-century prosodic theories. As Max Cavitch concisely put it in 2008, "poetry's liberation from the shackles of meter is one of the most important non-events in late nineteenth-century literary history."[3] It is a nonevent because meter is and always has been a discourse, not a set of constraints or restrictions. That is, "meter" is the name for a wide range of conflicting ideas about how languages, literature, and social identities are related. Scholars including Jason David Hall, Matthew Hart, Meredith Martin, and Yopie Prins have investigated how definitions of "meter," "rhythm," "prosody," and "versification" shifted throughout the nineteenth century and how these fields were imagined as forces that could construct and support idealized forms of racialized national identities.[4] As Prins's and Martin's work in particular has shown, although accentual-syllabic systems of scansion, based on the foot as the most basic metrical unit, have come to seem like the natural way to approach the formal study of English-language poetry, such systems only achieved hegemony in the twentieth century. That is, we may think today that there is a more or less scientific way to parse meter (a line of poetry can be broken down into its feet or into some kind of intervallic units, which are made up of differently accented syllables, which are determined by linguistic rules that are hardwired into the human brain and perhaps even into the human body via the rhythms of breath and heartbeat), but this is because scholars, critics, and poets in the twentieth century, motivated by a variety of ideological commitments, consolidated and flattened out what had been a set of wildly diverse approaches to English-language poetic meter into a unified(ish) system of foot-based prosody. By ignoring the fact that nineteenth-century prosody was always a field of cultural struggle, the great-divide narrative of modernist poetry, in which a stable metrical tradition and formal experimentation are opposed, "forget[s] to acknowledge or question the national and class [and, I would add, racial] ideologies" that have authorized this simplified version of literary history.[5] It has been said before in fields adjacent to modernist studies, but it needs to be said, often and loudly within modernist studies, that the vaunted break with "traditional" forms and the ensuing opening of form was in fact a narrowing of the prosodic field, motivated in large part by attempts to consolidate whitewashed English and American national identities.

Prior to this narrowing, there was no agreement about what constituted a "traditional" English-language meter or even about what meter measured; instead, there were heated debates about the roots of the English language and the racial and national identities of people who wrote and read English-language poetry. Because the English language developed from Germanic and Latinate sources, it is neither purely accentual nor purely syllabic. English-language poets can play with these and other systems, creating any number of idiosyncratic rhythms and forms. This means that English prosody has always been remarkably "free." As the Harvard professor John Livingston Lowes argued in his 1919 book *Convention and Revolt in Poetry*, versification in English could be said to be "absolutely incapable of formulation" because, while "there is one way, and only one, of correctly reading a Latin hexameter," there could be "three or four ways of reading an English blank verse line." According to Lowes, it was possible that "no two mortals ever read aloud any given long passage of [English-language] verse with precisely the same rhythms."[6] For critics like Lowes, who had been trained in the vicissitudes of English-language rhythms, the predominant issue raised by early debates about free verse forms was not a simple matter of formal constraint versus liberty but the much thornier question of what it would mean to loosen the rules of poetic form in a linguistic system that could already accommodate everything from Phillis Wheatley's couplets to Henry Wadsworth Longfellow's translation of the Icelandic *kalevala* form into the American epic

The Song of Hiawatha to Alfred, Lord Tennyson's translations of Latin alcaics to Walt Whitman's biblical cadences to Paul Laurence Dunbar's experiments with dialect poetry to Algernon Charles Swinburne's experiments with every linguistic tradition under the sun. To paraphrase Gertrude Stein's meditation on the difference between poetry and prose, there was nothing for free verse poets to cut loose from but rather a welter of prosodic debate to join.

What types of poetic theories and systems did critics develop to understand the place of free verse in this already complicated prosodic field? Why have we forgotten the multiplicity of these prosodic discourses, and how will recovering their histories inform current theories of poetics? As surprising as it might seem, this is a history about which we know very little. We have many accounts of the prosodic systems and poetic theories developed by individual poets who wrote in forms that we now recognize as free verse; scholars including Chris Beyers, Stephen Cushman, and Charles Hartman have been scrupulously attentive to the metrical systems and rhythmic ideals articulated by Walt Whitman, Ezra Pound, H.D., and T. S. Eliot, among others, and have provided suggestive answers to the question of what individual poets thought they were doing when they played with free verse forms.[7] But of course, poets were not the only cultural workers involved in theorizing, promoting, critiquing, and disseminating free verse poetry. *The Enclosures of Free Verse* shows that academic and critical debates about the connections between racialized identities and poetic forms actively shaped the reception of free verse poetry in the United States at the turn into the twentieth century and that these critical debates continue to insidiously influence how we talk about the relative values of various poetic forms, even though (or perhaps because) they are absent from most contemporary literary historical accounts of free verse.

Restoring these critical conversations to view is not a simple historicizing project; it is a matter of interrogating our own disciplinary reading practices and field formations. Part of the argument of *The Enclosures of Free Verse* is that it is not enough to historicize poems or to add new poets to our accounts of modernism or early twentieth-century literature, because it is possible to historicize a poem or to add poems to our syllabi without ever asking why we call those texts poems in the first place. It is harder to historicize a poetic term or form or genre without questioning how ideological investments have shaped and continue to shape what we read as poetry and how we read it— particularly what we read as *good* or valuable poetry. This is one of the fundamental insights of scholarship in historical poetics, which begins with the simple premise that terms like "poetry," "rhythm," "meter," and "prosody" change over time and that reading period theories of poetics can help us to see the various kinds of cultural and political work that poetry has done. Because prosodic debates turned on questions about the origins of languages and nations, they were (and are) always also debates about race, nationality, gender, class, and history. Or, put slightly differently, because poetic meter is an abstract set of ideas and not an empirically verifiable thing, the choice to champion one approach to meter over another always entails ideological commitments. If an investment in a prosodic system is an investment in a particular imagined community, as historical poetics scholars have argued,[8] then historicizing those prosodic systems is also a way to illuminate the racial ideologies that continue to undergird certain versions of literary history.

I am interested in bringing a historical poetics approach to bear on modernist claims about free verse forms because the overvaluation of modernist aesthetics has so thoroughly shaped the institutionally based study of twentieth- and twenty-first-century poetry and poetics. This is perhaps most evident in the overprivileging of "experimental" poetry in academic studies of modern poetry, which comes at the expense of attention to works that seem to be "merely" political or formally conventional or conservative. As Sarah Ehlers notes in her study of Depression-era poetry, there has long been a scholarly tendency to divide twentieth- and twenty-first-century poetry into that which fits into "mainstream versions of modernism" (formally innovative and self-evidently worth studying) and that which can be "revalue[d] . . . using evaluative schematics suitable to various political ideologies" (politically engaged but conventional/formally simplistic poetry that is not self-evidently valuable to literary critics).[9] Most often when scholars study modern poetry, they tend to "tur[n] their interpretive gazes to works that blend revolutionary politics with modernist aesthetic principles that conform more easily to evaluative standards," meaning that "it remains unclear how to theorize radical poetics outside of ideas about modernism, poetic expression, and formal mastery."[10] I take this to be a central theoretical question for studies of modern poetry and poetics because systems of aesthetic value encode and naturalize epistemological assumptions that can work to affirm the dominant order of things. The overvaluation of modernist aesthetics does not simply mean that we are failing to appreciate other systems of aesthetic value, in other words. Rather, we are failing to acknowledge how different aesthetics can open up new ideas of worlding outside of our current system of racialized capitalist modernity and how colonial modernity has depended on epistemicide to uphold racialized hierarchies of value.

Part of what is at issue in my account of the overvaluation of modernist aesthetics and the racialization of free verse is the particular field formation of modernist studies as it has developed in the contemporary university system, especially within the US academy. Modernist studies, of course, does not represent the whole of scholarship that has to do with modernism and modernity (although the flagship journal of modernist studies, *Modernism/modernity*, certainly makes a claim on both categories), but it does still powerfully shape how scholars decide what kinds of aesthetics are worth attending to. I am interested in how the reorientation of the field around a liberal multiculturalist model of difference in the 1990s (the "new modernist studies") effectively retrenched a narrow model of aesthetics and its attendant epistemologies even as it seemed to open the field so that the global field of literary cultures (at least those deemed sufficiently modernist) could be better represented. As Andrew Goldstone has shown in a quantitative study, in spite of the best efforts of the "new" modernist studies to expand the field beyond a narrow canon of high-modernist authors, modernist studies continues to be oriented around that narrow canon, in part because it is "a field in which it is hard to represent any object of study as interesting unless it can be represented as modernist," even as we have come to agree that "modernist" does not have one singular definition.[11] This is not to say that the scholarship that has worked to "replace a monolithic concept of 'modernism' or 'modern poetry' with a range of 'new modernisms' or plural 'poetries'" has not importantly brought attention to understudied artists and movements.[12] It is to say that the model of liberal inclusivity on which the new modernist studies was based—what Jodi Melamed identifies as a key part of "official antiracist discourses" that "have produced permissible narratives of difference that disseminate into and condition knowledge systems"[13]—failed to change fundamental assumptions about what constitutes aesthetic value (innovation, experiment) and about the positive valuation of the category of modernism within the field of modernist studies.

My project in this book is thus in part to "marginalize the modernist measure of value" for poetry that still dominates the field without relying on alternative categories that understand other measures of aesthetic value to be reaction formations to modernism (antimodernist, rearguard, low- or middlebrow, genteel, etc.).[14] Like Goldstone and others who have critiqued the limitations of modernism as an organizing category, I am pushing for something other than the expansive (colonial) model of modernist studies that continues to claim more and more new objects as worthy of study precisely because they are modernist ("difficult," "experimental," "innovative"). What would it look like for modernist studies to actively pursue "gaps in our thinking that might yield opportunities for *different* aesthetics that will no longer uphold racial hierarchies"?[15]

In the case of literary histories of modernist and contemporary poetry, I argue that, if we begin from an understanding of prosodic systems as multiple and contested well before the rise of modernist poetry, rather than pitting metrical "tradition" against rhythmical revolution, it will be possible to construct alternative genealogies and histories that might tell different stories about the metrical past and the metrical present than those to which we have become accustomed and to truly change the structure of literary histories of modernism. It is an ethical imperative to change those structures, for they depend to a great degree on the racist colonial idea that genres and forms develop progressively, just like the civilizations that produce them. Otherwise historically minded scholarship on modernist poetry still reflexively reproduces this unexamined colonial logic by hewing to an evolutionary narrative of prosodic development in which "traditional" meter is figured as a ghost or a vestige or a kind of literary atavism. To put this as bluntly as possible, to continue to narrate the advent of free verse as an evolution of poetic form or as a categorical shift away from "traditional" meter, without acknowledging the white supremacist colonial thinking that helped to create the idea of prosodic evolution, is to perpetuate white supremacy, in however subtle a form.

When I say that I want to truly change the structure of literary histories of modernism, I mean that I want to make it impossible to talk about the history of free verse in the United States as only or as primarily a story about formal innovation and to restore to view the longer history of the metaphor of freedom and bondage that gives free verse its name. This means returning to what has been repressed in studies of modernist poetics—namely, the complexity of nineteenth-century American poetry and poetics—in order to rethink our understanding of poetic influence and innovation in the early twentieth century. Since Houston Baker argued that "what exists on the antecedent side of black modernity is not a line of stodgy, querulous, and resistant premoderns but a universe of enslavement," scholars working on early twentieth-century poetry and poetics have often followed Baker in focusing on texts and aesthetic projects that were aimed at "mov[ing] clearly *up*, masterfully and re-soundingly away" from that "universe of enslavement."[16] Studies of modernist free verse, which tend to focus primarily on white poets, tell the story of the democratization of poetic form as part of the story of post-Reconstruction progressive reforms more broadly (movements for suffrage, labor, civil rights, decolonization), while studies of Black poets tend to focus on Harlem Renaissance and diaspora projects that were emphatically about "mov[ing] clearly *up* . . . [and] away from slavery," to return to Baker's phrasing. For very different reasons, studies of the poetry of the modernist era and of the Harlem Renaissance have thus taken it as a given that the nineteenth century was something that needed to be decisively left behind, aesthetically and politically. I am interested in how the partitioning work of the word "antecedent" in Baker's formulation keeps us from understanding the ongoing resonance of nineteenth-century (and earlier) structures in the modernist moment and in our own. What would studies of early twentieth-century poetry look like without that partition? What might we be able to see if we started with the idea that what exists on the "antecedent" side of white modernity is also a universe of enslavement, rationalized and ordered in part through what Ronjaunee Chatterjee, Alicia Mireles Christoff, and Amy R. Wong, following Kandice Chuh, name the "sorting mechanisms" of aesthetic judgments that function as "tools for racial demarcation"?[17]

Returning to nineteenth-century American prosodies and poetics to understand the development of free verse is a move that runs counter to most scholarship on the racialization of modernist poetry and poetics.[18] There has of course been much generative work on whitewashed critical genealogies of the poetic avant-garde; as Natalia Cecire notes in her account of experimental writing as "a white recovery project, . . . the quiet violences built into the discourse of the 'experimental' are well established at this point, thanks largely to the work of writers and critics of color, including Nathaniel Mackey, Fred Moten, Sonya Posmentier, Anthony Reed, Evie Shockley, Dorothy Wang, and Timothy Yu."[19] Much of the work that has challenged the whiteness of experimental writing and of the poetic avant-garde, however, has taken for granted the positive valuation of the category of experimental or formally innovative writing and has focused on poetic movements that took place in the latter half of the twentieth century (Language poetry and Black Arts poetry, for instance).[20] This means that early twentieth-century poets who worked against the racializing abstractions of form and rhythm that were crucial parts of critical discourse about free verse — especially poets who did so through "conventional" forms — continue to go unread. In focusing on poetic possibilities that were foreclosed by narratives of free verse as a liberating innovation in poetic technique, I hope to bring attention to the fact that these early twentieth-century alternative poetics — a rich archive of imaginative world building and "freedom dreaming," to use Robin D. G. Kelley's terminology[21] — continue to be overlooked by revisionist accounts that focus on poetic movements that took shape later in the twentieth century.

Indeed, it can be so difficult as to seem impossible to upend the idea that the advent of free verse as a unique formal innovation is the singular story of twentieth-century poetry and poetics in the Anglophone literary world. I want to underscore that, at the most fundamental level, my project in this book is to offer counterprogramming to the persistent framing of free verse as a real break with a unified metrical past. Even when scholars understand that this narrative is oversimplified, it remains a powerful framework for understanding historical changes in attitudes toward poetry during periods of intense political and social upheaval. My aim is to show that, from the outset, free verse in the United States was racialized as a white form and that this history of the racialization of "experimental" poetic form should lead to a revaluation of the ideal of modernist aesthetics that still organizes scholarship on modern and contemporary poetry and poetics.

The Racialization of Form and the Plasticization of Race

As I hope is clear from the preceding section, one of the orienting premises of this book is that prosody (and meter and rhythm and any other term that is variously and unevenly applied to the scansion of poetry) is not an empirical material thing in the world that can be neatly taxonomized but is rather a varied set of ideals, with multiple and conflicting ideological valences, constructed by different reading communities that may or may not be in conversation with each other. Put as simply as possible, prosody (and meter and rhythm . . .) means different things to different writers and readers at different points in history. Whereas previous studies of free verse attempt to classify kinds of free verse and to distinguish free verse innovations from older metrical forms, I attempt to read what specific communities of readers thought they heard and saw when they approached free verse poetry written at the turn into the twentieth century.

In this book's development of a new history of free verse, it pursues two major narrative strands. It looks to the US academy as a key source of racialized reading practices (which began to take root well before the New Critics attempted to deracinate and codify them as a scientific methodology) but also adds to recent work situated within critical university studies that is interested in attending to "other institutional and extra-institutional spaces for reading and teaching poetry."[22] As Andy Hines, among many other scholars, has reminded us, it is crucial both to understand "the disciplinary work of literary studies [within the university] in political and economic terms" and to "decenter the university as an exclusive site of knowledge production" in the pursuit of materially antiracist scholarly work.[23]

The Enclosures of Free Verse begins in the early twentieth-century US academy because this is where the theory that free verse was a return to Anglo-Saxon metrical principles and was thus a formal expression of white racial identity began to take shape. Philologically trained literary scholars were highly invested in the biological concept of plasticity (the ability to generate new species forms) for what they believed it could tell them about the origins of new literary forms like free verse. Particularly to scholars of Anglo-Saxon literature, who helmed the first English departments in the US and oversaw the development of professional organizations like the Modern Language Association, it seemed evident that the capacity for formal literary innovation was a racial instinct that linked an imagined group of people called Anglo-Saxons to contemporaneous white Americans. Throughout the 1910s and 1920s, literature professors in the United States helped to naturalize the idea that free verse was a form generated by whiteness, providing seemingly empirical support for the long-standing association of formal experimentalism with whiteness and formal imitativeness with Blackness and Indigeneity.

Beginning an account of modernist free verse from the early twentieth-century scholarly understanding of plasticity as a racial ability to produce new literary forms significantly changes what we are able to see about the politics of experimental form in this moment. Standard accounts of free verse tend to emphasize genealogies of the form, tracking the influence of late nineteenth-century French *vers libre* and the proto-modernist work of poets like Charles Baudelaire, Walt Whitman, and Stephen Crane on a cast of modernist poets that usually includes T. E. Hulme, F. S. Flint, Richard Aldington, Ezra Pound, T. S. Eliot, H.D., Amy Lowell, Carl Sandburg, William Carlos Williams, Marianne Moore, and Wallace Stevens and that is sometimes expanded to include Langston Hughes, Fenton Johnson, Sterling Brown, and James Weldon Johnson. These studies take it for granted that Whitman has always been an obvious starting point for studies of American free verse. But if we return to the records of the US academy in the early twentieth century, a much different story emerges. Prior to the 1910s, there was no scholarly consensus that Whitman had created a new form of poetry or that his work was worth attending to, and his poetry was often left out of national literary anthologies. It was not until scholars of American literature began in earnest the work of proving that their objects of study formed a coherent national tradition that scholars began to attempt to explain Whitman's meter in an empirical way.

These empirical investigations into Whitman's meter consistently portrayed Whitman as a key link in an Anglo-Teutonic metrical tradition, creating an imagined continuity of Anglo-Saxon culture that ran through contemporary American literature. To early twentieth-century critics, Whitman mattered not so much because he "broke the new wood," in Ezra Pound's phrase, but because his work seemed to prove their hypothesized connection between Anglo-Saxon racial identity and formal literary innovation.[24]

The most important thing to know about Anglo-Saxons is that they did not exist. I underscore this point here to highlight that the Anglo-Saxon poetic inheritance scholars created for Whitman and other free versifiers was, emphatically and completely, a fantasy. Linguistic, archaeological, and historical evidence shows that the habit of calling the people who inhabited the land we now call England before the Norman Conquest "Anglo-Saxons" is a vast and consequential oversimplification. "Anglo-Saxon" was an exonym that helped to create the illusion of linguistic, cultural, and political unity where there was in fact a heterogeneous mix of languages, cultural practices, and political institutions, growing out of constant trade, migration, and conquest. Using the term "Anglo-Saxon" to describe both pre–Norman Conquest England and the language spoken there, as has historically been the practice of literary scholars, makes it seem as though "Anglo-Saxon" was a meaningful ethnocultural unit and perhaps even an endonym, but this was simply not the case, as I discuss in more detail in chapter 1.[25] I want to be clear that throughout this book, when I refer to "Anglo-Saxons," the term should be understood to be under erasure.

Whitman's belated construction as the Anglo-Saxon father of American free verse arose from the hotly debated issue of how best to apply breakthroughs of evolutionary biology to the study of English literature. Articles in *PMLA* and *Modern Philology* in the 1910s explicitly connected the idea of racial plasticity (the ability to generate new species forms) to the idea of literary plasticity (the ability to generate new literary forms such as free verse). Plasticity seemed to scholars of Anglo-Saxon literature, conceived of as the beginning of a grand tradition of Anglophone literature, to have particular explanatory force. Plasticity, as Kyla Schuller and Jules Gill-Peterson note, "connotes a paradoxical state: the capacity to be formed by outside pressure, yet to maintain internal coherence all the while."[26] According to standard nineteenth-century accounts of Anglo-Saxons, Anglo-Saxons had marvelous powers of assimilation. They could, in other words, be molded by external forces (environment, contact with other cultures and races) but would maintain a core Anglo-Saxon identity in spite of these external influences. The idea that racial plasticity was key to generating new literary forms fit well with Anglo-Saxonist accounts of English literature, which sought to prove that there was a unique racial core of English language and literature that had somehow remained unchanged by the Norman Conquest and by longer histories of trade and migration. It did not take long for scholars to connect formal poetic innovations (blank verse, free verse) with this imagined Anglo-Saxon racial substrate and to extrapolate that Anglo-Saxon poetic rhythms could help contemporaneous white readers to strengthen their sense of racial identity. This Anglo-Saxonist white supremacist thinking about plasticity became the motor that drove the institutionalization of free verse — and, more broadly, of poetics as a key branch of literary theory—in English departments in the United States in the early twentieth century.

The ideas that Whitman was an Anglo-Saxon poet and that free verse was a return to Anglo-Saxon poetic principles emerged from the Old English scholar Francis Barton Gummere's highly influential communal origins theory. The communal origins theory of the evolution of poetry dominated literary study from the 1890s through the 1930s, with reverberations well into the present day. According to Gummere's theory, poetry began with the dancing and chanting of primitive "throngs," whose communal rhythms organized individuals into a group and provided the basis for the development of national and racial identities. Gummere was an ardent Anglo-Saxonist, meaning that he believed that Anglo-Saxon "throngs" provided the strongest foundation for English and American poetic traditions, due to the fantasy that Anglo-Saxons were inherently more democratic, freedom loving, and community minded than other "primitive" groups were. The communal origins theory was explicitly anti-Black and anti-Indigenous, since it posited that nonwhite throngs created rhythms that induced social disharmony and disintegration, as opposed to the rhythms of the socially cohesive Anglo-Saxon throng. In Gummere's telling, poetic meter was a disciplinary technology that could aid racial evolution; Anglo-Saxon rhythms would lead to a healthy national community, while nonwhite rhythms would lead to chaos. This fantasy of white poetic and democratic origins was used by Gummere's colleagues and students to construct a canon of American free verse poetry with Walt Whitman at the head. Indeed, F. O. Matthiessen went so far as to argue, in his field-shaping work *The American Renaissance* (1941), that Whitman had actually undergone a "crude re-living of the primitive evolution of poetry" from its "origin . . . in the dance, in the rise and fall 'of consenting feet' (in Gummere's phrase)" to the modern day.[27] Because Whitman's poetry was more in touch with the Anglo-Saxon foundations of English as well as with the rhythms of modern life, Matthiessen argued, it was uniquely suited to bind past and future into a new vision of the imagined community in verse. To early twentieth-century scholars, it seemed clear that free verse prosody could aid in the ongoing evolution of the Anglo-Saxon race as a uniquely democratic, freedom-loving group.

This imagined connection between Anglo-Saxon racial plasticity and the growth of free verse could perhaps have been a forgettable moment in the development of literary studies but for the fact that it quickly migrated out of scholarly journals and into more widely read publications, including the modernist little magazines and poetry anthologies most often associated with free verse. In these public-facing texts, the idea that formal innovation was a key Anglo-Saxon racial instinct became evidence that free verse was a fundamentally Anglo-Saxon form and that formal innovation and experimentation more broadly tended to be outcomes of the racial instincts of white people. I show that this understanding of racial plasticity as the generator of new literary forms guided the editorial principles of *Poetry: A Magazine of Verse* in ways that remain largely overlooked in extant scholarship.

Poetry has long been acknowledged as a key publication in the development of free verse forms and of modernist poetry more broadly. Founding editor Harriet Monroe's contentious collaboration with her foreign correspondent Ezra Pound is legendary, as is the magazine's early embrace of Imagism and of poetry deemed too "experimental" for many other established literary magazines. Along with *The Little Review* and *Others*, *Poetry* was instrumental in supporting the careers of modernist poets from Carl Sandburg to Richard Aldington to Countee Cullen to Marianne Moore. The wide range of poetic forms that *Poetry* published is often used as evidence that *Poetry* was a fundamentally cosmopolitan and inclusive magazine, and contemporary scholarly accounts often praise the magazine for publishing "nearly every key figure in Anglo-American verse of the period" and for achieving gender parity.[28] But these scholarly accounts have overlooked a crucial fact about the magazine's gender parity and its supposed radical openness to all kind of poets and poems: *Poetry* published zero Black women during Monroe's editorial tenure (1912–36). Contemporary scholarship repeats this erasure of Black women by focusing on the high percentage of women published in the magazine without considering the ways that gender categories are racialized. What can modernist scholars learn about *Poetry*'s understanding of poetic form as a racialized category if we begin an analysis of the magazine from the constitutive absence of Black women poets from its pages?

Focusing on this constitutive absence brings into view the anti-Black reproductive logic that drove *Poetry*'s editorial choices in its first decades of existence. It was not an accident or an oversight that *Poetry* published and reviewed work by Black men but not Black women but was rather an indication of a racialized understanding of modern poetry and of the work of cultural reproduction as an offshoot of biological reproduction. Monroe and her coeditors (especially Alice Corbin Henderson) offered their readers a white feminist interpretation of the academic arguments that free verse was an Anglo-Saxon form and that the ability to generate new literary forms—cultural plasticity—was rooted in the supposed biological plasticity of white bodies. While scholars like Gummere emphasized the masculine virtues of Anglo-Saxon culture as they were encoded in Anglo-Saxon poetry and its supposed descendants, Monroe and her collaborators emphasized the role of contemporary white women and children in carrying on and reproducing that Anglo-Saxon poetic tradition. Monroe and her coeditors consistently located the potential for the production of the most exciting new poetic forms like free verse within white women and children, especially when those white women and children were located on or had ties to plantations in the US South. *Poetry* was, in short, invested in free verse and in other modes of poetic experimentation precisely because they seemed to index the renewal and ongoing reproduction of whiteness as a mode of anti-Blackness in the early twentieth century.

The story I am telling about the racialization of free verse as a white form in the US academy and in key modernist publications needs to be told precisely because it has been overlooked for so long. In focusing on the foundational white supremacy of accounts of free verse poetry in the United States in the first half of *The Enclosures of Free Verse*, however, I risk recentering whiteness in discussions of modernist poetics. As I hope is clear throughout, I focus on the theorization of a white poetics to better see and to root out the traces of such thinking in contemporary approaches to poetics. I share Dorothy Wang's interest in the question of "why there exists a double standard in discussing the works of poets of color and those who are supposedly racially 'unmarked.'"[29] Wang identifies a critical tendency to read poetry by poets of color as "about" identity and to read poetry by white poets as "about" universalizable abstractions.[30] But as I show, from the beginning, "experimental" or "innovative" poetry in the modernist era was explicitly about white identity and was marked as such by critics and academics. Restoring this history of the racialization of free verse to view is one way among many to counter reductive accounts of the relationship between "experimental" or "innovative" poetic form and racialization.

Working the Trap: Black and Indigenous Engagements with Free Verse

The second narrative strand of this book turns from the narrow enclosures of white modernist poetics to poetic abundance—more specifically, to the varied generic and prosodic poetic projects undertaken by Black and Indigenous authors located outside the academy in the early decades of the twentieth century. Chapters 3 and 4 explore how two authors—Fenton Johnson and E. Pauline Johnson, respectively—held open space for alternative, expansive poetics that refused the enclosure of free verse and its accompanying abstractions. In very different ways, each of these authors has been figured as minor within modernist studies because they have been deemed insufficiently aesthetically "advanced" in spite of their centrality to key modernist publications (the little magazines *Poetry* and *Others* in Fenton Johnson's case; the influential anthology *The Path on the Rainbow* in E. Pauline Johnson's). I argue that what has been read as lack in their work—of complexity, of innovation—is in fact plenitude: a generic and formal dexterity that scholars of modernism no longer know how to read because we understand it to involve an unsophisticated replication of convention. For poets such as Fenton Johnson and E. Pauline Johnson, engaging with a broad array of "conventional" poetic genres and meters was a calculated strategy to evade and counter white reading practices that sought to enclose, exclude, and dispossess through processes of abstraction.

My choice to analyze the poetry of Fenton Johnson and E. Pauline Johnson as significant counterweights to the racialized discourse of free verse may seem idiosyncratic. As I tracked the racialization of free verse in the academy and in modernist little magazines and anthologies, however, Fenton Johnson's poetry stood out because he directly theorized free verse as a limitation for Black poets. Although scholars including James Smethurst and Lorenzo Thomas have been attentive to Johnson's importance for the development of modernist avant-garde poetry, these accounts rely on readings of his thirteen free verse poems, ignoring the two hundred "conventional" poems he published. Because this work takes it for granted that the "conventional" poetry is not worth reading, it misses the metacritique of free verse that Johnson developed over the course of his career. E. Pauline Johnson, meanwhile, came to the fore as I traced the connections some white critics drew between modernist free verse forms and ethnographic transcriptions of songs, prayers, and chants collected from members of Native American nations. E. Pauline Johnson was of course never recognized as a formally innovative modernist poet, and so I was struck by the fact that she was included in a notable modernist anthology, *The Path on the Rainbow*, which argued that white free versifiers were inheriting Native American poetic forms and perfecting them. While modernist scholars have been attentive to *The Path on the Rainbow*, none have engaged with the ways Johnson's "conventional" poems disrupt the settler colonial logic of the anthology. Whereas Fenton Johnson has been added to accounts of modernism as part of a liberal multicultural logic of inclusion, E. Pauline Johnson has been excluded as the negative, genteel core that modernism had to reject. It is my hope that centering the work of these two poets will make it easier to revalue the use of poetic conventions as something more than a choice to communicate clearly or transparently with a mass readership.

My exploration of Fenton Johnson's oeuvre takes a cue from Elizabeth McHenry, who argues that scholarly accounts of late nineteenth- and early twentieth-century African American literature have been limited by the organizing force of the Harlem Renaissance. As McHenry notes, "the literary projects of the early twentieth century are rarely allowed to claim their own independent space" and are instead addressed through a "'postbellum, pre-Harlem' time frame" that privileges texts that prefigure later modernist writing.[31] Building on queer studies work on failure as a productive rejection of hetero social norms, McHenry argues that "texts, genres, institutions, and forms of authorship that we have dismissed as unsuccessful, unproductive, unconventional, anomalous, or irrelevant" are in fact "an important archive of the queer literary practices through which African Americans rejected a system of racial categorization that deemed them socially intolerable, intellectually inferior, and politically unqualified."[32] Within modernist studies, "traditional" poetic genres and forms continue to be seen as "unsuccessful, unproductive, . . . [and] irrelevant," to use McHenry's terms, and thus go unread.[33] It is a foregone conclusion that any poet still writing in "traditional" genres in the 1910s and 1920s, without significantly transforming those traditions, was obliviously or willfully outmoded, clinging to a past they could not or would not recognize as past. Scholars of modernism tend not to stop to ask why a poet may have continued to engage with Tennyson or Frances Ellen Watkins Harper or hymnal meter or rhyme in these decades. But these unasked questions unlock an archive of imaginative, productive poetic refusals of the dominant order of things.

Fenton Johnson refused the dominant order of things by countering the modernist abstraction of genre into form. In his magazine *The Champion* and in his three published books of poetry, Johnson attempted to bring into view the unfinished business of the nineteenth-century poetic genres Black poets had used to organize specific reading publics and to envision Black liberation, highlighting what the white modernist privileging of form over genre risked forgetting or rendering illegible. Through close readings of Johnson's editorials and his generic poetry, I show how Johnson used the poems of Frances Ellen Watkins Harper, Albery Allson Whitman, and Black interpellations of the poetry of George Gordon, Lord Byron to give shape to the political anger that accompanied his hopes for racial uplift in the early twentieth century. Johnson powerfully redirected the prophetic visions of this abolitionist poetry to imagine what Black liberation in the twentieth century might look like. For Johnson, that liberation depended on generic mobility for Black authors and readers—the ability to lay claim to all kinds of particular generic poetic traditions and their accompanying modes of address to particular publics—from Black Romantic odes to Scots dialect poetry to midwestern American forms of free verse. To Johnson, this generic dexterity was integral to imagining potential future forms of Black community and Black liberation. This expansive generic work stands in marked contrast to Johnson's free verse poetry, which is characterized by constriction and constraint—formal, cultural, and geographical. If, for Robert Frost, writing free verse was like playing tennis with the net down, for Fenton Johnson, writing free verse was stepping into a net of "trapping fictions of blackness," to borrow a phrase from Jodi Melamed.[34] My analysis of Johnson's oeuvre thus begins to show how we might read free verse poetry differently—for the cultural possibilities its ascendance foreclosed as well as for those it seemed to open.

Perhaps nowhere is the foreclosure of poetic possibility more evident than in the realm of poetry written by Indigenous authors in the modernist era. This poetry, by and large, does not conform to the aesthetic and political standards that determine what we think of as significant poetry worth studying as modernist scholars; it is often metrically, generically, and formally "conventional," very often does not articulate a decolonial politics, and does not always register a sense of the value of modernity or modernism. The few notable attempts to credit early twentieth-century Indigenous poets with doing vital cultural work have still naturalized a division between complex, experimental poetry and simplified conventional poetry, thus continuing to privilege white modernist aesthetics and reifying a form/content split. For instance, Michael Taylor argues in his analysis of the poetry published in the *American Indian Magazine* that Zitkala-Ša and other early twentieth-century Native poets "compose[d] in rhyming couplets . . . because they privileged their politics over their poetics" and chose to "employ straightforward iambic tetrameter and rhyme" in order to privilege "clarity over artistic obscurity."[35] But what happens to our understanding of early twentieth-century poetry by Indigenous authors if we start from the premise that there is nothing particularly straightforward or clear about the choice to use iambic tetrameter or rhyme? As Michael Cohen argues, there are long, complex, multifaceted social and cultural histories behind each and every poetic convention, which Cohen terms "the social lives of poems." I am interested in how attending to the social lives of poems can help us to see that, if we have been trained as modernist scholars, we probably do not know how to read poetic convention. As Alex Socarides notes, "conventions are actually quite hard to find, and then, once found, are hard to read," precisely because they are supposedly transparent and obvious and because their social and political resonances change over time.[36] But learning to read "how conventions work necessarily inverts the significance that has long been placed on the poetic qualities of originality and experimentation" and "allows us to see anew that which we thought we knew and could discard."[37]

I turn to the influential 1918 anthology *The Path on the Rainbow* in order to reconsider "that which we thought we knew and could discard" within modernist studies—namely, formal and generic poetic conventions employed and Indigenized by Native American and First Nations authors. *The Path on the Rainbow* is certainly not the most famous modernist poetic anthology of the 1910s, though its popularity with various reading publics was enough to warrant new editions in the 1970s and 1990s, and it prefigured later anthologies of what became known as "ethnopoetics." The anthology also makes notable appearances in scholarship on the canonization of modernism. For instance, Jeremy Braddock explores how *The Path on the Rainbow* joins other "interventionist" anthologies of the late 1910s in figuring modernism "less as a canon of works than as a set of aesthetic and cultural practices."[38] Braddock notes that in the case of *The Path on the Rainbow*, these aesthetic and cultural practices are appropriative, as the anthology positions Native American oral art as the rightful inheritance of white free verse poets. The texts collected in *The Path on the Rainbow* as poems were almost uniformly written, translated, or transcribed by white settlers (most are nineteenth-century ethnographic texts), and the two that were not—E. Pauline Johnson's "The Lost Lagoon" and "The Song My Paddle Sings"—were singled out for being "neither original nor aboriginal."[39] Because Johnson wrote in recognizable poetic meters and genres, reviewers such as Louis Untermeyer and T. S. Eliot classified her work as inauthentically Indigenous. It seemed to modernist tastes to be too Victorian; her "time-dusty" "jingles" were "simply not 'primitive' enough to be considered 'modern,'" to borrow Michael Taylor's evocative phrasing.[40]

What interests me about contemporary scholarship that discusses *The Path on the Rainbow* is the fact that none of this scholarship reads Johnson's poetry, even as it registers the racism inherent in denigrations of her work. It is treated as a foregone conclusion by scholars of modernism that there is nothing of note in Johnson's outdated verse, in spite of generative work on Johnson's poetics by scholars of nineteenth-century and Victorian studies. By continuing to misrecognize Johnson's mastery of poetic conventions as a simplistic reproduction of outmoded poetic forms or as a sign of her successful colonization, modernist studies assessments of *The Path on the Rainbow* have continued to engage in dispossessive reading practices that strip Johnson's work of its nuance and complexity and that privilege settler narratives of progressive literary history. To be sure, modernist studies as a field has paid a great deal of attention to the way modernist primitivism produced modes of dispossessive reading. But less recognized is the way that approaches to poetic form continue to operate as such. Chapter 4 brings to the fore the argument that runs throughout this book: that learning how to read poetic form differently, in a way that does not dismiss convention out of hand or automatically valorize formal "experiment," is crucial to grappling with the settler colonial aesthetic logics that continue to structure the field of modernist studies.

In order to show how Johnson's "conventional" poems work against the primitivist settler colonial framing of *The Path on the Rainbow*, I first attend to Mary Austin's introduction, which teaches readers of the anthology to engage in what I am calling "dispossessive reading." I use this term to signal the ways that modernist reading practices work hand in hand with other forms of colonial dispossession to render Indigenous texts and textualized songs and rituals the property of white authors and readers. In Austin's case, dispossessive reading meant reading ethnographic translations of various kinds of oral expressions from many different nations and many different time periods as early forms of free verse—abstracting each expression from its historical and cultural context to make it fit into the Western literary category "poetry." Too, Austin abstracted meter into the more nebulous "rhythm," arguing that the rhythms of Native poetries were incapable of translation and hence were open to "interpretation" by white poets who could feel but not transcribe those racial rhythms. These abstractions allowed Austin and her collaborators to claim Native American poetry as the rightful inheritance of modern, non-Native, white North American poets, who were positioned as the salvage ethnographers who could preserve the poetic traditions of a vanishing race by translating them into contemporary free verse forms.

The question of E. Pauline Johnson's place within this settler colonial anthology offers an exemplary case of how modernist studies of poetry (especially poetry written by Indigenous authors) can benefit from a historical poetics approach to metrical forms. Though Johnson had no direct agency in the production of this collection, as this was a posthumous reprinting of her work, Johnson's deep engagement with poetic convention still unsettles the anthology's modernist abstraction of meter into rhythm, which in turn works against the anthology's settler colonial project of dispossession and appropriation. Both "The Lost Lagoon" and "The Song My Paddle Sings" use "conventional" nineteenth-century metrical forms to link queer eroticism with Indigenous mobility and Indigenous land claims. These poems' queer eroticism pushes back against the codification of heteronormative marriage as a tool of Indigenous dispossession in the late nineteenth and early twentieth centuries, and, within the pages of *The Path on the Rainbow*, their use of rhyme and tetrameter work against the idea that "authentic" Native poetry could only be textualized as free verse. The republication of these poems after her death continued Johnson's lifelong project of asserting that First Nations peoples were active shapers of modern life, operating well outside the boundaries settler nations attempted to impose on them—including the boundaries imposed by formal expectations that "authentic" Indigenous poetry should look like free verse.

Reading Otherwise

As I have outlined in this introduction, although scholars located in various fields have recognized in various ways that the agonistic construction of poetic "tradition" and poetic "experiment" that has shaped so much criticism about modernist poetry is just that—a construction that emerges from a white, Eurocentric view of literary history—we have only just begun to unpack how that construction ramifies in contemporary scholarship, particularly when that scholarship is located within modernist studies as it is practiced in the United States. As far as I know, this book is the first extended study of the explicit racialization of free verse as a white form in the United States, and this fact signals that the large-scale challenges to whitewashed Eurocentric accounts of modernism and modernity that have come out of postcolonial studies, African American literary studies, Native American and Indigenous studies, and Black studies have not yet fully upended older received narratives about the politics of modernist poetic forms. It is still possible to research the history of free verse and debates about modernist poetic formal innovation within teaching texts, handbooks, and encyclopedias of modernism without ever coming across any evidence that free verse was racialized as a white form. My goal with this book is to change that situation.

In this way, my project in this book accords with Brigitte Fielder's recent theorization of the metaphor of "recovery" in literary studies. Fielder argues that the metaphor of recovery is most generative when we understand that it "is not the archive itself but our various disciplinary engagements with it" that are in recovery when we engage with lost or ignored or neglected texts. For Fielder, this means that "recovery" work is about "accurately represent[ing] . . . historical relations of power and upend[ing] them through more rigorous attention to our body of texts."[41] I make the case that attending to the racialization of free verse in the early twentieth century can help us to see how our own aesthetic preferences remain shaped by those "historical relations of power," and I offer examples of what a "more rigorous attention" to both neglected and canonical texts might look like.

At its core, this is a book about how scholars read twentieth-century poetry now and how we might read otherwise in years to come. By showing that free verse in the United States was explicitly a white identity project from the outset, this book challenges us to read otherwise, in ways that do justice to the complexity of early twentieth-century poetry and poetics. Rather than understanding the story of modernist poetry as the story of the liberation of form from arbitrary constraints, I argue for an understanding of modernist poetry and poetics as a set of complex engagements with competing ideological investments in racialized ideas of rhythm, meter, and poetry. My aim is to highlight the kinds of poems and poetic theories that modernist studies, ethnic studies, and contemporary poetry scholars have not been equipped to read and to show how we might begin to read them without making them fit into our received narratives of revolution and rupture. And so, in the spirit of reading otherwise, I ask you to come with me to the twentieth-century US academy, where some of "our" contemporary critical reading practices begin to emerge.

CHAPTER ONE

Literary Theory's Fantasies of Whiteness

My account of the racialization of free verse as a white form begins with the Old English scholar Francis Barton Gummere. I begin with Gummere not because he was exceptional (he was typical of his era), nor because I think his work is inherently worth remembering (would that we could all forget it entirely!), but rather because I share Claudia Stokes's sense that "we can better handle the tools of our profession if we know more precisely the conditions of their origination," particularly when it comes to critical assumptions and premises that we may "unconsciously cling to." If, as Stokes argues, "our vision of the American literary past . . . is inevitably filtered through the lens of the literary nineteenth century that produced it," then how are the logics of nineteenth-century white supremacist thinking still structuring our studies of poetry and poetics in the US academy?[1] Gummere's example is particularly instructive, as can be seen in his shadowy presence in current accounts of poetic history. Take, for instance, the entry on "oral poetry" in the 2012 edition of the *Princeton Encyclopedia of Poetry and Poetics* (*PEPP*), which declares that "all poetry begins with oral poetry, the origins of which are found in the rhythms, sound patterns, and repetitive structures that reinforce and empower the words and actions of ritual."[2] The *PEPP* presents the claim that all poetry begins as ritual oral poetry as a fact without examining where the claim comes from, but the idea has a clear genealogy. The roots of this claim stretch back through Herder's idealization of folk poetry to the philological search for a proto-Indo-European language, but it was codified as a founding tenet of twentieth-century poetics by Gummere, who spent his career tracing the supposedly ritual, oral origins of poetry through its modern printed iterations. Consider the similarities between the 2012 *PEPP* definition of oral poetry just cited and Gummere's: "Who will deny that quite as early as any priest recited his prayer or buzzed his magic in solemn prose, there was a throng of folk dancing and singing with a rhythm as exact as may be?"[3] In Gummere's telling, as in the *PEPP*'s, "the actual habit of individual composition and performance has sprung from the choral composition and performance" of the throng's vocalized rituals.[4] At issue here is the categorization of varied cultural practices as *poetry*. Why do we still assume that it is accurate to classify oral rituals as poetry, or poetry in embryo?

As Aamir Mufti argues, this normative, developmental version of genre theory was part and parcel of "the revolution in knowledge practices and humanistic culture more broadly initiated by Orientalist philology," which functioned as part of "an articulated and effective imperial *system of cultural mapping*, which produced for the first time a conception of the world as an assemblage of civilization entities, each in possession of its own textual and/or expressive traditions."[5] The Orientalist remapping of the world, Mufti argues, aimed "to render legible *as literature* a vast and heterogeneous range of practices of writing from across the world and across millennia, so as to be able . . . to make them available for comparison, classification, and evaluation."[6] In other words, a diverse range of local, culturally specific activities was flattened into the Western bourgeois category *literature* and placed within a developmental, evolutionary framework that helped to justify colonial power relations between "primitive" societies and modern "civilizations."[7]

The organization of English-department curricula into historical sequences that began with Anglo-Saxon literature was a consequence and a continuation of this philological remapping of the world. Because both poetry and Anglo-Saxon culture were understood by philologists to be origin points in developmental narratives of civilization and of Anglo-American culture, respectively, philologists like Gummere were particularly keen to find the Germanic, pre–Norman Conquest roots of English meter as proof of the continuity of Anglo-Teutonic racial identity. Eighteenth-century works such as Thomas Percy's *Reliques of Ancient English Poetry* and his translation of Paul Henri Mallet's work as *Northern Antiquities* had helped to make the case that the Anglo-Saxon origins of England could be found in part by looking to the historical poetic record—particularly to folk poetry. Percy helped to advance the Herderian idea that popular ballads provided evidence of the "peculiar love of liberty which characterized the Gothic peoples" who, in his estimation, had founded England.[8] As Meredith Martin notes, Percy's work was "part of a general interest in pre-Chaucerian meters as unifying, folk-meters of the people."[9] Many of the founding assumptions of modern poetics emerged from this search for the Germanic, pre-Conquest roots of English meter, which seemed to scholars to be "more purely 'English' in some ways than the Latin forms imposed on English verse."[10] Gummere was quite explicit that metrical education in Anglo-Saxon prosody would lead directly to a strengthened sense of white racial identity and would better equip white readers to be good citizens of a white nation. His colleagues and students agreed and added to Gummere's theory the idea that free verse—especially Whitman's free verse—was a link in the chain of Anglo-Saxon literary and political greatness that Gummere described over the course of his long career. The fact that this story of the racialization of free verse as an Anglo-Saxon form is not common knowledge in contemporary scholarship signals a pressing need to better understand how such white supremacist thinking fundamentally shaped modern poetics from the outset.

My account of Gummere's communal origins theory and its role in the canonization of Walt Whitman as the father of American free verse in the US academy adds to recent generative work on the racialized reading practices of early twentieth-century literary critics, particularly those of the New Critics associated with the Fugitive and Southern Agrarian groups. Before the Southern Agrarians took their stand, before Cleanth Brooks and Robert Penn Warren taught generations of readers how to understand poetry, they learned from Gummere how to read poetic form as the sign of racial identity. The importance of this critical genealogy is often downplayed in institutional histories of English and of the US university system, which tend to move quickly past the formative decades of the late nineteenth century when philologists helped to remake literary study on the model of the empirical sciences. Accounts like Gerald Graff's and Michael Warner's emphasize that philologists in newly formed departments of national languages and literatures in the late nineteenth century helped to give literary study the prestige of a science by presenting literary study as a matter of "advancing and debating hypotheses within a scientific community," so that, as Elizabeth Renker argues, "the philologist emerged as the scientist of English who would carve out a space of professional authority in the new university culture."[11] However, few institutional histories spend time with the specific hypotheses and debates that constituted the first versions of modern literary theory. Consequently, such accounts are able to argue that the romantic racialism that characterized nineteenth-century philology was quickly overcome in departments of English.[12] A closer look at philological theories of literary and national development in the early twentieth-century academy, however, brings into view a much different story. As I will show, dwelling with the specific hypotheses of philologically trained scholars of literature opens up a longer view of philologically based literary study as a mode of anti-Black and colonial worlding and raises questions about the lingering effects of such worlding on contemporary literary study, particularly in the realm of poetics.[13] This book does not offer a comprehensive institutional history, but I argue that the small slice of the history of modern literary study I present is central to understanding how, as David Lloyd argues of aesthetics, "race operates as a discretely structuring assumption" of Anglo-American poetics and especially of Anglo-American prosody.[14]

This chapter has three interlinked aims, corresponding to the three following sections: (1) to demonstrate the hegemony of Gummere's communal origins theory in the first English departments in the United States and to contextualize Gummere's theory within larger disciplinary debates about the capacity of different races to produce new literary forms; (2) to show how Gummere turned Anglo-Saxonism into a set of anti-Black, anti-Indigenous metrical principles, abstracting imagined social relations into verse traits and helping to popularize the idea that premodern European communal ideals could be realized in modern metrical discourse; and (3) to show how the communal origins theory became the basis for the institutionalization of free verse in the US academy, starting with the canonization of Walt Whitman in the 1910s. Together, these sections begin to make the case that early twentieth-century academic discussions of free verse baked a white supremacist theory of poetic development into our contemporary approaches to poetics.

The Inescapability of the Communal Origins Theory

Francis Barton Gummere was integral to the development of modern literary theory—and especially modern poetic theory—in the US academy. His career spanned decades, and his theories influenced the teaching of poetry at all levels, from elementary schools to PhD programs to Chautauqua circuits to university extension courses. A few details from Gummere's career help to give a sense of his stature in his time. In 1895, the brand-new English Department at the University of Chicago offered Gummere its very first professorship in literary theory and interpretation because of his groundbreaking work on the communal origins theory. When Gummere turned down the position to continue teaching at Haverford, Chicago hired Richard Moulton because his work on the "ballad dance" stemmed from Gummere's theory of communal origins. Harvard also unsuccessfully attempted to hire Gummere away from Haverford in 1901.[15] Gummere was elected president of the Modern Language Association (MLA) in 1905, and he published widely in and served on the boards of the most prestigious journals of the era, including *PMLA*, *Modern Philology*, *The English Journal*, *Modern Language Notes*, and *The American Journal of Philology*. Discussions of Gummere's communal origins theory dominated the pages of these earliest professional journals, and a significant number of the early presidents of the MLA weighed in on the subject (importantly, thirty-nine out of the first fifty-nine presidents of the MLA were scholars of Anglo-Saxon literature and/or were trained in Germanic philology).

Gummere's influence on American literary cultures and reading practices (especially scholastic ones) cannot be underestimated. Steve Newman notes that Gummere's textbook *A Handbook of Poetics for Students of English Verse* "was widely adopted, reaching a third edition in five years."[16] Along with his contemporary George Lyman Kittredge, Gummere also helped to keep the communal origins hypothesis alive in classrooms from elementary schools to universities for decades through service on the National Education Association's Committee of Ten, which shaped the study of English in elementary and secondary schools.[17] Gummere's centrality to early twentieth-century literary theory can perhaps be most easily seen in one of the first textbooks meant to introduce students to literary studies as a discipline. In *An Introduction to the Methods and Materials of Literary Criticism: The Bases in Aesthetics and Poetics* (1899), Charles Mills Gayley and Fred Newton Scott (themselves foundational figures in English and rhetoric and composition, respectively; I discuss Scott in more detail in the third section of this chapter) explained to students that while there were many possible methods of literary study, every scholar of literature "should naturally first acquaint himself with the history of literature, with the development of its kinds." Once the student had acquired "a fair knowledge of the scope and the evolution of a literary species, he may proceed to an inquiry into the laws that regulate its evolution," and outward from there to comparisons of different "literary species" of various national literatures, and, finally, of "literary art with other forms of art."[18] They explained that students who were seriously interested in "the comparative study of literary origins and development" would have to read widely in sociology, law, anthropology, and ethnology, paying particular attention to Herbert Spencer's *Data of Ethics and Principles of Sociology*; E. Leveleye's *Primitive Property*; Sir Henry Maine's *Village Communities, Early History of Institutions*, and *Ancient Law*; T. H. Huxley's explanation of "biology" in the *Encyclopedia Britannica*; and Edward Tylor's *Primitive Culture* and *Anthropology*. A synthesis of these fields may have seemed daunting, but according to Gayley and Scott, Gummere had come close to achieving such a synthesis.[19] Indeed, they argued that Gummere's interdisciplinary thinking was so exemplary that they "would unhesitatingly commend to the attention of students whatever he may publish upon the subject . . . [of] the origins of poetry."[20] Gummere was, in other words, *the* source to turn to for students and scholars interested in theorizing poetry and poetics in the early twentieth century.

Gayley and Scott's reliance on a vocabulary of evolution (e.g., their use of "species" rather than "form") to describe literary study was not arbitrary. As Nancy Glazener notes, for literary scholars in this moment, "evolutionary metaphors that cast genres as species evolving from each other, developing alongside each other, or competing with each other" were so common as to be ubiquitous.[21] By the late 1890s, philological and ethnological inquiry had already seemed to have proved empirically that languages and societies, respectively, evolved over time and that literature, as a linguistic and social product, would naturally reflect that evolution. Indeed, Richard Moulton, Gummere's counterpart at the University of Chicago, argued that the incorporation of evolutionary theory into literary study was the defining factor of modern criticism; he claimed that "the failure to recognize literature as a thing of evolution was the fundamental error of the literary theory that dates from the Renaissance," because such theory posited static, ideal literary forms rather than recognizing the "natural evolution" of literary genres.[22] While scholars working on the problem of the evolution of literary forms were generally careful to note that evolution was an analogy, since literature is a social product and not a biological organism, they were also enchanted by the idea that they could discover the laws of literary evolution in the same way that biologists seemed to be discovering the laws of genetic inheritance. This means that during this period, scholars of literature were reading widely in biology, as Gayley and Scott's suggested reading list shows, and borrowing terms from the emerging science of genetics to understand the evolution of literary forms and of national literary traditions. As one might suspect, this means that notions of racial heredity quickly became part of these scholarly conversations about the development of literary forms, in which Gummere played a foundational role.

Institutional histories of English and comparative literature often dismiss the impact of romanticized thinking about race on these disciplinary formations, but such thinking was integral to the development of literary theory in this moment.[23] As Kyla Schuller reminds us in *The Biopolitics of Feeling*, early twentieth-century discussions of evolution were still likely to consider the impact of environment and geography—and hence of race—on heredity. Schuller notes that "the term *gene* was coined in 1908," but it was not until the 1930s that we saw "the consolidation of modern hereditary theory," which overshadowed previous Lamarckian ideas about how experiences and environment could shape heredity and species change.[24] Leading scholars of literature like Gummere, Gayley, and Scott were quick to make connections between racialized identities and the ability to generate new literary forms.

This means that literary scholars in this moment were thinking very explicitly about plasticity, as Kyla Schuller and Jules Gill-Peterson define it: "the capacity of a given body or system to generate new form."[25] Schuller has tracked how sentiment was used as a disciplinary force to counter the perceived volatility of plastic, impressible bodies and the populations made up of those bodies, but sentiment was not the only disciplinary technology employed to theorize population management and racial evolution; so too was metrical discourse, particularly when it focused on secondary education.[26]

A search of the *Princeton Prosody Archive* shows not only that literary scholars in this moment were invested in the explanatory force of the biological concept of plasticity but that they put forth a theory of English poetry that depended on the perceived superior plasticity of Teutonic or Aryan races. Put slightly differently, literary scholars in this moment understood the ability to generate a new literary form to be connected to the racial plasticity of a national population. Monographs, textbooks, and elocution manuals alike noted that the English language and its verse forms—especially blank verse, frequently conceived as a precursor to twentieth-century free verse—were fundamentally more plastic than other languages and that this plasticity was tied to a racialized national identity. Writing in 1903, the Stanford professor Raymond Macdonald Alden, for instance, quoted approvingly J. A. Symonds's argument that "English blank verse is perhaps more various and plastic than any other national metre" and that this plasticity indicated the English "national literary spirit—uncontrolled by precedent or rule."[27] The perceived plasticity of English was almost always tied to an imagined Germanic racial heritage, showing that, although literary scholars in this moment often used the term "plastic" simply to mean flexible, they were also thinking about plasticity as an index of racial identity. For instance, Sir Israel Gollancz, professor at King's College, London, wrote in 1921 that blank verse, "which was originally a purely academic important from Italy, . . . became the *plastic* instrument able to bear the *impress* of varied human emotions, only when it had become, as it were, thoroughly Teutonised."[28] Such a "rediscover[y] [of] that freedom which characterized the Old English metre" was, according to Gollancz, "the English spirit resisting slavery to an academic convention, and naturalizing an alien metre."[29]

Gollancz's use of the terms "plastic" and "impress" highlight the imbrication of accounts of the development of literary forms and of biological models that understood race to be an outcome of "unevenly distributed plasticity."[30] The influence of the idea of impressibility as Schuller describes it—bodily responses to the environment creating identifiable populations that collectively make up an evolving race — can also be seen in John Preston Hoskins's account of national literary development. Writing in *PMLA* in 1910, Hoskins, a professor of German language and literature at Princeton University, explains that "different [national] standards of literary form" were the "outcome of the varying biological heredity and of the diverse experience which these nations undergo in the course of their development."[31] Indeed, Hoskins went so far as to argue that an author's "social heredity," or the "great body of traditions, conventions, forms, ideas, etc." available to them, was simply "environment stored in symbolic form."[32]

As these examples show, it was a common assumption among literary scholars in the early twentieth century that the ability to generate new literary forms was directly tied to the plasticity of the racial groups that created them. In this view, some racialized bodies had a greater innate capacity to generate new forms, biological and literary, than others — an idea that shaped how philologically trained scholars approached their search for the origins of poetry and its development into discrete national traditions. Indeed, in Hoskins's account of how biology provided models for literary critics, he argued that it was precisely historical investigations into the conditions that produced poetry — investigations generally undertaken by Anglo-Saxonist philologists such as Gummere — that would provide insight into the twinned evolution of literary forms and of racialized national identities. Hoskins explained that "social heredity" properly belonged to "the sphere of historical investigation" and that matter such as "ideas, ethical convictions, religious beliefs, types of character, actions, incidents" could "be historically fixed and defined," so that literary scholars could see how new forms emerged from a combination of socially inherited tradition ("ideas, ethical convictions, religious beliefs") and of new elements "drawn directly from contemporary life."[33] According to Hoskins, such historical investigation would allow scholars "to gain a true knowledge of the process of literary variation" as a kind of social and racial evolution by tracking changes in the elements of literary forms over time.[34]

John Matthews Manly, chair of the English department at the University of Chicago from 1898 to 1933, shared this view, arguing that it was possible to look to the beginnings of specific genres to trace their evolution into new literary forms: "Perhaps the only way in which we can avoid deception is to begin with the mediaeval drama when it was unmistakably drama, and carefully go back to the time when it came into existence . . . Tracing backward the history and form of these groups, we find that they are real groups."[35] This was precisely the approach Brander Matthews took in his series *The Wampum*

Library of American Literature; Matthews promised that each volume in the series would trace "the development of a single literary species" over the course of its evolution.[36] This search for what Manly called "germs or embryos" of literary forms thus seemed to literary scholars to offer insight into literary, historical, and racial development as interconnected phenomena.[37]

Gummere devoted his life to this search for poetic, and thus racial, origins. Like the majority of his peers who helped to create modern English departments as we know them today, Gummere began his career as a philologist, earning his PhD at the University of Freiburg in 1881. He wrote a dissertation on the development of metaphor in Anglo-Saxon poetry, which helped to cement the idea that the historical study of poetic meter was especially well suited to uncovering the origins of English literature. After Eduard Sievers argued that he had "revealed the regular metrical principles of Germanic verse" in the 1880s, scholars of poetry attempted to "illuminate the relative chronology of Old English poetry by an intelligent application of the powerful sound laws and rules of meter" that Sievers and others had "discovered."[38] As Ashley Crandell Amos notes, nineteenth-century scholars "attempted to identify specific linguistic changes that might serve, like chemical reagents, to put a text in chronological perspective."[39] Allen Frantzen shows that the seemingly scientific methods of these philologically trained metricists "were produced by . . . [the] originary myths prized by nationalist cultural historians," but by being "presented as regulated systems, and set in an institutional situation, . . . [such] methods would eventually be presented with all the prestige and certitude attached to science."[40]

This scientific prestige and certitude were bolstered by philologists' engagement with contemporaneous anthropological and ethnological theories. In Gummere's case, studying Anglo-Saxon versification seemed to prove that the "core" of the English language was Germanic, and studying anthropological accounts of so-called primitive societies seemed to prove that poetry was originally the product of a primitive "throng" that sang and danced together. Gummere believed that the rhythm of these communal dances provided the basis for social consent and group cohesion, and he extrapolated that nationally and racially specific rhythms could concretize what he called, a hundred years before Benedict Anderson, "imagined communities." In his view, Anglo-Saxons had a particular talent for creating what he called "democracy in verse," which helped them to "realize the imagined community."[41] In contrast, he argued that racial groups he viewed as less plastic and hence less capable of progressive evolution, including, in his terms, "mere hordes" of "American Indians" and "African savage[s]," tended to produce rhythms that led to less advanced communities and societies.[42] This led Gummere to understand pedagogical approaches to poetry to be directly tied to a form of population management. In his view, teaching white children to internalize the supposedly democratic rhythms of Anglo-Saxon poetry would counter the potentially degrading effects of other races on Anglo-Saxon US citizens and their culture. Gummere thus helped to popularize the idea that meter and rhythm were tools that could be used to "orchestrat[e] a people's sensory experience [in order to] direct their development" along racial lines.[43] Meter was, in other words, understood by Gummere and his peers to be a potential aid to racial evolution—a kind of eugenic technology that could be used in any educational setting.

Gummere believed that his theory was a necessary corrective to the work of John Stuart Mill, whose definition of poetry as "feeling confessing itself to itself in moments of solitude" threatened to obscure the communal, social origins of the art form. Gummere feared that the popularity of Mill's definition, which, as Virginia Jackson argues, had become the dominant paradigm for understanding lyric poetry by the late nineteenth century, would distort the record of literary evolution by overemphasizing the modern forms and functions of poetry.[44] He explained that in the modern era, "a solitary habit of thinking has made itself master of poetry, particularly the lyric," so that contemporary critics had lost sight of poetry's origin in shared, communal forms.[45] Such a loss seemed to Gummere to be catastrophic; if racialized cultural identity was an effect of shared poetic rhythms, as he believed it to be, then uncoupling rhythm from poetry, as Mill's definition did, would lead to poetry's cultural irrelevance and, potentially, to the disintegration of the state as an imagined community of white citizens. For scholars such as Gayley and Scott, the evolutionary study of poetry represented an important advance in modern literary criticism, but for Gummere, it represented a crucial intervention in modern social life. He dreamed that what he saw as the best of Anglo-Saxon social organization could be realized in modern metrical discourse, if students could only be properly trained to feel the core Anglo-Saxon rhythms of the English language.

Gummere began developing his case against Mill as an undergraduate at Harvard University under the tutelage of Francis James Child, the foremost ballad theorist and anthologist in the nineteenth century. Child believed that the poems that were closest to their origins in oral performance, such as Old English ballads, could be seen as survivals of a time before "book-culture." Child traced the "survivals" of this oral culture in popular printed ballads; though he believed that these poems had been corrupted in the act of being collected and printed, his philological training led him to believe that they could still teach scholars the otherwise unknowable history of a preliterate people. As Michael Cohen explains, "in Child's ballad discourse, popular ballads and preliterate folk were origin points in developmental narratives about cultures and nations."[46] Gummere believed that the validity of his mentor's work had been proved by contemporaneous ethnological studies, including those of Daniel Brinton, whose career as a professor of American linguistics and archaeology at the University of Pennsylvania overlapped with Gummere's tenure at Haverford.[47] Brinton, much like his more famous contemporaries James Frazer, Leo Frobenius, and Edward Tylor, believed that ethnological inquiry could provide insight into the origins of human culture. In books like *Aboriginal American Authors and Their Productions* (1883) and *The Basis of Social Relations: A Study in Ethnic Psychology* (1902), Brinton endorsed popular theories of orthogenesis and recapitulation, arguing that man as a species evolved through discrete stages of civilization and that the traces of early stages of evolution were preserved in more highly evolved organisms and institutions. The ethnological study of "savage" or "primitive" social groups thus provided unique insight into the origins of human culture, because "in such [primitive] conditions . . . we are nearer the origins of arts and institutions."[48]

Gummere looked to Brinton's studies of what was categorized as Native American poetry to prove that the oral poetry of primitive tribal groups was especially useful for bearing witness to social structures and customs that had passed away in seemingly more evolved stages of civilization. Gummere argued that Brinton's studies showed that "primitive conditions" of literary production necessarily led to communally produced poetry, performed by the social group as a unit, and that this communal performance led to a certain type of social cohesion no longer found in modern societies. According to Gummere, Brinton's work on the "incessant refrain" of Native American poetry, which was danced and chanted by entire tribal groups, proved that the repeated refrain served a clear social function—to produce "consenting cries and movements" that synced individuals into a unit, thereby concretizing the group's identity. Primitive poetry, according to Gummere, could thus be defined as a "consenting and cadenced series of words," in marked contrast to Millian definitions of poetry as the expression of an isolated individual.[49] Gummere argued that in light of this ethnological proof, it was a scandal that "nearly all writers on poetry have neglected . . . the communal basis of the art."[50] Whatever poetry had become, its evolution began with communal rhythms. And in the case of English-language poetry, he believed, those communal rhythms had been based in what he saw as racially superior Anglo-Saxon rhythms and cultural values.

Brinton and other ethnologists emphasized the importance of the "group-mind" in primitive societies and artworks, but Gummere took the hypothesis of the group-mind a step further to argue that the rhythms of communal poetry were not merely reflective of but responsible for the formation of a group's tribal identity. Brinton's study of the "ethnic psyche," or the mind-set of primitive man, for instance, seemed to prove that primitive life was "made up of a number of experiences common to the mass but not occurring in any one of its individual members" and that the phenomenon of this "group-mind" could be explained as "the actual agreement and interaction of individuals resulting in mental modes, tendencies, and powers not belonging to any one member."[51] Gummere argued that the "agreement of individuals" could only be brought about through "tribal incantation and choral singing," which he called "the original social fact," explaining that P. M. A. Ehrenreich's ethnological research on what Ehrenreich called the Botocudo people ("Botocudo" is a Portuguese exonym applied to different Indigenous peoples of the area that became the Mato Grosso state of Brazil) had proved this to be so.[52] Ehrenreich claimed that the oral poetry of this group was produced

> on festal occasions [when] the whole horde meets by night round the camp fire for a dance. Men and women alternating . . . form a circle; each dancer lays his arms about the necks of his two neighbours, and the entire ring begins to turn to the right or to the left, while all the dancers stamp strongly and in rhythm the foot that is advanced, and drag after it the other foot. . . . Throughout the dance resounds a monotonous song to the time of which they stamp their feet. . . . Now and then, too, an individual begins a song, and is answered by the rest in chorus. . . . They never sing without dancing, never dance without singing, and have but one word to express both song and dance.[53]

Gummere interpreted Ehrenreich's account to mean that "the primitive horde in festal dance and song [found] by increased ease of movement and economy of force, by keener sense of kind, by delight of repetition, the possibilities of that social consent which is born of rhythmic motion."[54] Ethnological accounts like Ehrenreich's seemed to prove that a group's identity as a coherent social body did not precede their festal dances; rather, it was produced as a result of their rhythmic motions, which helped to create a physical instantiation of collective tribal identity. Gummere explained that the group in Ehrenreich's account demonstrated "the rude fashion of imagining a community by converting the concept of it and the yearning for it into external acts, which, in turn, fortify and extend the concept itself," meaning that "rhythmic utterance and rhythm itself" were "not so much the outcome as the occasion of social union."[55] Gummere concluded that organized social relations never existed a priori with any so-called preliterate people but were instead the result of the "loud and repeated crying of a throng, regulated and brought into consent by movements of the body, and getting significance from the significance of the festal occasion."[56] In his account, rhythm was not a linguistic effect but rather an embodied racial characteristic that helped to confirm the identities of discrete tribal groups. Members of "preliterate" societies did not simply recognize their membership in a group because they sang that group's songs; rather, the rhythms of communal, oral poetry created the group as it sang. Put another way, racialized cultural (or, in more "evolved" groups, national) identity was an effect of poetic rhythm.

Gummere argued that, taken together, ethnological and philological studies revealed "the spectacle of a long evolution," from "the uncertain, tentative beginnings of social life, [where] we see human beings acting, alike in the tasks and in the pleasures of their time, with a minimum of thought and a maximum of rhythm," to "a highly developed society, where the monotonous whir of machinery has thrust out the old cadence and rhythm of man's labour, where strenuous and solitary wanderings replace the communal dance, and where every brow is marked with the burden of incessant thought."[57] Theorizing in a Herderian vein, Gummere posited that the evolution of poetic form revealed the price that modern cultures had to pay for adopting the twinned phenomena of printed literature and industrial capitalism. The poetic art of preliterate cultures may have been simple and repetitive, but it "bea[t] with the pulse of a whole race" and became "racial or national, . . . 'popular' in its best sense." As soon as Christian scribes had begun to "cop[y] . . . exercises from a dead page" without a "sense of race," rhythm as the defining factor of poetry had begun to be lost to sight. This loss was intensified with the rise of the capitalist marketplace, which encouraged individual authors to produce ever more technically accomplished, bloodless poetry in an attempt to gain fame and fortune with a novelty-seeking public. What had been "poetry for the ear" gradually became "poetry for the eye," and in its translation to the page, poetry lost the "racy," embodied vitality that had been its birthright.[58] According to Gummere, modern printed poetry helped to fracture the once coherent social body, and the loss of rhythm in contemporaneous definitions of poetry was one symptom of that fracture. Restoring to view the Anglo-Saxon rhythms he believed to be the core of English poetry would, Gummere believed, help to create the community he imagined of Anglo-Saxon Americans, particularly if young white children could be educated to feel those rhythms together in classroom settings.

"A Race of Scholars": Anglo-Saxonism as Metrical Principle

Gummere's invocation of "Botocudan" dancers and his nostalgia for an imagined precapitalist past may make it seem as though he was a cultural relativist, interested in the communal poetry of any and all societies equally. But Gummere's use of the terms "race" and "racy" in his description of premodern communal poetry was not accidental. Like many of his philologically trained peers, Gummere was an Anglo-Saxonist (a term I use, following Reginald Horsman, Hugh MacDougall, and Allen Frantzen, among others, to mean "the use of Anglo-Saxon culture and texts for ideologically motivated and political ends")[59] who believed in a highly romanticized, mythologized vision of a Germanic race, conceived as a superior world-conquering race, and he argued frequently that Anglo-Saxon communal ideals were the only possible foundation for a "healthy" democracy in the United States in the twentieth century. Indeed, Gummere turned Anglo-Saxonism into a set of metrical principals, abstracting imagined social relations into verse traits and solidifying core strains of anti-Blackness and anti-Indigeneity in American poetics that would prove to be central to theorists of free verse. In Gummere's history of poetry, what mattered was white bodies moving together rhythmically. Bodies that were coded as nonwhite merited only footnotes in his larger body of work, but his theories became the lens through which white and nonwhite poets alike would be understood in the modernist era, as I show in chapter 2. In this section, I explain Gummere's theory of English poetry as a racial formation of whiteness—a theory that was necessarily and foundationally anti-Black and anti-Indigenous and that imagined poetic rhythm as a kind of eugenic technology.

When I say that Gummere abstracted social relations into verse traits as part of his theory of poetry as a racial formation of whiteness, I mean that he explicitly argued that material conditions of Anglo-Saxon life were embedded in modern metrical forms, in the same way that past geological conditions could be registered in a fossil.[60] In *The Beginnings of Poetry* (1901), Gummere argued that there was ample evidence "that beating and stamping, earliest forms of work, plus the human voice which followed the rise and fall of labour, are the basis of metrical 'feet'; . . . iamb and trochee are stamping measures, spondee a measure of striking or beating, still easy to note where two hands strike in rhythm; that dactyl and anapest can be heard at the forge of any blacksmith." Even if one disagreed that the transfer of bodily rhythms into metrical rhythms had been so literal, Gummere argued, no one could deny "the vital fact of rhythm as the pulse of earliest human labour and play, of earliest poetry, of earliest music."[61] In Gummere's view, this primitive rhythm was "an exact rhythm, the rhythm born of consent"; it was the force that helped to create imagined communities, and as such, scholars needed to understand rhythm "as one of the greatest factors in social development," even under the supposedly more complex, less rhythmically exact modern era.[62] Gummere's explanation of rhythm as a force of "social development" indicates his interest in using metrical education as a type of population management—an interest seen most clearly in his pedagogical writings.

In Gummere's metrical imaginary, because historical social relations could be indexed by verse traits (the rhythms of labor were encoded in iamb, trochee, spondee, and so on), contemporary social relations could also be changed through programs of metrical education. He believed that contemporary Anglo-Americans could access their racial roots through the concerted, programmatic study of Anglo-Saxon meter and rhythm and hence become better democratic subjects, since Anglo-Saxon culture was believed to have been fundamentally and ideally democratic. (This played into the popular idea that the descendants of these Anglo-Saxons in England and the United States had directly inherited the institutions, characteristics, and "civilizing mission" of their ancestors.)[63] Gummere advanced the perceived connection between Anglo-Saxon poetry and modern democracies in a series of articles about the necessity of teaching philology in elementary schools as well as in his textbook *A Handbook of Poetics for Students of English Verse*, a widely adopted text that was first published in 1885 and that was reprinted multiple times throughout the early twentieth century.[64] In these texts, Gummere tied metrical traits directly to supposedly racial traits and political formations, and he argued that metrical education would help to train what he called "a race of scholars" who could strengthen the Anglo-Saxon foundations of the United States' version of democracy.[65] This argument culminated in his 1910 book *Democracy and Poetry*, which made a full-throated case for the necessity of metrical education as a means of ensuring that Anglo-Saxon cultural traits and political institutions persisted in the United States. Modern white citizens could not return to prior stages of human development, but they could, Gummere believed, realize premodern forms of Anglo-Saxon sociality in modern metrical discourse.[66] In Gummere's telling, meter provided a tool for ensuring the ongoing vitality and purity of Anglo-Saxon racial identity in the twentieth-century United States. In this way, Gummere helped to promote the idea that metrical education could be a form of population management that would encourage the growth of supposedly racially healthy traits and social systems.

While Gummere's insistence that elementary-school students should learn philology may seem outlandish, he was very much in step with much of the pedagogical thinking of his time. As Angela Sorby notes, the rise of mandatory public schooling in the postbellum United States was meant "not only . . . to educate children, but . . . to remake them, so that the next generation could build a united America unfettered by sectional, ethnic, or racial conflict." In practice, this often meant inculcating students with "a reductive Anglo-Saxon version of American history" and a sense of "civic virtue" as a universal concern.[67] Sorby tracks how some of Longfellow's poems were used to teach children the values of assimilation and national belonging; Gummere's work shows how some pedagogues thought they could teach students to feel not just American but Anglo-Saxon, by reading accentual poetry so as to feel its rhythms in their bodies, binding them together into a white imagined community.

In Gummere's 1901 *Handbook*, he explained to students that while they may have been confused by competing ideas about whether English poetry was accentual or quantitative, the core of English poetry was accentual, and the accentual nature of Anglo-Saxon poetry helped students to see the racial traits of the Anglo-Saxons who produced it. In explaining the difference between accentual Anglo-Saxon verse and quantitative Greek and Latin verse, Gummere argued, "this choice of accent rather than quantity lay . . . in the passionate and vehement nature of our Germanic race. Our ancestors were disposed to extremes, and lacked the quiet, artistic sense that adopted the placid rhythm of Greek verse. The German could not *linger* on his verse-accent; he put into it all the strength of which he was capable."[68] Not only could racially inflected temperamental traits be seen in Anglo-Saxon verse, according to Gummere; so too could students trace the movements of Anglo-Saxon bodies in the beat of English accentual verse. This was because, Gummere argued, Anglo-Saxons were more in tune with the rhythms of the body and less interested in abstraction than were cultures that had developed quantitative verse. He explained that the "double beat of left-right" Anglo-Saxon dance steps gave us the "alternation of stronger right and weaker left [which] gave the accented and the unaccented beat (=syllable) of the foot. With the end of the *verse* (*verto*), the dancers *turned* again to repeat their forward-and-back."[69] In Gummere's telling, the literal foot became the abstracted metrical foot as Anglo-Saxon culture started to become influenced more and more by classical and Romance languages and cultures. Teaching students to read poetry for accent, Gummere believed, could thus also teach students to see the Anglo-Saxon bodies that had created the accentual system in the first place and to appreciate the Teutonic "raciness" that was at the root of Anglophone poetic rhythms.

In the *Handbook*, Gummere does not extrapolate about the future of Germanic rhythms and Anglo-Saxon racial traits and political institutions in the United States. But ten years later, in *Democracy and Poetry*, he more clearly spelled out the connections he assumes in the *Handbook* between Anglo-Saxon racial identity, Anglophone poetry, and twentieth-century political institutions in the United States. In this book, Gummere explains that "the central democratic idea" is "the active and supreme function of the imagined community."[70] By this, he means that the highest communal ideal is a democracy in which each individual understands their freedom to be possible only because of their commitment to and work for the collective; in a real democracy, "free individuals combin[e] in service and allegiance to an imagined state."[71] He explains that "the standing peril of democracies" is "their own lapse into ochlocracy, into the rule of the mob," but that "constant vision of the imagined community keeps this peril afar off."[72] This is why, for Gummere, poetry is vitally important to social life and not simply about aesthetics or form. Poetry is "the visionary power" that creates true "belief in the imagined community, that sort of fiction which is more real than fact." That is, a community, in Gummere's view, is "made real by the dreams and imagination of its own members."[73] Poetry—especially poetry in which the accentual beat of Anglo-Saxon bodies harmonizing in a group can be felt or heard—helped the "American freeman" to take up his central task: "to see his ideal community steadily and whole, and to put its yoke upon his own neck."[74] *Democracy and Poetry* was thus not just a catchy title to Gummere; democracy was only possible because of the rhythms of poetry, the art form that he believed encouraged social consent and communal cohesion. The rhythms of accentual Anglo-Saxon verse, which he believed to be the backbone of Anglophone poetry, showed readers how to subsume their needs to those of the collective, since Anglo-Saxons were believed to be inherently loyal to their community and to have sown the seeds of all future democratic institutions.[75] Anglo-Saxon poetry thus seemed to Gummere to be a "notable case of democracy in verse" and "a fair attempt to realize the imagined community" and hence a guiding light for contemporaneous citizens of a white democracy.[76]

Gummere's metrical imaginary, in which Anglo-Saxon rhythms would help white Americans to see their civic duty to other white Americans, was, as might be expected, fundamentally and explicitly anti-Indigenous and anti-Black. While Gummere rarely wrote about nonwhite poets, since he was most interested in the value of texts like *Beowulf* for the white twentieth-century reader, he did frequently disparage Native American and African societies specifically as part of his ongoing argument that Anglo-Saxons were superior to other races. We can thus see in Gummere's work the results of the shift Reginald Horsman traces in eighteenth-century Anglo-Saxonist scholarship from "merely praising Germans or Saxons to attacking other peoples," which "transform[ed] the whole Anglo-Saxon movement into a matter of innate racial distinctions."[77] Whenever Gummere described Anglo-Saxons, he consistently turned to imagined racial hierarchies that were animated by a settler colonial logic of conquest. According to Gummere, the heroic Anglo-Saxon ancestors of the "English-speaking race" had conquered and enslaved Indigenous peoples as part of their rise to world domination, signaling that settler colonialism was a proper inheritance of Anglo-Americans and a sign of a "dominant" race. Following the popular idea that the "parent stock" of Anglo-Saxons was the imagined Indo-European-speaking Aryan race, Gummere argued the earliest Germans had "broken . . . from that mysterious East which has sent out wave after wave of western conquest; and must have driven away, or possibly enslaved, the primitive tribes which held the land, . . . an indigenous race, smaller and darker than the Germans" who were most likely "a hunting folk low enough in the scale of civilization, who 'had neither wool, salt, nor wagons with wheels, and could not count to one hundred.'"[78] This racial hierarchy and relation of justified colonial dominance, according to Gummere, still obtained in the present. He insisted repeatedly that "the primitive Aryans, the parent stock of our race," could be shown through "conservative inference from the facts of philology" to have been "on a higher plane of civilization than the North American Indian," because "the Aryan was no longer a mere hunter; he knew horses and cattle, though the latter were used mainly for the yoke."[79] Such a comparison was also impossible, according to Gummere, because it "confound[ed] what the Germans call *Uncultur* and *Vorcultur*." That is, primitive Germanic tribes were part of a "developing, ardent, ambitious race, destined soon to become a dominant race," and had "pass[ed] through the clan-stage to higher forms of national life," while "American Indians . . . [would] never come to anything better than a raw clanship and remain mere hordes."[80] In Gummere's imagined history, Anglo-Saxons had developed into white Americans, while "American Indians" had not developed and hence had been destined to be conquered by the descendants of the Aryans.

Gummere's anti-Black racism was tied to the settler colonial logic that animated his discussion of Indigenous peoples. Following the racial science of his era, Gummere argued that agriculture and individual property ownership distinguished "developing" races from races that were incapable of development. Indeed, he claimed that philological research had shown "own" to be "a very old Germanic word," meaning that "we may be sure that our ancestors were not in that delightful condition of certain African tribes where nobody owns anything and everybody steals what he can."[81] Because of this relationship to property, Gummere argued, the primitive German was "a person . . . whom no amount of ethnology is going to put on a par with the modern African savage."[82] Gummere was interested in developing a theory of Anglo-Saxon poetry, and so he spent little time discussing the implicit relationship between poetic rhythms and imagined communities he posits for Native American and African social groups. It would not take long for critics and scholars following in Gummere's wake to theorize these relationships, however, as I discuss in subsequent chapters.

Put slightly differently, Gummere's work helped to bake anti-Blackness and anti-Indigeneity, as the necessary foundations of American whiteness, into American poetics in this moment. If *only* Anglo-Saxon rhythms could concretize the imagined community, as he believed, then competing rhythmical traditions would necessarily detract from that desired social cohesion. White editors in the modernist era were quick to expand on and further develop this idea, as we will see.

The Afterlives of the Communal Origins Theory

Gummere was not without his critics, but even those critics had to acknowledge his tenacious hold on the scholarly and pedagogical imaginations of his contemporaries. His most notable opponent was Louise Pound, who, in a series of articles and books published in the 1910s, 1920s, and 1930s, took Gummere to task for the romanticism of his hypothesis and for what she saw as his total lack of evidence for his claims. In an article published in *PMLA* in 1919, for instance, Pound argued that, although the "belief in dance origins . . . has current American acceptance," this theory was "neither borne out by the evidence, nor intrinsically probable."[83] Pound's intervention was crucial in a number of ways; her work insisted on rigor over fantasy, and it turned scholarly conversations away from searches for "original" texts or the Germanic "core" of English literature and toward the idea of textual multiplicity and variation. But her work also highlights how the communal origins hypothesis was never entirely discredited, especially in literature classrooms. Writing in 1929, Pound noted that although she had shown that it was without basis, the theory remained "persistent," especially in the high school English classroom.[84] Pedagogically focused journals such as *The English Journal* frequently ran pieces by high school teachers explaining how they taught communal composition in their classes, most often by having students chant, stomp, and clap together.[85] Steve Newman notes that Gummere's domination of textbook publication helped to keep the communal origins hypothesis in the classroom and that his understanding of poetic origins was integral to Robert Penn Warren and Cleanth Brooks's approach to poetry in their coauthored textbook *Understanding Poetry*. Indeed, as this section shows, Gummere stamped the study of poetry and poetics inside and outside the US academy for generations to come. Here I trace the influence of the communal origins theory on the canonization of Walt Whitman and on understandings of free verse as a return to Anglo-Saxon prosody. Gummere inspired early academic proponents of Whitman to imagine him as an inheritor of Anglo-Saxon greatness, setting up the idea that free verse was an Anglo-Saxon poetic form. Scholars explicitly connected the perceived racial plasticity of Anglo-Saxons with the perceived plasticity of free verse forms, cementing an association between whiteness and formal experimentation that persists to this day.

It is perhaps the most deeply ironic twist in the twisty afterlife of the communal origins theory that it was used to canonize Whitman as the poet of US democracy in the 1910s and 1920s, given that Gummere believed that Whitman was the epitome of antidemocratic individualism. (According to Gummere, Whitman adhered strictly to the doctrine, "say what you will, of what you will, how you will," without attending to the needs of his imagined community.)[86] As I have argued elsewhere, Whitman's canonization as a formal innovator happened surprisingly late.[87] It was not accepted within academic circles that he had even written poetry until the 1920s, and even then, debates about the metrical nature of his poetry abounded, perhaps helping to explain Joseph Csicsila's observation that "anthologists were surprisingly slow in their recognition of Whitman as one of America's truly finest writers."[88] Whitman simply proclaimed that he had created a new form of national poetry, and his defenders in the 1880s and 1890s did little to justify his metrical project. They tended to assert that Whitman was an important innovator and defender of democracy without providing proof of their own, simply quoting Whitman's poetry in the belief that it spoke for itself.[89] But as scholars of American literature set out to prove that their objects of study formed a coherent national literary tradition in new departments of English in the early twentieth century, critics began to attempt to explain and categorize Whitman's metrical innovations in a systematic way. Fred Newton Scott was one of the first academics to argue that Whitman had successfully created an entirely new, and entirely American (read: Anglo-Saxon), verse form—an argument he elaborated in "A Note on Walt Whitman's Prosody," published in *The Journal of English and Germanic Philology* in 1908.

Scott, like Gummere, was an influential figure in English studies in the early 1900s. He served as president of the Modern Language Association in 1907 (two years after Gummere's presidency), founded the department of rhetoric at the University of Michigan, cofounded the National Council of Teachers of English and the Linguistic Society of America, and authored an impressive number of textbooks, critical studies, and scholarly articles, including the widely used *Introduction to the Methods and Materials of Literary Criticism*, cited earlier in this chapter for its praise of Gummere's work on poetics. Scott was particularly interested in the problem of differentiating the rhythms of poetry from the rhythms of prose, and his work in this area led him to believe that he had discovered the solution to the problem of Whitman's irregular form. Surprisingly, Scott believed that the solution to the problem of Whitman's form could be found by combining aspects of Gummere's communal origins theory with aspects of Gummere's arch-nemesis J. S. Mill's definition of poetry as "feeling confessing itself to itself." He believed that Gummere was correct in arguing that poetry had begun as a social practice grounded in rhythm but that it had evolved into an individualistic expressive art form with little connection to early communal rhythms, meaning that Mill's definition was an accurate description of modern poetry. In eliding the distance between Gummere and Mill, Scott ignored the fissures and pressure points in prosodic discourse, thereby contributing to the growing sense that there was one "right" way to read poetry rather than multiple ways to approach different genres and metrical forms. Scott saw poetry as a unified, coherent genre (as opposed to a supergenre or a collection of many different genres), and he believed, like the overwhelming majority of his peers, that academic investigators could discover the "primal causes" and universal principles that governed its evolution.[90]

Scott explained that the rhythms of prose and of poetry could be differentiated cleanly by looking at their functions. Speakers who wanted to communicate information had to factor in the response of their audience, which, he argued, led to a back-and-forth communication and so to "a swaying, fluctuating movement of a seemingly irregular kind." Speakers who wanted to express emotion, on the other hand, had only to account for their own feelings and so tended to produce "a fairly regular series [of sounds] subject to changes in tempo and pitch corresponding to the successive moods of the speaker" (notably, in making this argument, Scott cited Darwin's theory of evolution and Karl Groos's study *The Play of Animals*, which proposed that play served an evolutionary purpose).[91] If written prose and poetry had developed as modes of communication and expression, respectively, as Scott believed both Mill's and Gummere's work proved, then it stood to reason that the rhythms of prose would be made up of long nonrepeating units, based on the back-and-forth movement of communicative speech, while those of poetry would be made up of short recurring units based on the more regular movement of individualistic expressive speech. In premodern poetry, Scott explained, the short units of poetic rhythm corresponded to the stamping feet and clapping hands of the throng described by Gummere. In modern poetry, the units of rhythm were derived from "changes in tempo and pitch corresponding to the successive moods of the [individual] speaker," meaning poetic rhythm was "shaped by purely physiological or psychological causes."[92] To Scott, this theory seemed to prove that the most fundamental units of English-language poetry were not syllabic units (iambs, dactyls, anapests, etc.), as many prosodists believed, but rather temporal units derived from the rhythms of the human body. Syllabic units could be rightly understood as abstractions imposed on those basic bodily rhythms — abstractions that could easily distract poets and their audiences from what he saw as the real rhythms of poetry, which were the rhythms of the body in motion. In this analysis, Scott concurred with Gummere that the accentual principles of Anglo-Saxon verse, pre–Norman Conquest, were the core of English poetry, while classical metrical terms were mere overlays.

Scott argued that the discovery of these universal rhythmical rules, founded on the rhythms of the body, meant that the answer to the question of how to interpret Whitman's idiosyncratic cadences was finally at hand. He posited that Whitman's unusual long lines were the result of a blending of the wave-like rhythms of prose (which he called "motation") and the steadier rhythms of poetry (which he called "nutation"). According to Scott, Whitman's natural "delight in large *free* movements and rushes of sound made him impatient of the *short* units, the quickly recurring beats, of the nutative rhythm. He wished to embody in his verse the largo of nature," and so he "sought to make [these natural sounds and movements] the very foundation of his prosody, the regulative principle of his rhythm."[93] Whitman had asserted that his poems were the best expression of democratic freedom, but Scott believed he had found scientific proof that Whitman's poetry was indeed more "large" and "free" than the "short," cramped, and stifling movements of "regular" meter. Scott thus helped to naturalize the opposition between "traditional" foot-based systems of prosody and the more "organic" forms of meter that Gummere had argued were essentially Anglo-Saxon.

At the same time, Scott's theory was able to locate the genesis of this new metrical freedom in the language of the American people, thus implicitly making the case for the study of American literature as a subspeciality for scholars of English. He explained that Whitman's hypersensitivity to the unique beauty of American speech helped him to see that he had to create an entirely new idiom in order to adequately express its "peculiar genius" and that it was his ear for "the pitch-glides and speech-tunes" of prose that allowed him to develop his new, hybrid poetic form.[94] Scott's account of Whitman's speech-based rhythms seemed to provide particularly compelling evidence that American poetry had finally become an organic expression of a unified national culture rather than an imitation of British poetry. As such, the poetic tradition that Whitman inaugurated could help to maintain the unity of the nation, creating a feedback loop between national identity and its literary expression. In Scott's opinion, as in Gummere's, social and artistic institutions were intertwined. He argued that poetry and government were ruled by the same principles, explaining that "the relation between art and nature is like that between a people and its government. . . . The people can become free and remain free, only by submission to restraint. They can preserve their coherence, their communal individuality, their organic life and opportunity for unlimited expansion of that life, only as these things incessantly find expression in traditional, law-observing, law-embodying institutions."[95] Prior to Whitman, no American poet had been able to devise a poetic law that could give expression to the American people's unique "organic life," and so American literature had failed to successfully cohere as a national tradition. The realization that Whitman had been creating within the bounds of rhythmic law rather than simply "yawping" without a sense of poetic rules meant that he could take his rightful place as the fountainhead of a modern American literary tradition and that scholars of American poetry could finally prove that their discipline was a vital area of research.

Though Scott followed Gummere in arguing that a nation's literature and its identity were inseparable, his sense of the relationship between poetic rhythm and identity was slightly different. Gummere believed that national identity was an effect of rhythm, but Scott understood rhythm to be a figure for the functioning of a nation. If Scott's conflation of prosody and social relations was less absolute, it was no less powerful, for Whitman's prosody as a figure for the body politic provided a model for reconciling the potential chaos and heterogeneity of a truly democratic society with the supposed lack of freedom in any other social system. Scott put forth this model in parable form, explaining, "when I read Whitman's poetry in light of [the] conception" of Whitman's prosody as an interweaving of the long, irregularly recurring rhythms of prose and the short, repeating rhythms of poetry,

> a fantastic myth passes through my mind. I seem to see in Whitman some *giant-limbed* old heathen god who has descended to the earth fain to take part in the dance of mortals. He begins by practicing the waltz, but soon tires of the mincing steps and quick gyrations. He wants a larger, freer movement. He then tries marching and running and leaping, only to find that what his soul hungers for is the undulating movement of the waltz. So, devising a kind of colossal minuet, with woven paces and with waving arms, he moves through it with a grandiose, galumphing majesty peculiar to himself, flinging his great limbs all abroad and shedding ambrosia from his *flying locks*, yet with all his abandon keeping time to the music, and in all the seeming waywardness of his saltations preserving the law and pattern of the dance.[96]

Importantly, Scott codes Whitman as Anglo-Saxon in this passage. As a devoted reader of Gummere's work, Scott would have been familiar with Gummere's (and with other Anglo-Saxonists') descriptions of the physicality of early Germanic peoples. According to Gummere, "all agree" that German men were "huge of stature" and that the "conspicuous feature" of the early Germanic man was "his flowing locks."[97] Gummere explained that "the German cherished his flowing hair; it was his outward and visible sign of freedom, a precious thing," for "to be a roundhead was to be a slave."[98] The Germanic freeman was thus "distinguished by his long, flowing hair, and by his arms, the so-called folk-weapons."[99] In characterizing Whitman as a "giant-limbed" heathen god with "flying locks" and "waving arms," Scott draws on common Anglo-Saxonist myths in order to drive home that the American throng is tied to Anglo-Saxon ancestors and that

American literature is a vibrant branch of a long Anglo-Teutonic tradition of democracy in verse.[100]

Scott advanced this parable of Whitman the dancer god as the foundational myth that the United States had been searching for since its colonial days. The motative movement of prose, with its potentially lawless irregularity, stands in for the heterogeneous individuals that make up the American people. These fractious individuals are brought under control by the regular, lawful nutative steps that allow bodies to move together in "the rhythm of consent" that Gummere had theorized, thereby becoming a unified people. For Scott, the "discovery" of Whitman's prosody was also the discovery of the first American throng. By following the lead of their giant dancing Teutonic leader and thereby finding their rhythm, he believed, the American people had found a way to overcome the social divisions and pressures that always threatened a democratic society. The "waywardness" and "abandon" of willful individual subjects would be harmonized in the pattern of the "colossal minuet" that was *Leaves of Grass*. For Scott, Whitman was useful not so much as the familiar figure of metrical revolution, the Whitman who liberated the line and "broke the new wood" for Ezra Pound, but as the figure of metrical reconciliation, the benevolent dancing giant who would bring his national community together.

Scott's vision of an Anglo-Saxon Whitman appealed to many scholars writing in Scott's wake, who began in earnest the work of fitting Whitman into a coherent Anglo-Teutonic metrical tradition. There are many possible reasons why the Anglo-Saxon Whitman would have seemed generative to scholars of American literature, but perhaps most importantly, Anglo-Saxon culture was perceived to have been consummately masculine and vigorous, making an Anglo-Saxon Whitman the masculine poet who could help to counter what Elizabeth Renker calls "the many-sided problem of the institutional femininity of American literature as a classroom subject and the cultural femininity of American literature as a body of texts."[101] Whatever the reason, the next few decades saw an outpouring of scholarship that seemed to prove that Whitman's seemingly idiosyncratic forms and the later free verse experiments they inspired were in fact deeply traditional and reached back to Anglo-Saxon precursors.

One of Scott's students, Ruth Mary Weeks, was one such Whitman proponent. Weeks had studied under Scott at the University of Michigan in the 1910s, and in her 1921 article "Phrasal Prosody," she took up the argument Scott had advanced in "A Note on Walt Whitman's Prosody." Weeks argued that Whitman's free verse and the free verse that followed were not aberrations or breaks with a metrical past but rather a step toward an ultimate poetic harmony that would reconcile "Procrustean classic" meters with the innovative rhythms of modern life. Weeks held to the Gummerian view that poetic rhythms evolved in tandem with the rhythms of everyday life, so that "primitive" poetry was strongly rhythmical and communally oriented, while modern poetry was irregularly rhythmic and individualistic. These idiosyncratic rhythms were an inescapable part of modern life, but they needed to be reconciled with the needs of the American community if poetry was to become a useful force in contemporary life. Drawing on Scott's preferred metaphor, Weeks argued that "the new day has new needs; the long free stride of democracy cannot accommodate itself to classic dancing measures," and that Whitman had created the new measure of modernity by taking the "vocal wave" as his "rhythmic unit."[102]

Unlike Scott, however, Weeks believed that the vocabulary of "traditional" metrical poetry, based on syllabic feet, was compatible with Whitman's "new rhythmus." She argued that Whitman had "attempted to use the various types of [vocal waves] as other poets use arbitrary groups of syllables to produce rhythmic effects," shifting the emphasis from the syllabic unit to what she called the "phrasal unit." Whitman had invented many types of "phrasal feet," she explained, including the "trochaic emphasis foot," and Amy Lowell's "delicate trochees," Carl Sandburg's "resounding dactyls and amphibrachs," Edgar Lee Masters's "hesitating minor iambs," and Ezra Pound's "mixed measures" were simply "perfecting this new and more flexible rhythmic unit."[103] To Weeks, preserving the vocabulary of "classic meters" as a means of describing free verse was important because it hinted at the ongoing evolution and the ultimate unity of poetic verse forms. She explained that free verse would not overtake "classic" meter but would instead dialectically incorporate it, helping poets to develop "a richer, more pulsing measure than we have known, various yet sustained, combining syllabic and phrasal accent, pitch, time, pause, and rhyme—all the rhythmic values of spoken English"—into a singular "rhythmus." Free verse was not a disruption or a break with the past but "a new and beautiful note [in] the composite chord of the coming poetic harmony."[104] What place nonwhite poets have in that coming harmony is unclear in Weeks's work, but one suspects, given the naming of Lowell, Masters, Sandburg, and Pound as exemplary, that this is a harmony exclusive to white poets.

Weeks extended Scott's utopian horizon beyond national boundaries; in her opinion, the rhythms Whitman invented had the potential not only to unify the heterogeneous national body of the United States but, more broadly, to reconcile the past with the present, bringing the evolution of social life to a new pinnacle. If the gains of modern civilization had been offset by the loss of "the habit of social experience" that primitive civilizations had manifested in their tribal dances, as Weeks, like Gummere, believed, then modern man needed the "golden strand of meter" to bind that ancient, communal mode of sociality to the present.[105] Because rhythmic and social harmony were one and the same, Weeks argued, a completely harmonized poetry could overcome the fragmentation and alienation that had been ushered in by mechanized print and hastened by the industrial revolution.[106] Whitman's free verse pointed the way to this new incarnation of an Ur-rhythm, but only as part of a holistic vision of poetry that included both the embodied rhythms of free verse and the more abstract patterns of "classic" meter as integral parts of modern culture.

Scott and Weeks helped to spawn a spate of articles and book chapters arguing that Whitman had actually rediscovered the essential Anglo-Saxon principles of English prosody and in so doing had paved the way for a more "natural" and "organic" mode of modern American poetry. Writing in 1923 in *Studies in Philology*, John Erskine argued that Whitman's prosodic contribution had been to overturn the fetishization of end rhyme, which, following Gummere, he explained away as "an import into English verse from Romance poetry." According to Erskine, Whitman knew that "the art of verse is for the ear, not for the eye," and so he returned to the principles of oral poetry that had ordered English verse before the invasion of Romance-language poetic conventions and classical metrical terminology.[107] In a 1929 article, also written for *Studies in Philology*, Lois Ware concurred, explaining that Whitman was not an unconventional or shockingly innovative poet, as was popularly believed. Instead, he had returned to Old English conventions — "particularly to alliteration, assonance, repetition, parallelism, and, to a less extent, to the refrain."[108] This was not metrical apostasy but rather a return to pre–Norman Conquest principles of versification. Writing for *American Literature* in 1939, Sculley Bradley also advanced this view, explaining that critics of Whitman had been "too little acquainted with the true nature and history of English rhythm to recognize, beneath the disguise of innovation, the rugged face of a well-known English ancient."[109] Because "so much emphasis has been laid upon the classical ancestry of our English prosody," Bradley argued, "criticism has frequently lost sight of the earlier and very strong Germanic and Old English ancestry" of Whitman's prosody.[110] Bradley explained that Whitman had returned to the Old English practice of "regulat[ing] rhythm by the interval of elapsed time between stresses," which made an "appeal to the ear rather than to the eye." In this way, Whitman avoided "predetermined metrical pattern" and wrote instead according to the principles of English "oral tradition."[111] Indeed, Bradley argued, Whitman had rediscovered the Anglo-Saxon "hovering accent," which had been theorized extensively by Gummere. Bradley argued that Fred Newton Scott had misnamed this hovering accent, or the distribution of stress "along the word, or a pair of words, or even a short phrase," by calling it "pitch-glide" but that, at root, Scott had also seen that Whitman was returning to Old English rhythmical principles rather than inventing new rhythms.[112]

Perhaps most notably, the idea that Whitman had returned to Anglo-Saxon rhythmical principles provided F. O. Matthiessen with his justification for including Whitman as a key figure in *The American Renaissance* (1941). Matthiessen argued that Whitman mattered because he had actually undergone a "crude re-living of the primitive evolution of poetry" from its "origin . . . in the dance, in the rise and fall 'of consenting feet' (in Gummere's phrase)" to the modern day. According to Matthiessen, Whitman understood that words had to be "grasped" with the senses before they could be effectively deployed, and this understanding allowed Whitman to move away from what Matthiessen called the "conventional" poetry "of instructed imitation" to "the internal pulsations of the body, to its external movements in work and in making love, to such sounds as the wind and the sea."[113] Whitman's poetry was consequently "more authentic than something Longfellow read in a book and tried to copy" and was thus far more suited to founding a truly native poetic tradition.[114] Matthiessen argued that "Whitman's native instinct had rediscovered something similar to what [Gerard Manley] Hopkins believed he had found by learning Anglo-Saxon: that before the language had bent itself to classical influence, . . . it was 'a vastly superior thing to what we have now.'"[115] Because Whitman's poetry was more in touch with the Anglo-Saxon foundations of English as well as with the rhythms of modern life, Matthiessen argued, it was uniquely suited to bind past and future into a new vision of the imagined community in verse.

Conclusion: Communal Origins Today

While it is beyond the scope of this chapter to trace the Anglo-Saxonization of Whitman after Matthiessen, I hope that I have convincingly made the case that the establishment of Whitman's poetry and of subsequent American free verse as Anglo-Saxon forms was central to their canonization by academics in the early twentieth century. It is of course impossible to say whether

Whitman would have occupied such an important place in twentieth-century academic accounts of American poetry had he not been imagined as a link in a chain of Anglo-Saxon greatness, but the fact that his canonization did depend on this myth should matter to our contemporary accounts of poetic innovation. I hope too that my discussion of the construction of Walt Whitman as an Anglo-Saxon poet has shown some of the ways in which Gummere's ideas were decontextualized, deracinated, and turned into seemingly scientific, disinterested truths about prosody later in the twentieth century.[116] To return to where the chapter began, perhaps the most surprising measure of Gummere's influence is that he still figures prominently in relatively recent editions of *The Princeton Encyclopedia of Poetry and Poetics* (1993, 2012). In addition to being an uncited source for the ideas in the entry for "oral poetry" in the 2012 edition, Gummere is cited in nine articles in the 1993 edition, and while the entries for "incremental repetition" (a term Gummere invented), "ballad," and "hovering accent" do note that Gummere's theories were contested, other entries simply cite Gummere as a source or position his work as exemplary. The entry for "foot," for example, explains that "one disadvantage" of scansion by foot is that it "works only on regular verse—Gummere made this crucial point a century ago," while the entry for "meter" includes the sentence, "As Gummere said over a century ago, the old terms for the various feet are best used simply to characterize the general movement of verse."[117] Gummere's presence in the 2012 edition has been reduced to five appearances, but he is still cited as a reliable source of information about meter, genre, and form. There is also, notably, still a Francis B. Gummere professorship at Haverford College.

Remnants of Gummere's thinking remain with us in other ways. I have been making the case that Gummere and his peers baked evolutionary theory into academic accounts of poetry and poetics by building on eighteenth- and nineteenth-century philological accounts of English and on early twentieth-century biological accounts of racial evolution to position contemporaneous Anglophone poetry—especially free verse—as the lineal descendant of Anglo-Saxon poetry. Thus, the idea of an unbroken continuity of poetic expression from oral rituals to modern print has been and continues to be presented as an obvious evolutionary truth rather than as the modern invention of eighteenth- and nineteenth-century race science that it is. This retroprojection matters because, as Gérard Genette argues in *The Architext*, it allows "literary theorists [to] . . . 'bury' their own difference—their own modernity"—which is also to say, their own colonial interests.[118] Put slightly differently, it is important to understand that the construction of a poetic tradition that stretches back to ritual oral performances, Anglo-Saxon or otherwise, is a critical fiction rooted in particular historical moments because it can also help us to see how the philological remapping of the world described by Aamir Mufti contributed to what Cedric Robinson describes as "the West's suppression of Europe's previous knowledge of the African (and its own) past."[119] In other words, the insistence of Gummere and his peers that modern English literature could be traced back to Anglo-Saxon literature depended on a suppression of the histories of migration, miscegenation, and cultural intermixing in the areas that eventually became European nations—a suppression that continues today, as has been evidenced by recent controversies within the organization known until 2019 as the International Society of Anglo-Saxonists.

It bears repeating here that Anglo-Saxons did not exist and that the Anglo-Saxon poetic inheritance that scholars like Scott created for Whitman and other free versifiers was, emphatically and completely, a fantasy. As mentioned in the introduction, "Anglo-Saxon" was an exonym that helped to create the illusion of linguistic, cultural, and political unity where there was in fact a heterogeneous mix of languages, cultural practices, and political institutions, growing out of constant trade, migration, and conquest. As David Wilton has shown, while Continental authors used "Anglo-Saxon" to refer to the people who inhabited what is now England, "the pre-Conquest English people simply did not refer to themselves as 'Anglo-Saxons.' . . . They did occasionally . . . use *seax* as an inclusive ethnonym, but more commonly compounded that root to refer to smaller ethnic groups. Instead, the terms they overwhelmingly used as an inclusive ethnonym for themselves were *englisc* and *angelcynn*."[120] After the Norman Conquest, the term fell out of usage until the end of the eighteenth century, when "'Anglo-Saxon' [began] to be used to mark contemporary English culture as distinct from others."[121] As Wilton notes, this usage is a direct result of the fact that, "in the nineteenth and early twentieth centuries, the study of 'Anglo-Saxon' was thought to be essential for establishing the empirical and civic legitimacy of American academic institutions and English departments in particular."[122] Nineteenth- and twentieth-century usages of the term "Anglo-Saxon" were always ideologically motivated.

This brings us back to the way that the study of English poetry and poetics, from Anglo-Saxon epics to modernist free verse, was understood to function as a positive spur to the racial development of white Americans. As Allen Frantzen notes, "From the very beginning of college and university education in America, philology, including Anglo-Saxon studies and covering the earliest phases of English literature, was inextricable from the civic goals of the English department. . . . At the MLA meeting of 1902, James Wilson Bright, author of an Old English grammar and reader, a version of which is still in wide use, declared that the philologist should take part in 'the work of guiding the destinies of the country,' since 'the philological strength and sanity of a nation is the measure of its intellectual and spiritual vitality.'"[123]

The idea of "the philological strength and sanity of a nation" sounds like a white supremacist talking point because it was one. As Mary Rambaran-Olm has argued, "white supremacist movement[s] in Euro-America [have] used the term 'Anglo-Saxon' to justify racial violence and colonial genocide for at least 200 years. . . . The term's association with whiteness has saturated our lexicon to the point that it is absurdly misused in political discourse."[124] Though it may seem obvious now that a department of literature would want to cover all of the literature written in a particular language from its historical origins to the contemporary moment, and hence that English departments must begin their coverage with Anglo-Saxon or Old English texts and that these texts came from earlier modes of oral composition, the choice to narrate history in this way was always part of Anglo-Saxonist ideology, rooted in the story of normative human development that had been popularized by Germanic philology. Even though it was recognized in the eighteenth century "that the Old English language itself did not form a single seamless whole but instead included several different stages and dialects," as Ashley Crandell Amos notes, the philological remapping of the world made it possible to collapse these differences into the imagined continuity of national literary traditions.[125] From the primitive throng to Whitman to modern free versifiers, it seemed, ran "the directness and the virility of the native stock," as the Harvard professor John Livingston Lowes put it in his 1919 study *Convention and Revolt in Poetry*.[126]

How did this Anglo-Saxonist version of literary history shape how readers and poets approached free verse in the 1910s and 1920s? Thus far, I have focused on readers located in the US academy, but as we will see in chapter 2, this mythology of an Anglo-Saxon poetic lineage was also central to nonacademic readers in this era, providing a basis for later identifications of experimental writing with white writers. I turn now to the story of how these critical fictions about the development of English poetry migrated out of scholarly monographs and into the pages of one of the most influential little magazines of the modernist era: Harriet Monroe's *Poetry: A Magazine of Verse*.

CHAPTER TWO

Poetry Magazine's Plantation Imaginaries

Poetry: A Magazine of Verse is in many ways an anomaly among modernist little magazines. Unlike its relatively short-lived peers *Others* (1915–19), *Blast* (1914–15), and *The Little Review* (1914–29), *Poetry* still exists, over one hundred years after Harriet Monroe founded the magazine with money she personally raised by canvassing wealthy Chicago businessmen. *Poetry*'s openness to poetic experimentation and its publishing record are legendary. It is often credited as being a key champion of free verse and of the so-called New Poetry of the 1910s and is frequently credited with publishing virtually every major name in modernist poetry (W. H. Auden, Basil Bunting, Hart Crane, Countee Cullen, T. S. Eliot, Langston Hughes, James Joyce, Marianne Moore, Ezra Pound, Dorothy Richardson, Edna St. Vincent Millay, Wallace Stevens, W. B. Yeats . . .). Given this illustrious publishing record, it is perhaps unsurprising that scholarship on *Poetry* tends to overlook what the magazine did *not* publish in its first decades of existence: poetry by Black women.

This chapter begins with the absence of Black women poets from *Poetry*'s pages in order to explore the structural imbrication of gender, race, and poetic form in modernist periodicals and poetics and in modernist studies more broadly. It is particularly crucial to revisit *Poetry*'s role in racializing free verse now, as laudatory narratives about *Poetry* have crystallized into critical consensus in encyclopedic publications such as *The Oxford Critical and Cultural History of Modernist Magazines* (2012), risking a continued misunderstanding of the racial politics of free verse. These critical narratives tend to valorize what is seen as the cosmopolitan inclusiveness of little magazines like *Poetry* and to portray their support of experimental poetic forms and of diverse authorial identities as interconnected endeavors. Many of these narratives of the inclusive little magazine emerged from feminist recovery work that sought to restore to view the major role played by women editors in developing modernism, against the Pound- and Eliot-centric models of earlier studies.[1] While I want to be clear that this recovery work was generative and necessary, I also want to highlight that, by and large, such work has not theorized gender as a racial formation. The failure within modernist periodical studies to think about gender "as an always racial and racializing construction," to use

C. Riley Snorton's formulation, has helped to contribute to the erasure of the white supremacist history of free verse in the United States.[2]

Scholarly work on *Poetry* magazine is particularly illustrative of the consequences of analyzing gender and race as separable formations. Prior to the feminist recovery work of scholars including Jayne Marek, Ann Massa, Claire Badaracco, Robin Schulze, and John Timberman Newcomb, among others, *Poetry* and its founding editor, Harriet Monroe, were often portrayed as genteel or provincial or anti- or other than modernist. Post-1990s scholarship on the magazine has shown that dismissals of *Poetry* were driven by misogynistic attitudes toward Monroe and her coeditors Alice Corbin Henderson and Eunice Tietjens on the part of both fellow modernist-era writers like Ezra Pound and by mid-twentieth century academics.[3] Scholarship working to counter these misogynist dismissals has emphasized the magazine's radical openness to a variety of poetic experiments, its admirable cosmopolitanism and inclusiveness, and its foresight in printing poets who would go on to become central to twentieth-century poetry.[4] For instance, Marek's foundational revisionist account of *Poetry* argues that the magazine "provided a democratic space that encouraged inclusiveness and extensive scope in modernism" and that among its "most significant contributions" to modern poetry was its "encourage[ment] [of] an international sensibility."[5] John Timberman Newcomb argues that the magazine "proposed poetry in the twentieth century as a sharing of self and other, familiar and new, native and foreign, across a world understood as irrevocably modern and inextricably interdependent."[6] Most revisionist accounts of *Poetry* make claims that the magazine published "nearly every key figure in Anglo-American verse of the period," as Newcomb puts it, and many present lists of the poets the magazine published as evidence of *Poetry*'s radical inclusiveness.[7] Helen Carr's entry on *Poetry* in *The Oxford Critical and Cultural History of Modernist Magazines*, to take one example, celebrates the magazine's "considerable" "openness to . . . a range of experiment and change" and provides the following list of contributing authors as evidence of the magazine's inclusivity:

T. S. Eliot, John Gould Fletcher, Robert Frost, Vachel Lindsay, Amy Lowell, Edgar Lee Masters, Marianne Moore, Carl Sandburg, Wallace Stevens, . . . William Carlos Williams . . . W. B. Yeats, Arthur Symons, Edwin Arlington Robinson, . . . Ernest Rhys, . . . Orrick Johns, Alfred Kreymborg, Sara Teasdale, Edna St Vincent Millay, . . . John Reed, . . . Padraic Colum, Joseph Campbell, F. S. Flint, Ford Madox Ford (then Hueffer), James Joyce, Isaac Rosenberg, Walter de

la Mare, D. H. Lawrence, Frederic Manning, John Rodker, . . . Anna
Wickham . . . W. H. Auden, Louise Bogan, Hart Crane, Countee
Cullen, William Empson, Robert Graves, Meridel Le Sueur, Archibald
MacLeish, Dorothy Richardson, Laura Riding, Allen Tate, Robert
Penn Warren, Yvor Winters, . . . Louis Zufoksky, . . . George
Oppen, Carl Rakosi, Charles Reznikoff, Kenneth Rexroth, and . . .
Basil Bunting.[8]

The persistent scholarly focus on form as a measure of poetic diversity
has allowed us to read lists like Carr's as heterogeneous and has resulted in
scholarship that repeats *Poetry*'s total erasure of Black women from the poetic record. During Harriet Monroe's editorial tenure (1912–36), Georgia
Douglas Johnson, Jessie Redmon Fauset, Anne Spencer, Gwendolyn Ben-
nett, Helene Johnson, Lucy Ariel Williams (also known as Ariel Williams
Holloway), Clarissa Scott, and a young Gwendolyn Brooks, among others,
wrote and published extensively, and yet *Poetry* did not publish or review any
work by any Black women during these years. This fact is not remarked on in
scholarship on *Poetry*; instead, critics have tended to praise the magazine for
gender parity. Newcomb, for instance, notes approvingly Mary Biggs's finding that "during the years of Monroe's editorship . . . 46 percent of the poets who appeared in *Poetry* were women," which Biggs calls an "equality of
literary opportunity that [women] had not had before and have probably not
had since."[9] The example of recovery work on *Poetry* thus helps to show that
modernist periodical studies—and the studies of free verse that rely on
those modernist periodicals as primary sources—has not yet fully engaged
with key Black feminist, queer, and trans theorizations of gender as a racial
formation, allowing instead the inclusion of white women into a literary
work or genre to signal a progressive approach to gender. But as decades of
Black feminist scholarship has shown, "antiblackness constitutes and dis-
rupts sex/gender constructs," to use Zakiyyah Iman Jackson's formulation.[10]
I take as axiomatic Jackson's statement that "any study that attempts to provide an account of how racialization operates must offer an explanation of
the intransigent, recursive, self-referential, and (re)animating power of abject constructions of black gender and sexuality," and I read the erasure of
Black women authors from the modernist poetic record as one effect of such
abject constructions.[11] I thus return to *Poetry*'s archives to think about how
the anti-Black "symbolic order" that Hortense Spillers names the "American
grammar" continues to shape discussions of modernist poetic form in ways
the field of modernist studies has by and large not yet acknowledged.[12]

Thinking with Black feminist and trans formulations of gender as a racialized construct, I propose that reading *Poetry* from the constitutive absence of Black women poets during its first few decades of existence brings into view the anti-Black reproductive logic that drove *Poetry*'s editorial choices. This reading of *Poetry* can help us to better understand the all too often overlooked racial politics of experimental poetic forms in the early twentieth century. I argue that Monroe and her coeditors (especially Henderson) offered their readers a white feminist interpretation of popular contemporaneous arguments that free verse was an Anglo-Saxon form and that the ability to generate new literary forms — cultural plasticity — was rooted in the supposed biological plasticity of white individuals. While scholars like Gummere and Scott emphasized the masculine virtues of Anglo-Saxon culture as they were encoded in Anglo-Saxon poetry and its supposed descendants, as I discussed in chapter 1, Monroe and her collaborators emphasized the role of contemporary white women and children, figured as emblems of reproductive futurity, in carrying on and reproducing that Anglo-Saxon poetic tradition.[13] Monroe and her coeditors and contributors consistently located the potential for the production of the most exciting new poetic forms — free verse among them — within white women and children, especially white women and children who were located on or had ties to plantations in the US South. *Poetry* was, in short, invested in free verse and in other modes of poetic experimentation precisely because they seemed to index the renewal and ongoing reproduction of whiteness as a mode of anti-Blackness in the early twentieth century. I show that Monroe and her collaborators engaged with Anglo-Saxonist prosodic histories and with plantation imaginaries to construct experimental poetry as key to the reproduction of whiteness.

In order to bring *Poetry*'s racial/gender politics into focus, this chapter proceeds through two sections. The first explores Monroe's pedagogical ambitions — particularly her single-minded focus on teaching prosodic history as the history of Anglo-Saxon innovation. Monroe's investment in the idea that free verse was a return to Anglo-Saxon rhythmical principles has been almost completely ignored in scholarship on *Poetry*, but this understanding of the history of poetic innovation was key to Monroe's editorial decisions. Most crucially, as I show in the second section, Monroe's Anglo-Saxonization of free verse was part and parcel of *Poetry*'s dismissal of almost all Black poets — but not Black folk materials — from the magazine's pages. I analyze how *Poetry* drew on ideas about the superior cultural and biological plasticity of Anglo-Saxons to position Black folk art as formless and in need of shaping by white interpreters, especially by white women and children, who were understood to be the most plastic members of the most plastic race.[14] It did so in part by imagining a future for American poetry in which white plantation and "jazz" poets like Julia Peterkin and Vachel Lindsay would have internalized Black poetic rhythms so that they could become the property of white children, who were positioned as figures of modernity and futurity. Against the prevailing scholarly consensus that *Poetry* was an inclusive and cosmopolitan little magazine that promoted formal experimentation above all, I argue that *Poetry*'s editors adhered to a racializing logic in which the production of new poetic forms and the production of whiteness were coterminous.

Harriet Monroe's Pedagogy of Whiteness

Harriet Monroe saw it as her mission to bring scientific truths about poetry, which she believed were only just being discovered in the 1910s, to her reading public. Critics have noted Monroe's desire to enlarge the audience for poetry, but less often noted is her desire to teach her audience how to understand the past, present, and future of English-language poetry as a racialized tradition.[15] The magazine's famous motto — "To have great poets there must be great audiences too" — meant to Monroe that the audience must be in "a reciprocal relation" with the artist.[16] As she explained in a 1911 essay in *The Atlantic*, this meant that audiences needed to understand the aims and methods of poets, for "the highest art . . . comes only when profound energy of creation meets profound energy of sympathy."[17] Unlike fellow little magazines such as *Others*, which pointedly avoided editorial explication and theorization of the poetry they published, *Poetry* devoted up to half of each issue to writing about poetry. *Poetry* was interested in teaching its readers about poetry, poetics, and methods of reading in a way that rival publications were not, and its "comments" section covered everything from how to scan free verse to how to understand Serbian ballads as part of a world literature.

Poetry was successful in its pedagogical aims, becoming a significant influence on the teaching of poetry in universities and colleges. This was possible partly due to what Claudia Stokes identifies as "the permeability of the literary academy" in the early twentieth century.[18] Literary studies in this era overlapped and intertwined with what Nancy Glazener calls "public literary culture" — women's clubs, Chautauqua circuits, and other modes of "informal adult education."[19] Monroe took advantage of this institutional permeability, intentionally pursuing alliances with university professors, whose emerging status as professionalized experts helped to sanction her own expertise. Monroe and other members of *Poetry*'s editorial staff were active in public lecture circuits at universities around the country, frequently performing the role of professional authority to a range of publics. Monroe alone was invited to speak at "the Universities of Illinois, Chicago, Northwestern, Baylor, Indiana, de Pauw, Texas, [and] New Mexico," as an ad for her lectures noted, and a 1926 speaking tour took her to Georgetown College in Kentucky, Tulane University, the University of Arizona at Tucson, the University of Washington in Seattle, and a meeting of the American Association of University Women in Spokane.[20] When Monroe pitched an anthology of the New Poetry to Edward C. Marsh at the Macmillan Company in 1915, she presented it in explicitly pedagogical terms. She wrote that *Poetry* magazine had "aroused great interest among colleges," intimating that students were in need of a guide to experimental modern poetry and that *Poetry*'s editors — not university professors — were the people to provide that guide.[21] The magazine also provided a much-traveled bridge between amateur and professional readers of literature by publishing reviews of scholarly monographs and accounts of how poetry was being taught in various colleges and universities. In so doing, the magazine helped to bring debates about the origins of poetry to a wider public than was reached by *PMLA* and *College English*.

Poetry presented the university as the source of important truths about the history of poetry and prosody but positioned the magazine itself as the source for true information about the modern poetry the academy neglected. Monroe and her coeditors capitalized on the organization of departments of national literatures, which generally taught very little contemporary writing, to position *Poetry* as the solution to a perceived educational crisis. It is well documented that contemporary literature was generally viewed as the domain of literary clubs and societies within the relatively young modern language departments in US universities in the 1910s; contemporary writing was believed to have a life of its own outside the university. But Monroe and her coeditors painted the lack of contemporary poetry in the university classroom as a scandal, particularly around the time they were developing the anthology of the New Poetry. In the January 1915 issue of *Poetry*, for instance, Alice Corbin Henderson argued that "a scientific department conducted as a literary department is conducted, with no consideration of the achievements of the last thirty years, would be a disgrace to any college."[22] The ads Monroe circulated for her lectures likewise played up *Poetry*'s status as the single source for information about modern poetry. An ad from the 1910s declared that "probably no one else has had so good an opportunity as the editor of *Poetry* for thorough acquaintance with . . . the New Movement in

Poetry. The magazine, which began as a pioneer in a new field, is now the recognized centre of influence in this art."[23]

Monroe's attempt to create educational resources for the study of modern poetry and poetics through strategic alliances with and critiques of the academy is central to understanding the role of the prose editorial apparatus in each issue of *Poetry*. Carr notes that "Monroe and her editorial team" used this space to "trenchantly set out the case for the new in poetry" and argues that Monroe was "very open about what kind of shape that 'new poetry' would take, whether drawing on ballads or jazz like Lindsay, or the free verse speech rhythms of Sandburg, or the pared down *vers libre* of Imagism, or Wallace Stevens's elegant and elusive stanzas."[24] But openness is far from the whole story here, as the invocation of Vachel Lindsay as a "jazz" poet indicates. Throughout Monroe's tenure as editor, the editorials in *Poetry* drew on contemporaneous academic theories about the origins of poetry to make the case that the "new" in poetry came from a return to "pure" racial sources and that it was the job of white poets to refine these racial materials into a new modern literature. Like the academics discussed in chapter 1, Monroe and her editorial colleagues understood literary and racial evolution to be connected, and they upheld the primitivist, Gummerian ideal that modern metrical discourse could help return an alienated and overcivilized society to the vitality of premodern cultures while maintaining a core white racial identity.

Monroe was interested in the idea that there were innate connections between racial groups and particular poetic experiments—an idea that emerged out of debates about communal origins in the US academy in the 1910s and 1920s, as we have seen. Part of Monroe's desire to engage with these arguments came from her sense that scholars were at last nailing down fundamental truths about rhythm and meter in English poetry.[25] This mattered to Monroe because, she believed, contemporary poets could create better, more culturally significant poetry if they better understood the core principles behind the development of poetic forms. As Monroe argued in 1918, a renewed interest in scientific studies of poetic rhythm in universities meant that "the poet of the future, . . . proceeding upon exact knowledge, will greatly develop and enrich our language-rhythms. . . . The poet hitherto has worked in the dark. . . . Henceforth science will lend her lamp; she will hand him the laws of rhythm just as she hands to the painter the laws of light and color, or to the architect the laws of proportion and stress."[26]

The laws Monroe believed scholars were finally uncovering had everything to do with how academics were imagining a white American race in this moment. As I argued in chapter 1, in the 1910s and 1920s, literary scholars were still interested in the search for poetic origins that had so occupied Gummere from the 1870s on precisely because it seemed to promise "exact knowledge" of the history and laws of English and American poetry and the racialized people who produced such poetry. While much changed in scholarly discussions of communal origins in the 1920s as disciplines emerged and shifted, as I discuss in more detail in this chapter, certain key tenets remained constant. The idea that human cultures evolved stadially, for instance, was an especially sticky one in poetics, where a Hegelian theory of the evolution of genres continued to hold sway. That is, the idea that all cultures necessarily developed through the same stages of expression, from a communal, oral epic poetry to individualistic lyric poetry, remained popular as *Poetry* began to make its case for the what it saw as the truth about poetic laws.[27] The frequency with which *Poetry* put forth this evolutionary version of poetic history is startling, and it speaks to the way Anglo-Saxonist ideas about racial evolution and temporality shaped conversations about free verse poetry. Particularly in the early days of *Poetry*, Monroe gave the Gummerian, Anglo-Saxonist version of English poetic history in as many venues as she could.[28] In short, this version of history had it that, as Gummere had argued, Anglo-Saxon poetry had been unalienated, free from arbitrary conventions, "vital," and "racy," as opposed to text-bound, overly classicized, imitative, formally constrained modern poetry. Contemporary free versifiers were rediscovering this Anglo-Saxon heritage. It was not a coincidence that the rediscovery of the Anglo-Saxon roots of free verse was primarily happening in the United States, according to proponents of this version of literary history, because white Americans were simply the latest wave of Aryan migrants who continued their world-conquering march westward. In this vision of poetic history, a return to the metrical principles of premodern Anglo-Saxon poetry could also help modern readers return to the unalienated communal sociality that Anglo-Saxons had enjoyed. Poets and readers could, in other words, recapture a premodern vitality in modern metrical discourse, reshaping alienated social relations through art. Crucially, it was believed that the superior "absorptive" powers of Anglo-Saxons positioned them as the only racial group that could take up all that was good about cultures that had not or could not attain the level of development Anglo-Saxons had supposedly reached—especially African American and Indigenous cultures—without absorbing what were perceived to be the inherently antisocial and antiprogressive elements of these cultures. Free verse, as another chapter in an Anglo-Saxon poetic history, was thought to be the proof of a new high point in the development of the "world-conquering" Aryan race.

It bears repeating that this highly selective Anglo-Saxonist version of poetic history was an invention of the nineteenth century. As Meredith Martin has shown, the popular nineteenth-century genre of the metrical history (versified accounts of English history meant to help students remember the succession of English kings, among other historical episodes) helped to cement the idea that English meters and an English national identity—rooted in an imagined pre-Norman, Anglo-Saxon past—were inextricably linked and developed progressively. As Martin notes, these metrical histories generally "began before 1066, returning to a pre-Norman past, rewriting the Battle of Hastings as 'the Norman yoke,'" while also "appealing to vernacular and less complicated verse structures, mostly ballads and tetrameters," thereby helping to imagine Anglo-Saxon accentual verse "as a native and natural form in English."[29] (It also bears repeating that this narrative of the naturalness of Anglo-Saxon accentual meter relies on the "suppress[ion] [of] the internal 'others' of Saxon-derived dialects" as part of "the process of standardizing English grammar.")[30] Metrical histories, along with a generalized enthusiasm for all things Anglo-Saxon and the expanding role of public education, helped to popularize the idea that "pre-Chaucerian meters"—especially Anglo-Saxon accentual meters—were "unifying . . . folk-meters of the people."[31] By the end of the nineteenth century, it was widely accepted that both English meter and English national identity were "progressive, chronological, and tied to a glorious past of either classical or ancient English origin."[32]

The idea that this past was specifically Anglo-Saxon picked up steam toward the end of the century, as Anglo-Saxonist nationalist movements became more influential.[33] The Anglo-Saxonist version of metrical history was ideologically appealing because it seemed to show that English meters—and the people who developed them—were freer and more democratic than classical meters and cultures. This was the argument Lindley Murray made in his best-selling *English Grammar* (first printed in 1795 and reprinted in 1824; sixteen million copies were sold in the United States alone).[34] Murray argued that English went beyond and improved on classical prosody because of the native instinct for accent. As Martin notes, Murray made the case that "our accent allowed English feet pleasure and freedom, as opposed to those fixed Greek and Latin feet."[35] Histories of meter like Murray's were "evolutionary narratives of England's progress," and these progressive narratives appealed to prosodists in the United States who wanted to see their country as further improving on English metrical and political institutions.[36]

Harriet Monroe is not often thought of as a prosodist, but she wrote pro-lifically about English prosody. And like her nineteenth-century counter-parts, Monroe connected metrical and national development and repeatedly narrated versions of the Anglo-Saxonist history of English meter. One of her earliest iterations of this history appeared in the September 1915 issue of *Poetry*, in an article titled "Chaucer and Langland." Monroe argued that the titular poets represented the Gallic and the Teutonic influences on Anglo-phone literature, respectively, and that, while Chaucer's refined, cosmo-politan sensibilities had been the major influence on English poetry through at least the nineteenth century, Langland's Teutonic influence was finally be-ing felt in modern free verse. In Monroe's words, "English poets have done [Chaucer's] will for centuries" in "prefer[ing] rhyme and the three-time iam-bic measure to the alliterations and assonances, and the harsh irregulari-ties, of the pounding four-time measure derived from . . . Saxon tradition."[37] But this Norman-inflected Chaucerian tradition of prosody was, according to Monroe, waning thanks to the influence of Walt Whitman's free verse. Fol-lowing Fred Newton Scott and other academics who had argued that Whit-man was a link in the chain of Anglo-Saxon greatness, Monroe argued that Whitman was "the first great modern poet . . . to put aside altogether the renaissance patterns" and that, while "he did not consciously return to the music of the sagas—the Gothic motive, as it may be called—yet his free verse is more allied to Langland than to Chaucer; it has more in common with the old Anglo-Saxon bards than with Shakespeare or Milton or Swinburne."[38]

Not incidentally, in making the case that modern free verse was a return to Anglo-Saxon rhythms, Monroe drew on popular myths about Anglo-Saxon democracy. Following the widespread Anglo-Saxonist myths that Germanic peoples were inherently more democratic than other "races" and that they had a talent for spreading this democracy worldwide, Monroe argued that Langland had been "a great democrat" who "made the crowd the subject of his epic" and "a great seer" who "looked forward to the end of [the] miseries [of the poor], not through mythical compensations in heaven, but through increase of justice on earth," in contradistinction to the aristocratic Chau-cer, who "took the world as it was."[39] The return of modern poets to the Teu-tonic tradition represented by Langland meant also a continuation of the spread of Anglo-Saxon democracy worldwide. She argued that Chaucer had led his successors to "accep[t] his aristocratic point of view . . . and almost entirely ignor[e] the burden-bearing poor" but that "Langland is like to bridge the centuries and clasp hands with the poets of the future, the prophets of the new era, toward which the world is marching through blood and fire."[40]

Thus, the "world-encircling language" of English was returning to its Germanic roots and, in the process, to Germanic democratic ideals.[41] According to Monroe, this return to Anglo-Saxon poetic culture was poised to become dominant worldwide: "the impetus toward free verse . . . which is evident in so much modern poetry—French and Italian as well as English"—showed that "Langland and his Old-English predecessors will have increasing influence," so that "we shall have a new realization of their power of imagination and of the splendor and variety of their rhythms."[42] This mattered not only because Anglo-Saxons were believed to have a unique talent for democracy but also because Anglo-Saxons (and their poetry) were believed to have been fundamentally communal. In the Gummerian framework, such premodern civilizations created strongly rhythmic, communally oriented art, which had the potential to help modern alienated readers overcome the shattering individualism of the modern era. It may have seemed as though Chaucer had won "the war of *kultur*" that had been "fought on English soil," but, according to Monroe, the rise of free verse showed that it was Langland, the Anglo-Saxon democrat, who would at last prevail.[43]

The argument that modern free verse was a return to an Anglo-Saxon tradition was not a one-time event for *Poetry*; it was something Monroe attempted to drill into readers, both inside and outside the pages of her magazine. I offer here an incomplete sampling of essays in which *Poetry*'s editors connected modern free verse with Anglo-Saxon poetry. This cataloguing is important because the frequency with which Monroe and her collaborators made this argument has been so completely written out of contemporary scholarly accounts of *Poetry* and of free verse. Monroe and Henderson used the introduction to their anthology of the New Poetry (1917), for instance, which Monroe had pitched as a guide to modern poetry for college students, to again highlight the Anglo-Saxon roots of free verse. The introduction repeated the argument that "Chaucer may have had it in his power to turn the whole stream of English poetry into either the French or the Anglo-Saxon channel. . . . He naturally chose the French channel, and he was so great and so beloved that his world followed him" and that if Langland "had had Chaucer's authority and universal sympathy, . . . Shakespeare, Milton and the rest might have been impelled by common practice to use—or modify—the curious, heavy, alliterative measure of *Piers Ploughman*, which now sounds so strange to our ears."[44] Any time that poets attempted to "restore" the "direct relation" with contemporary life that pre-Chaucerian poets had enjoyed, according to Monroe and Henderson, poetry as an art form experienced a revitalization that made it relevant and popular to readers once more. They again singled out Whitman as the poet who had most recently reinvigorated poetry and called on poets and critics "to inquire . . . into the origins of English poetry, in the effort to get behind and underneath the instinctive prejudice that English poetry, to be poetry, must conform to prescribed meters."[45] In their account, English poetry was, at its core, a free and open art form that admitted many different kinds of "free" verse, while French poetry was responsible for duping readers into thinking that poetry should be metrically regular and derived from textual rather than oral literary traditions. Monroe and Henderson argued that American poets would lead the way out of this Francophone metrical cage.

In 1918, Monroe reviewed the Columbia professor William Morrison Patterson's *North American Review* article "New Verse and New Prose" and "rejoice[d] that he agrees with us in linking up the present free-verse experiments with the ancient Anglo-Saxon rhythms, an authentic but long-neglected tradition to which the present editor has paid tribute in her introduction to *The New Poetry—an Anthology*."[46] Glenway Wescott's 1921 review of new translations of classical verse posited that H.D. "writes English as hard as Anglo-Saxon, and cultivates no continental suavities," once again implicitly making a connection between Anglo-Saxon poetic rhythm and contemporaneous free verse.[47] In the April 1923 issue, the Northwestern University professor of philosophy Baker Brownell published a piece called "Kinaesthetic Verse," in which he argued that "our traditional poetry" had "appreciated [the] fundamental muscularity of words" until Chaucer eclipsed Langland in popularity. The pre-Chaucerian "muscular values" of words had been lost to view in the course of the development of printed poetry, according to Brownell, leading to an underestimation of the importance of the Langland tradition of "muscular" verse. Modern poetry was, however, a return to this Anglo-Saxon sense of poetry, and "what has seemed to conservatives a breakdown of poetry"—free verse—"is a change in emphasis from sound to the muscular experience of words."[48]

The tone of Margery Swett's 1924 article "Free Verse Again" shows just how widely accepted *Poetry* thought this argument about the Anglo-Saxon roots of free verse should be. Swett explained, with some aggravation, that she had been commissioned by Monroe to write about free verse because, although "the subject of free verse was treated by *Poetry* so thoroughly at various times . . . that the editor had thought the topic exhausted," it had "been revived with a certain energetic eloquence, and recent letters seem to imply that *Poetry* is still expected to act as champion." And so Swett dutifully reminded *Poetry* readers that "free verse is older than the English tongue," repeating Monroe's earlier position that "the iambic measure with rhyme was a French fashion domesticated in England by Chaucer, whose genius made it the standard form in English, but that the Anglo-Saxons had preferred alliteration in a much freer metrical scheme." Modern free verse, according to Swett, had to be understood as the endeavor of "an individual or a race [to] be free to express itself in its own rhythm and idiom."[49] The following year, Monroe returned to the idea that prosody was connected to racial identities and that free verse was specifically the expression of the Anglo-Saxon race. Indeed, Monroe outright analogized free verse to race, arguing, "Scientific tests and measurements show me no essential difference between the wild one [meaning free verse] and the rest of the tribe. Free verse and all varieties of metrical verse seem to me blood brothers and sisters, and the differences between them—mere matters of costume and manners—cannot affect the racial strain."[50] Monroe then reiterated that English was "more or less derived from the speech of the barbarians whom Caesar fought," meaning Germanic tribes.[51] According to Monroe, free verse was fundamentally a racial expression—the form proper to Anglo-Saxons and their descendants. Throughout the 1910s and 1920s, *Poetry*'s editorial apparatus made it clear that free verse was an Anglo-Saxon form. It was, in short, the poetry of white people.

It is not an overstatement to say that *Poetry*'s adherence to Anglo-Saxonist metrical histories shaped everything about its editorial decisions and its theorizations of poetry and poetics, from its embrace of free verse and of white "interpretations" of Indigenous songs to its ambivalent approach to Black poetic forms. Perhaps most shockingly, editorials in *Poetry* explicitly and uncritically invoked the myth of Aryan migration and used this framework as a way to understand modern poetry as a global phenomenon led by the United States. As Reginald Horsman has explained in his classic study of Anglo-Saxonism in the United States, nineteenth-century philologists had helped to popularize the idea that "a specific, gifted people—the Indo-Europeans [also known as Aryans]—[had] spilled out from the mountains of central Asia to press westward following the sun, bringing civilization, heroism, and the principles of freedom to a succession of empires."[52] In the United States, this myth was used to justify the imperial expansion of the country, particularly its genocidal treatment of Indigenous peoples and its military incursions into the Caribbean and the Pacific. *Poetry*'s editorials invoked this myth throughout Monroe's tenure. In a review of John Neihardt's *The Song of the Indian Wars* in the March 1926 issue, for instance, Berenice Van Slyke explained that, while it may have seemed odd to Neihardt's readers that he used Greek titles in a poem about Native Americans, "Mr. Neihardt may reasonably say that in the great wave of Aryan migration of which these Indian wars are only an incidental adventure, we are cousin to the Greeks."[53] By situating the United States' military actions against Native American nations as part of "the great wave of Aryan migration," Van Slyke explicitly and economically makes the case that white American settlers were but the latest wave of westward Aryan migration, thereby perpetuating popular nineteenth-century ideas about US empire as natural and inevitable and justifying the domination of a "weaker" race by a "world-conquering" race. The same sentiment appeared in Margery Swett's 1925 review of Clifford Gessler's *Slants*, which featured poetry about Gessler's adopted home of Hawai'i. Swett explained that "wanderlust is rich in the blood of Americans, we are a nation built by those who push farther and still farther West until some reach, on an island in the Pacific, the last outpost of our frontiers, the place where West meets East."[54] Like the authors of nineteenth-century metrical histories, Van Slyke and Swett naturalized a connection between the advance of poetic form and the advance of empire.

Even in moments that have been read as evidence of *Poetry*'s liberal cosmopolitanism, Monroe reiterated her commitment to this Anglo-Saxonist worldview. For instance, scholars tend to read the fact that *Poetry* published Rabindranath Tagore in the early 1910s as evidence of what Newcomb calls the magazine's "intercultural modernity" and "commitment to cultural reciprocity."[55] But even this commitment to cultural exchange was tinged by racial Anglo-Saxonism. Monroe explained in 1913 that she was so enthusiastic about Tagore in part because "the important revelation in this great Hindoo's [sic]" work was "not the antagonism but the sympathy between the two vast branches of the Aryan stock."[56] That is, Tagore was important to *Poetry* because his work seemed to show the imagined lost ancestral connection between the branch of Aryans who became Anglo-Saxons (otherwise known as "Indo-Europeans") and the branch that stayed in Asia.

Editorials in *Poetry* often argued that American free verse, as a return to Anglo-Saxon racial instincts, provided evidence that the Aryan migration westward had indeed been successful and that Anglo-Saxon Americans could become indigenous to their settled lands. Editorials that made these arguments almost ritualistically repeated the Anglo-Saxonist metrical history outlined earlier in an effort to prove the existence of a distinctly American, distinctly modern poetry rooted in this Anglo-Saxon past. In the August 1917 issue, for instance, in response to a *Yale Review* article by Henry Seidel Canby on "the American impulse to take to the woods," Monroe tied the Langland-versus-Chaucer version of literary history to a mythology of American pioneer culture.[57] Monroe begins the essay by invoking her reaction to the Anglo-American myth of the first Thanksgiving, explaining that she "had always read the story with solemn sympathy for the pilgrims until that hardy woodsman, Hamlin Garland, pointed out how absurd it was to starve in those forests filled with game. 'The fools,' he said, 'they hadn't sense enough to learn of the Indians. . . . But their sons learned.'"[58] The rest of the essay constructs a kind of double history for American poetry that roots it both in Anglo-Saxon racial traits and in stolen land and appropriated cultural practices. According to Monroe, the first Anglo settlers of the lands that became the United States had failed to "learn of the Indians" about the lands they settled, getting caught up instead in imitating European arts and cultural practices. In leaning so heavily on texts and ignoring the landscape around them, these settlers forsook their innate Anglo-Saxon ability to capture the vitality of lived experience in oral poetry. The present generation of poets, however—especially those writing free verse—had turned back to nature for inspiration and hence were tapping into the imagined spontaneity and naturalness of early Anglo-Saxon poetry. Monroe explained that "the dust of civilization" had covered over the Anglo-Saxon ability to truly capture "the power and grandeur of the wilderness" until Henry David Thoreau and Whitman began to "shake off" that dust by experimenting with freer metrical forms.[59] She tied modern poetic experiments to Anglo-Saxon nature poems, arguing that "perhaps it remains for our poets to feel wild immensities on land as the old Anglo-Saxon poet felt them at sea. They made a good beginning with Whitman."[60] Good free verse was a return to an Anglo-Saxon aesthetic born out of an Anglo-Saxon experience of the natural world. Monroe explained that imitative art was "infinitely confusing and wearying," but "the wilds" offered "refreshment," which could lead to "an art more indigenous and original, more truly our own, than all the feudal operas we sing or the Doric-temple railway stations we build."[61]

In addition to being proof of a return to an Anglo-Saxon aesthetic feeling for nature, free verse also indicated to Monroe that American settlers had finally "learned of the Indians." According to Monroe, the most vital experiments in free verse, the most successful efforts to "feel wild immensities on land as the old Anglo-Saxon poet felt them at sea," could be found in the poems from Indian motives of Dr. Gordon, Miss Skinner, Mrs. Austin, Alice Corbin and others, as well as in direct translations by Natalie Curtis and other students; in John Gould Fletcher's poems of Arizona and other wild places; in C. E. S. Wood's *Poet in the Desert*; in Edith Wyatt's spacious poems of the Great Lakes and the western heights; in Vachel Lindsay's poems of Kansas and the plains. And the spirit of it, though not precisely the locale, one finds in such a poem as Mr. Frost's *Snow*; in certain things by Mr. Masters, Mr. Sandburg, Mr. Johns; and in H.D., who, however preoccupied with Greek symbols, is essentially a poet of wild nature, a daughter of the pioneers.[62]

Monroe connected an American "pioneer" spirit with Anglo-Saxon nature poetry, arguing that these instances of free verse based on "Indian motives" and the American landscape would ultimately lead American poets to "bear great gifts to the mother tongue and those who speak it" and to "achieve a real refreshment, perhaps a re-creation, of the race."[63] Modern poetry mattered as a reinvigoration of the Anglo-Saxon race, a return to the creative vigor of these imagined ancestors, and the creation of a culture that would supplant and perfect "primitive" Native American cultures. In rediscovering the Anglo-Saxon roots of free verse, this narrative went, contemporary poets had also discovered how to mold Indigenous sources of inspiration in order to claim them as the property of white poets.

Monroe and her collaborators embraced Indigenous cultures as proper sources of inspiration for white American poets in part because, in the 1910s and 1920s, it seemed to many white Americans that the United States' genocide of Indigenous peoples had been successful. Indigenous peoples were not an active threat to empire; they were also not US citizens until 1924, and hence incorporation into *Poetry*'s version of American poetic history happened on much different terms than did the incorporation of other groups who were citizens. There is much more to be said about *Poetry*'s and other modernist institutions' extractive approaches to Indigenous expressive cultures—indeed, so much more that I return to this topic in chapter 4. While *Poetry*'s settler colonialism was inextricably intertwined with its anti-Blackness, the magazine's editorials had to work much harder to deal with the place of Black songs and poems in an American tradition than they did to incorporate Indigenous songs and poems, which the magazine took to already be the rightful property of white poets. I turn now to the tortured logics Monroe and her coeditor Henderson used to claim Black folk materials as essential to the construction of modern American poetry while at the same time barring almost all Black authors—and all Black women authors—from publication in their magazine's pages.

Form, Formlessness, and the American Folk

As scholars including Martin, Yopie Prins, and Jason Rudy have shown, metrical histories such as the Anglo-Saxonist metrical history outlined earlier provided powerful organizing structures for theorists who wanted to strengthen a sense of national identity.[64] Martin notes that, in the context of England in the era between 1860 and 1930, "the desperation to provide rules for English meter is often powerfully allegorized, for poets and prosodists, as akin to providing rules for civilizing and educating the unruly masses of the quickly developing welfare state."[65] In the United States in the Jim Crow/modernist era, prosodical histories analogously seemed to offer a way to make sense of the complicated racial makeup of an imagined American community. The long-standing idea that metrical history could be a civilizing force became, in *Poetry*'s pages, a way to turn Black expressive cultures into the property of white American modernist poets—especially when those poets were white women and white children, who functioned within the magazine's pages as figures of futurity and potential.

The way that *Poetry* approached the poetic traditions of different racialized communities reflected a number of developments in ethnography, anthropology, and folklore studies in the 1910s and 1920s—fields that Monroe and Henderson were keenly attuned to.[66] The search into the origins and laws of poetic rhythms and forms that was taking place across these emerging disciplines, where Gummere's communal origins hypothesis was being challenged and revised, seemed both to confirm the Anglo-Saxonist version of literary history and to open a window onto a new phase of that history. For Gummere and his generation of scholars, "genuine" folk poetry was what they called a "closed account." That is, the material conditions that had given rise to what scholars deemed "genuine" English and Scottish folk ballads no longer existed, and hence genuine folk poetry could no longer be produced. As Gummere's mentor Francis James Child had argued, the culture that had produced genuine ballads "was produced by a singleness of faith, feeling and social class that was no longer possible" under the conditions of modernity.[67] This premodern culture had "facilitated a ballad poetry of unalienated simplicity which modern poets aware of their individual creativity could no longer reproduce."[68] Modernity had ushered in the collapse of what had been cohesive, collaborative communities that produced art collectively into a mass of individuals competing for fame as singular authors.

The increasing availability of ethnographic reports about "primitive" cultures in the 1910s and 1920s, along with the emergence of anthropology and folklore as academic disciplines, began to change this view of ballads and folk poetry as a closed account. As Regina Bendix notes, after Child's and Gummere's generations, "younger scholars collected songs, including ballads, in the United States" and started to "refus[e] to classify them as spurious, even if they did not conform to [the Harvard School's] arbitrary ballad criteria."[69] Instead of categorizing *poems* as genuine or imitative, focus shifted to categorizing *cultures* as "genuine" or "spurious," to use the anthropologist/linguist (and frequent *Poetry* contributor) Edward Sapir's influential formulation.[70] Gummere and like-minded scholars had believed there was no return to a premodern mode of sociality, but Sapir's idea of "genuine" cultures, in which "nothing is spiritually meaningless," helped to spur thinking that there were still pockets of premodern, unalienated sociality even in the modern world.[71] "Genuine" cultures were also "primitive" cultures, which were believed to have materially preserved a premodern stage of human development. The Gummerian search for poetic origins that had been focused on the philological authentication of texts thus became a search for cultural and racial authenticity, as Bendix (along with many scholarly accounts of modernist primitivism) so thoroughly documents.

The problem for white editors, scholars, and critics of poetry in this era was thus what to do with the materials ethnographers were collecting, particularly since so much energy was focused on collecting African American folk materials. As Henderson argued, these folk materials constituted a "genuinely racial and distinctly valuable contribution" to an American literary tradition," but they also seemed threatening to Henderson because of their nonwhite origins.[72] The threat and promise of primitivism for white modernists is of course well-trod scholarly territory.[73] However, the way that Monroe and Henderson used ideas about plasticity—the perceived ability of differently racialized bodies to produce new cultural and biological forms— to neutralize that perceived threat has not been fully appreciated. Building on their pet argument that free verse was a return to Anglo-Saxon racial rhythms, Monroe and Henderson repeatedly argued that the supposed genuineness of Black folk cultures mattered only when they were taken up by white poets, who could give form to these materials in ways that Black poets seemingly could not. Put slightly differently, Monroe and Henderson struggled with the question of how Black folk materials (everything from Paul

Laurence Dunbar's dialect poetry to spirituals to folk tales—anything that could be theorized to be originally authored by an imagined Black folk) fit into a white American poetic tradition.[74]

Poetry was obsessed with Black folk cultures of the US South, which it took to be simultaneously the foundation of much of American culture and an aesthetic failure—everything and nothing, a vital source of raw material that Black poets had been unable to make coalesce into recognizable aesthetic forms. According to *Poetry*, it was instead white women with ties to plantations who were capable of creating forms from this raw material, making explicit a connection between the production of new, experimental poetic forms and the reproduction of whiteness as a mode of anti-Blackness. If Black folk materials seemed to threaten a coherent American poetic tradition with their supposed formlessness, then white reinterpretations of those folk materials seemed to head off that threat, creating form and order from a "genuine," "primitive" source that could not be refined by the people who produced it. This, I am proposing, is why *Poetry* repeatedly returns to the plantation as the source of modern American poetry: In the editors' understanding of poetics, only whiteness can produce form, and the production of new forms is the hallmark of good modern poetry.

Poetry's investment in the US South is routinely overlooked, but the South—particularly a romanticized vision of the plantations of the antebellum South—was one of the magazine's key fixations. While *Poetry* published only four Black poets during Monroe's editorship (Fenton Johnson, Countee Cullen, Langston Hughes, and Santie Sabalala), the magazine frequently reviewed books by Black male poets, and in nearly every one of these reviews, the magazine stressed the inability of these poets to turn Southern Black folk materials like spirituals into new poetic forms. The first book by a Black author to be reviewed in the magazine was Fenton Johnson's *Songs of the Soil* (1916; I discuss this book in more detail in chapter 3), which was reviewed by Henderson. Henderson's review began with the claims that, "although indirectly, the negro has contributed not a little to certain developments of American art, particularly in music, musical shows and folk-stories. But he has himself benefited very little, or been very little concerned individually with the achievements that bear the imprint of his race."[75] According to Henderson, Black folk culture was a vital source for American art, but individual Black artists had not succeeded in making that folk culture into meaningful new poetic forms. Henderson drew on the long tradition of portraying Black artists as fundamentally imitative to argue that the dialect Johnson used in *Songs of the Soil* was merely an imitation of Paul Laurence Dunbar, who had merely imitated Thomas Nelson Page and Joel Chandler Harris.[76] Henderson urged Johnson and other contemporary Black poets to "discard this prop [dialect] and invent a new and individual idiom based upon the characteristic speech of [their] people."[77] There was, in Henderson's telling, no such thing as a formal poetic innovation that had been created by Black poets.

The argument that Black poets were imitative rather than innovative was repeated almost as often as the argument that free verse was an Anglo-Saxon form in *Poetry*'s pages. In an omnibus review of works by James Weldon Johnson, Charles Bertram Johnson, Waverley Turner Carmichael, and Joseph S. Cotter (which notably took up less than half a page, while reviews of single books by white authors in the same issue ran up to five pages), published in 1920, Helen Hoyt explained that "the Negro race has given so much musically to America that we look eagerly for signs of what we may expect in poetical contribution. But a mere half-century after the Emancipation is too soon to make even a forecast."[78] The brief notice mentions that James Weldon Johnson's *Fifty Years* "is the most important of the volumes here grouped," but beyond that, the only mention of the other books is a quotation from Charles Bertram Johnson, which Hoyt uses to argue that "even Paul Laurence Dunbar's achievement of a few fine poems . . . does not quite satisfy the aspirations of his race."[79] A 1920 review of Countee Cullen's first book, *Color*, argued that "the many elements [of poetic craft] which have entered that reservoir below the threshold of [Cullen's] consciousness have undergone as yet no thorough chemistry."[80] A 1926 "News Note" about the "Negro Poets' Number" of *Palms*, another modernist little magazine published out of Guadalajara, Mexico, argued that the issue's introduction by Walter White misrepresented the state of Black poetry by portraying it as innovative.[81] The anonymous author of the note explained that White's introduction "mentions the achievements of the American Negro in all of the arts and near-arts, declaring that 'in no one field . . . has so much been done as in poetry,'" which the author argues is an erroneous point of view, "since it seems to us that up to a few years ago little poetry of striking interest had been written by the Negro, except a few poems by Dunbar."[82]

Poetry's stance about the fundamental imitativeness of Black poets did not waver even in the 1930s, when the power and originality of the work emerging from artists associated with the Harlem Renaissance seemed to many critics to be undeniable. A dismissive "Brief Notice" of Sterling Brown's *Southern Road* in the May 1934 issue, for instance, argued that "a negro student who has progressed in his poetical technique to the point indicated by the youthful stanzas in *Part Four* of this volume, can no longer consider himself a primitive, and must achieve, in attempting to go back to his racial beginnings, no more than a mongrel effect. He has followed Housman, Shakespeare, and other masters of English lyricism too far. His salvation lies in following them farther."[83] According to the reviewer, Brown remained imitative and had failed to create anything new, linguistically or formally. Harold Rosenberg's 1936 review of James Weldon Johnson's *Saint Peter Relates an Incident: Selected Poems* was similarly damning, arguing that "it is possible to respond favorably to [Johnson's] verses" only "when the great folk-song tradition of his people flows over his poetry, as in some of the dialect poems."[84] In *Poetry's* telling, the individual Black poet consistently failed to raise folk art into a new poetic form.

Poetry was also consistent in its argument about who was capable of creating new poetic forms from Black folk materials: white women. In a review of James Weldon Johnson's *God's Trombones* in 1927, Harriet Monroe predictably argued that, in Johnson's work, "the authenticity is less complete, the art less perfect" than in Joel Chandler Harris's work. She then lamented that Johnson had not "let himself go a little more rashly; for the creation myth, as I heard Lucine Finch repeat her old mammy's version, was more powerfully poetic than Mr. Johnson's."[85] Lucine Finch was a white writer from Alabama who toured the United States performing what she called "Mammy Stories," apparently in a more properly "poetic" form than Johnson's. Reviews of other white women writing poetry based on Black folk materials were similarly glowing. Eunice Tietjen's 1916 review of Ruth McEnery Stuart's *Plantation Songs and Other Verse*, for instance, argued that Stuart had written "negro dialect songs of the best type, gay, humorous, rollicking and tender, full of sympathy and rioting with color. It is safe to predict that some of these . . . will be chanted and loved in nooks and corners of the earth for many a long year. . . . Uncle Remus himself might have written the negro songs!"[86] Monroe's 1927 review of Beatrice Ravenel's *The Arrow of Lightning* likewise singled out its fine "Negro numbers," which seemed to Monroe to "have a fresh lyric quality" that poems by Black poets apparently lacked.[87]

Even when the magazine published a positive review of work by a Black poet, it still managed to make a connection to white women on Southern plantations. *Poetry's* review of Langston Hughes's *Fine Clothes for the Jew*, published in 1927, was written by Julia Peterkin, who praised Hughes's poems because some of them struck her as "curious examples of the Negro rhythms to which I am accustomed on our plantation."[88] Indeed, Peterkin was a favorite contributor to *Poetry* precisely because of her perceived access to the genuine folk culture of the antebellum plantation. As was noted in the November 1923 issue of the magazine, which featured free verse poetry in dialect by Peterkin, "Julia M. Peterkin . . . has resided since her marriage in Lang Syne Plantation, at Fort Motte, S.C.," where "for years she has studied the habits of life and speech among the Negroes on the estate."[89] Peterkin's dialect poetry is the closest *Poetry* under Monroe came to publishing work by a Black woman; Peterkin's "Venner's Sayings" purported to be a free verse "transcription of the utterances of the most ancient member of the colony, . . . a very dark African woman nearly a century old, who has remained on this Lang Syne plantation, slave and free, ever since her birth."[90]

Peterkin was in many ways *Poetry*'s ideal writer. She seemed to have access to a pocket of Black culture that existed out of time (according to *Poetry*, the isolation of the Lang Syne Plantation meant that "the three hundred or more black people living there, being descendants of the first families imported, have retained their primitive customs and superstitions to an unusual degree," and Peterkin took transcriptions of individual speech patterns and stories and turned them into free verse, thereby giving a modern form to the supposedly timeless formlessness of "authentic" Black folk culture.[91] In Peterkin's poetry, it seemed that the authentic American poet could remain white even as the plantation remained the source of new poetic forms. Peterkin allowed Monroe and Henderson to imagine that white women had "picked up the thread where the primitive Negro poet dropped it," as Henderson put it in a 1920 article on American folk poetry, taking Black women's lives as literary property while barring Black women poets from the pages of *Poetry*.[92]

Perhaps the clearest statement of the idea that new poetic forms—and renewals of white American identity—emerged from the plantation was published in the first of two "Southern Numbers" that *Poetry* put out in April 1922 (the second was published in May 1932; both featured exclusively white poets). In this issue, Monroe gave a whopping thirteen pages to DuBose Heyward and Hervey Allen's manifesto "Poetry South" (most essays in the magazine were between two and six pages), which forcefully argued that the plantation was the source of the most vital modern poetic forms. Heyward and Allen argued that Northern American poets had rightly been searching for original poetic forms ("creative art from its very nature must be original") but that they had wasted their time by "ceaseless[ly] experiment[ing] with alien forms."[93] They explained that because "the South is still predominantly agricultural . . . the plantation of one kind or another is still the economic, vital unit," meaning that "when the plantation poet speaks," it will be in order to "reflec[t] in simple measures the patriarchal life remnant about him."[94] According to Heyward and Allen, the plantation was the direct source of new poetic forms that would be indigenous rather than "alien."

The fact that *Poetry* identified the plantation as a key source of new poetic forms, combined with its repeated insistence that white women were the best plantation poets, indicates Monroe and Henderson's investment in literary plasticity—the production of new poetic forms—as a function of racial plasticity. Or, put slightly differently, the magazine aligned the future of American poetry with figures of white reproductive futurity even as it recognized the importance of Black folk art to American poetry. The way that Monroe and Henderson connected the production of new poetic forms to figures of white reproductive futurity is perhaps most apparent in their treatment of Vachel Lindsay. *Poetry* was an early and vocal champion of Lindsay—an enthusiasm that critics tend to read as a lapse in judgment on Monroe's part. But such a reading misses how central Lindsay was to Monroe and Henderson's vision of a future-oriented, experimental white poetic tradition. Throughout the 1910s and 1920s, *Poetry* made the case that Lindsay was one of the few poets to have successfully used Black folk materials to create a distinctly American poetry and that this mattered specifically to young white children who were learning poetic rhythms from his salutary example. The investment in teaching *Poetry*'s readers to understand the Anglo-Saxonist version of prosodic history that I traced earlier in this chapter thus eventuated in a second pedagogical project: teaching readers to understand that the telos of that metrical history was modern American poetry, built in part from Black folk materials but authored exclusively by white poets.

To give a sense of how enthusiastic *Poetry* was about Lindsay, during Monroe's twenty-four-year tenure as editor, the magazine published fifty-two poems and seven prose pieces (books reviews, essays, letters) by Lindsay. Lindsay mattered so much to *Poetry*'s editors because he seemed to have successfully domesticated what was threatening to white thinkers about Black poetic rhythms, thereby incorporating an "inheritance" of Black folk materials without making Blackness essential to an American identity. Henderson argued, in her 1920 assessment of the state of "The Folk Poetry of These States," that Lindsay had "improvised upon Negro themes precisely as the sophisticated musician improvises upon folk-melodies" so successfully that "the genuine folk-quality in his Negro poems is indisputable."[95] And, even more importantly, in Henderson's telling, Lindsay's poetic transmutation had made these materials digestible for white children, teaching them to internalize "primitive" rhythms so they could one day make refined art from those raw rhythmic materials.

In Henderson's review of Lindsay's *The Congo and Other Poems* from March 1915, she argued that Lindsay's poetry mattered because its "growth has been peculiarly independent of foreign influence"—it was distinctly American.[96] And this distinctly American poetry was already subtly working to influence a new generation of white American poets. Henderson claimed to "know several small children to whom that poem ["Dirge for a Righteous Kitten," panned by many reviewers] is as meat and drink, and who, with this as a starting-point, have quickly assimilated all the deep round vowel sounds and rolling bass of *The Congo* as well as the light graceful step of *Judith the Dancer*—again not a bad thing for the future of poetry in these states!"[97] Henderson's food metaphors invoke what Kyla Wazana Tompkins identifies as "the theme of the black body as food . . . in American culture," which indexes the "white desire to consume and internalize blackness."[98] Citing bell hooks, Tompkins notes that "in 'eating the other' the white self affirms liberal interiority through the metaphor of assimilation and digestion," so that "blackness is the precondition . . . on which whiteness is made material."[99] In Henderson's metaphor, Lindsay provides white children with the meat and drink that will help them to grow and materialize their own poetic abilities. Their white subjectivity is constituted by their "assimilation" of the supposedly Black sonic landscape of Lindsay's *The Congo*, but this assimilation also obliterates Blackness, which is subsumed in Lindsay's white body and in his young readers' white bodies. As Tomkins argues, "the white desire to devour black subjectivity also indicates the desire to annihilate it, to recognize the black subject only in terms of her capacity to regenerate whiteness."[100] This is precisely what Lindsay seemed to offer to readers of poetry: the capacity to regenerate whiteness through the assimilation and obliteration of Black culture. This process of assimilation and obliteration, in *Poetry*'s telling, was the key source of new, innovative poetic forms like free verse in the early twentieth century.

This violently rapacious desire is evident in the essays and notes Lindsay published in *Poetry*. In a piece titled "Mr. Lindsay Protests Against Jazz" in the February 1923 issue, Lindsay explained that he "very much resented being called a 'jazz poet,'" because "jazz is hectic, has the leer of the badlands in it, and first, last and always is hysteric. It is full of the dust of the dirty dance. The saxophone, its chief instrument, is the most diseased instrument in all modern music; it absolutely smells of the hospital." According to Lindsay, jazz had "blasphem[ed] . . . the beautiful slow whispered Negro spirituals," so that contemporary Black art had failed to make good on the authenticity of Black folk forms.[101] Lindsay's description of jazz echoed the common folkloristic logic, identified by John W. Roberts, in which "the discovery of new forms of vernacular creativity among African Americans comes to be seen as a sign of pathology rather than of vital creative energy within African American communities."[102] According to *Poetry*, Black folk materials could only become part of modern poetry if they were sanitized through their assimilation by white poets and readers—especially young white poets and readers. For Henderson and Monroe, as for Gummere, the metrical, rhythmical training of white children promised to direct the racial evolution of white Americans.

Rethinking Race and Poetic Form

I have focused on unpacking *Poetry*'s pointed exclusion of Black women from its pages and on secondary scholarship's continued erasure of that erasure, not to call out individual prejudice but to highlight the necessity of a deeper investigation into the structural imbrication of gender, race, and poetic form in modernist periodicals and in modernist studies more broadly. I have been making the case that feminist recovery work has often privileged gender as an analytic lens without considering gender as an always raced and racializing category. Similarly, studies of race and modernism often overlook the ways that race is a gendered and sexuating category. Thus, on the one hand, there have been compelling accounts of Monroe and Henderson's important editorial contributions to modernist poetry and poetics, cited in the introduction to this chapter, and on the other, there have been incisive studies of Monroe and Henderson's eugenicist, anti-Black, and anti-Indigenous thinking by Robin Schulze, Elizabeth Barnett, and Michael P. Taylor, respectively. Scholarly attention to Monroe and Henderson's editorial importance and their primitivist acts of cultural appropriation have been salutary, but they have also missed the fact Monroe and Henderson promoted free verse as a specifically Anglo-Saxon form. Similarly, the link *Poetry* cemented between white women and children and free verse has been noticed but not fully unpacked in scholarship on modernist poetry. For instance, in Suzanne Churchill and Ethan Jaffee's entry on the "New Poetry" in *The Oxford Critical and Cultural History of Modernist Magazines*, they note that "unreserved enthusiasts proclaimed that the rhythms of free verse were more natural than metrical poetry," citing the *Poetry* contributor Constance Lindsay Skinner's stance that "children and humble folk without 'learning' naturally sing their way into the rhythms of the psalms." Churchill and Jaffee note too that "the idea that free verse was a natural expression of the human body generated a slew of somatic metaphors. Free verse was called 'barefoot' and 'corsetless.' . . . These somatic metaphors associated the emancipation of poetry with the discourses of feminism and women's suffrage."[103] But of course, these somatic metaphors were racialized and were eugenic as often as they were (purportedly) liberatory.

In *Poetry*'s telling, Black authors generally, and Black women authors specifically, were barred from a poetic modernism focused on new poetic forms like free verse from the outset because they were understood to be the experimental subjects of plantation modernity rather than experimental writers or cultural innovators. If the plantation, as a "laboratory space," to use Brit Rusert's terms, where all kinds of experiments with "the possibilities and limits of sex, gender, and reproduction" were conducted, was the source of raw material for new poetic forms, as Monroe and Henderson argued it was, then Black women and men could only ever be the producers, not the refiners, of that raw material.[104] (As Amy Clukey notes, "the promise of the plantation" is precisely to "cultivat[e] raw materials for commodity production.")[105]

This is the crucial backstory to *Poetry*'s famed gender parity. And this is why, even during the height of the Harlem Renaissance, *Poetry* almost entirely ignored or dismissed poetry by Black male authors and did completely ignore all poetry written by Black women. Indeed, rather than give space to the many poetic innovations of Black writers of this era, the magazine published multiple special features on white children's poetry, along with an entirely white "Women's Issue."[106] Unpacking *Poetry*'s racial/gender politics more fully thus helps to provide a deeper historical understanding of the long association of experimental literary form with whiteness and can help us to imagine what antiracist literary histories of experimental poetic modernism and of modernist little magazines might look like. Rather than reading modernist periodicals in search of the formal innovations they championed, we might look instead for the structuring absences and racializing, sexuating logics at play in the development of modernist periodicals and poetic cultures.

Thus far, I have analyzed the production of free verse as an Anglo-Saxon form in the US academy and in *Poetry* magazine. It remains to be seen how Black and Indigenous poets navigated this white supremacist framing of free verse and poetic innovation. I turn now to the only Black poet to have free verse poems published in both *Poetry* and its avant-garde counterpart *Others*: Fenton Johnson.

CHAPTER THREE

Fenton Johnson's Poetic Genealogies

In the November 1918 issue of *The Crisis*, Alfred Kreymborg, editor of the avant-garde little poetry magazine *Others: A Magazine of the New Verse*, published a poem titled "Red Chant." The poem begins by addressing Kreymborg's fellow poet Fenton Johnson:

> There are veins in my body, Fenton Johnson—
> veins that sway and dance because of blood that is red.
> There are veins in your body, Fenton Johnson—
> veins that sway and dance because of blood that is red.

The poem ends by exhorting Johnson,

> Let us go arm in arm down State Street—
> let them cry, the easily horrified:
> "Gods of my fathers,
> look at the white man chumming with the black man!"[1]

Kreymborg's direct address to and fantasized walk with Johnson indicates Johnson's significance for white artists who styled themselves as the poetic avant-garde in the early twentieth century. Indeed, Johnson was one of the few Black poets whose work appeared consistently in the "experimental" little magazines most closely associated with free verse. Johnson was the only Black author to have work published in both *Poetry* and *Others* (he was also the only Black poet *Others* published), and his free verse poems were widely anthologized, with "Tired" remaining a classroom staple to this day. It is thus striking that, although Johnson sometimes appears briefly in accounts of experimental writing,[2] Johnson almost never figures significantly in histories of free verse or of modernist periodicals or modernist poetry more generally, unless those histories are specifically about African American literature and modernism.[3] Johnson tends to be treated as a minor figure whose experimental work was promising but who ultimately disappeared after becoming increasingly embittered with the literary world. But Johnson's complex engagements with multiple poetic cultures deserve much more than a footnote or a passing mention. I argue in this chapter that standard critical approaches to modernist poetic forms have rendered Fenton Johnson's serious theorization of poetry and poetics illegible to contemporary critics.

While scholars including James Smethurst and Lorenzo Thomas have argued that Johnson is a foundational figure in modernist literature, even scholarship like theirs that works to restore Johnson to his proper stature tends to dismiss the large body of poetry Johnson wrote before he started writing free verse. These accounts attend solely to Johnson's formally "experimental" writing, which consists of thirteen free verse poems published in *Poetry* and *Others*. The bulk of Johnson's poetry is left out of this scholarship, and so the close to two hundred poems collected in Johnson's three published volumes of poetry, *A Little Dreaming* (1913), *Visions of the Dusk* (1915), and *Songs of the Soil* (1916), go unread, dismissed as conventional or uninteresting or even "insipid," in the more caustic assessment of James P. Hutchinson.[4] For instance, Thomas, one of Johnson's most careful and illuminating readers, makes the case that "race consciousness . . . informs much of [Johnson's] poetry regardless of the poetic fashion he decided to employ," and yet Thomas rejects the possibility that Johnson's "three published volumes of dialect and conventional lyrics" could be more formally complex than has previously been understood.[5] Thomas goes so far as to argue that Johnson's third volume, *Songs of the Soil*, "can be understood as a necessary clearing of the throat, a last glance at dialect verse that allows Johnson to proceed with the experiments that would yield his best poetry."[6] The phrase "conventional lyrics" conflates the many different formal and aesthetic traditions Johnson engaged in his published volumes and helps to maintain the sense that his free verse was experimental while his earlier work was not. Similarly, while Smethurst argues that "Black writers of the Nadir" including Johnson were crucial to the development of what was retrospectively named literary modernism, suggesting the ways that literary historical periodization can obscure the complicated political and cultural work of "conventional" literary genres and forms, he still correlates convention with conservatism.[7] In reviewing the legacy of Johnson's *Champion* magazine, for instance, he argues that the works it published, "including Johnson's stories and poetry, remained relatively conservative formally," and hence Smethurst turns away from this work toward Johnson's seemingly more significant free verse poems in order to make the case that Johnson "helped build the infrastructure of the new avant garde [sic]."[8]

In the rare cases when scholars do attend to *A Little Dreaming*, *Visions of the Dusk*, and *Songs of the Soil*, they generally proceed by picking out poems that can be read as precursors to Johnson's more famous free verse poems so as to claim him as an avant-garde poet who consciously left behind Victorian and Romantic aesthetics.[9] Few critics have asked which specific nineteenth-century genres, forms, and traditions Johnson engaged with in his books of poetry.[10] Put simply, the critical insistence that Johnson was most important as an avant-garde modernist poet misses the opportunity to investigate what, exactly, specific nineteenth-century poetic traditions seemed to offer to Johnson as a poet invested in theorizing race through experimentation with a wide array of genres and forms throughout his career. As it turns out, understanding Johnson's engagement with nineteenth-century poetry is crucial to a fuller understanding of his free verse.

Scholarship on Black Victorianism and Black Romanticism has shown that Victorian and Romantic poetry were integral parts of politically engaged African American literature well into the twentieth century. Daniel Hack, building on work by Frances Smith Foster, Carla Peterson, Ann DuCille, and Vanessa Dickerson, among others, has shown that "Victorian literature . . . was called upon repeatedly and revealingly by African American authors and editors through the turn of the twentieth century" in "a self-conscious tradition" of citation, rewriting, and recirculation.[11] While Hack's concern is not the modernist era, his work yet reminds us that the common conflation of the descriptors "Victorian" or "nineteenth century" with value judgments like "outmoded" or "conservative" within modernist studies of poetic form covers over the ways that "African American writers and intellectuals in the nineteenth and early twentieth centuries . . . leveraged nineteenth-century . . . literature in their very efforts to cultivate racial solidarity, to claim a distinctive voice, and to establish a distinct tradition of literature."[12] Similarly, Matthew Sandler reminds us that "Romanticism did not disappear from African-American culture with the onset of the twentieth century" and that the works of the Harlem Renaissance, "the little magazines and salons of the New Negro movement," and Black music coming out of the Jim Crow South all owed significant debts to Romantic models of poetry and language.[13]

In Johnson's case, engaging with nineteenth-century poetic genres and conventions—especially those genres and conventions that were central to nineteenth-century abolitionist activism—was key to countering white modernist constructions of literary history like those found in *Poetry* magazine, which pointedly skipped over the poetry of the nineteenth century. Johnson focused on specific genres like the ode and the historical epic to show that these genres had been and continued to be key to organizing specific publics around shared political goals and were thus central to the continuously unfolding and unfinished project of global Black liberation. Johnson's historiography went against the grain of both Black and white accounts of American literary history; as Meredith McGill notes, "for the most part, modernist poets had little interest in engaging either the history of slavery or the [nineteenth-century] poetry that opposed it."[14] This meant that accounts of African American literary history in the modernist era tended to follow the pattern identified by Joan R. Sherman, in which "black poetry began with Phillis Wheatley, . . . disappeared for over one hundred years, and only reemerged with Paul Laurence Dunbar."[15] Throughout Johnson's career, he resisted this critical disappearance of nineteenth-century poetry—especially the revolutionary abolitionist poetry of Black Romantics like Frances Ellen Watkins Harper, who lived until 1911, just one year before *Poetry* magazine was founded, and only two years before Johnson published his first book.[16] In his magazine *The Champion* and in his three published books of poetry, Johnson attempted to bring into view the unfinished business of the nineteenth-century poetic genres and conventions that Black poets had used to envision Black liberation, highlighting what the white modernist abstraction of genre into form risked forgetting or rendering illegible. To Johnson, an investment in nineteenth-century poetry was precisely an investment in poetic experimentation and in what he saw as the linked toppling of white supremacist regimes of value. It is my contention that Johnson was not clearing his throat to make way for modernism in his early works; he was imagining new world histories and futures, in part by rewriting nineteenth-century poetic genres for a new political era.

In this chapter, I attend to Johnson's magazine *The Champion* and to his three published books of poetry so as to consider Johnson as a serious poetic theorist in his own right. Each of the three sections in this chapter shows how Johnson thought about connections between literary history, poetic experimentation (in the broadest possible sense: experimentation with established genres and forms as well as with emerging forms), and the overcoming of white supremacist thinking in the cultural and social life of the early twentieth-century United States. In the first section, I explore how Johnson used his monthly magazine to counter the white supremacist poetic histories that were being put forth in the pages of *Poetry* in the 1910s and to construct global Black literary lineages. The Afrocentric literary histories published by *The Champion* help to illuminate what made Romantic poetry a vital resource for Johnson. In the second section, I show how Johnson used the poems of Frances Ellen Watkins Harper, Albery Allson Whitman, and Black interpellations of the poetry of George Gordon Lord Byron to give shape to the political anger that accompanied his hopes for racial uplift in the early twentieth century. Johnson redirected the prophetic visions of this abolition-ist poetry to imagine what Black liberation in the twentieth century might look like. For Johnson, that liberation depended on generic literacy and mo-bility for Black authors—the ability to lay claim to all kinds of specific ge-neric poetic traditions, from Black Romantic odes to dialect poetry to free verse, in order to represent the fullness of Black diasporic life and the po-tential for future forms of Black liberation. As I show in the third section, attending to Johnson's overlooked program of generic and formal virtuosity gives us a new way to understand Johnson's free verse poetry. Against criti-cal accounts that position Johnson's turn to free verse as the full flowering of his poetic talents, I argue that, read through the lens of Johnson's early books, we can see that Johnson's turn to free verse instead marked the di-minishment of his poetic ambitions. Whereas his "conventional" work was extraordinarily formally mobile and expansive in vision, Johnson's free verse was marked by constriction and constraint—formal, cultural, and geograph-ical. Ultimately, I show how a historical poetics approach to free verse might help us to begin to read this form differently—for the cultural possi-bilities it foreclosed as well as for those it seemed to open up.

Chicago's *Champion*

Though *The Champion* only ran for a little over a year (September 1916–April 1917), it was, as Richard A. Courage and James C. Hall argue, "a signal contribution to early twentieth-century African American cul-tural production—rich in intellectual content and attentive to the diversity of the pan-African world."[17] As Johnson wrote in the introductory issue, the magazine was "born of the desire to serve a struggling race impartially" and had "the aim to make racial life during this twentieth century a life worth liv-ing" by "impress[ing] upon the world that it is not a disgrace to be a Negro, but a privilege."[18] *The Champion* covered everything that could fall under the heading of "Negro achievement," to borrow the subtitle of the first issue. Each issue included illustrations, a "Pictorial Review of Recent Race Events," short news items, fiction, poetry, cultural criticism, and athletic news (covered by Johnson's cousin, the track star and world record holder Binga Dismond). The list of contributors to *The Champion* was impressive; as Courage and Hall note, Johnson was adept at "engag[ing] leading African American intellectuals across the country as contributors and editorial collaborators."[19] For instance, *The Champion* had the distinction of running Marcus Garvey's first US publication ("West Indies in the Mirror of Truth" was published in the January 1917 issue).[20] Johnson's achievements with *The Champion* were all the more remarkable because his sole source of financial support appears to have been his wealthy uncle, the famed banker Jesse Binga, at a time when many successful Black periodicals "had the benefit of close association with organizational structures that provided editorial support, capital investment, and a ready audience of individuals associated with a distinctive ideological position or investment in a specific pathway to racial uplift or civil rights."[21]

In part because *The Champion* was a general interest magazine for middle-class Black readers, while *Poetry* specialized in poetry and poetics and catered to white readers, scholars generally do not discuss the two publications together. But Johnson was aware of all that was happening in *Poetry*'s Cass Street office, which was located just over seven miles away from *The Champion*'s State Street headquarters, and Johnson shaped aspects of *The Champion* in response to *Poetry*. Indeed, Johnson visited *Poetry*'s office at least once, as his correspondence with Monroe indicates, and he often used *Poetry* as a benchmark for Black creative achievement. For instance, in the March 1917 issue of *The Champion*, Johnson wrote, "we desire to see Colored Chicago lift herself out of the slough of esthetic despond," and he argued that "the same agencies that produced Harriet Monroe's 'Poetry' Magazine should go into the highways and byways and discover those who can best give the world pictures of both the realistic and the emotional side of Negro life in this unique city."[22] Even as late as the 1930s, in an unpublished poem titled "Rosemary for Chicago Poets," Johnson gave Monroe top billing as a force in the Chicago literary scene:

> Can you forget the glorious days
> When Harriet Monroe's eyes as fire
> Burning from a volcano on Cass Street
> Consumed half a world grown dead?[23]

As is clear from the records he left, Johnson read *Poetry* attentively, making it all the more notable that, from the very first issue of *The Champion*, it began countering the Anglo-Saxonist literary history that *Poetry* put forth.[24] While Monroe and Henderson argued that Black American culture was fundamentally composed of imitations of European cultural forms and that contemporary Anglophone poetry (especially free verse) could be traced back to a vigorous Germanic past, *The Champion* argued for the primacy and superiority of African cultures in the development of Western civilization. *The Champion* took every opportunity to publish historical counterprogramming to *Poetry* that reminded its readers that the history of poetry—indeed, the history of Western civilization—was always already Black history.

The inaugural issue of *The Champion*, published in September 1916, included a historical survey by George W. Ellis titled "The Outlook of the Negro in Literature," which argued that the alphabet itself was a Black invention, making all literature foundationally Black. Ellis, who had served as a diplomat in Liberia and who had penned the scholarly work *Negro Culture in West Africa* (1914), explained that "Diodorus ascribes the very origin of philosophy and science to the Negro in Ethiopia before even the appearance of Egyptian civilization," a view "confirmed by Lucian," Volney, and, more recently, the anthropologists Giuseppe Sergi and William Z. Ripley.[25] According to Ellis, without the "alphabet and hieroglyphics" developed first in Ethiopia, there would simply be no "science, art, philosophy and religion"—no modern world at all.[26] William Ferris, a graduate of Harvard and Yale and author of the monumental work *The African Abroad, or His Evolution in Western Civilization* (1913), repeated this message in the December 1916 issue of *The Champion*, arguing that "we now know that what is called the Aryan or white man's civilization in its first principles was worked out by black men in the Negroland and Kingdom of Meroe in Africa in the valley of the Nile and transmitted to Ethiopia, thence to Egypt and from Egypt to Greece and from Greece to Rome."[27]

Ellis and Ferris, in these and other articles, participated in what Wilson Jeremiah Moses, following St. Clair Drake, calls "the African American vindicationist tradition," which sought "to establish the credentials of the black race by showing that it had contributed to civilization in the dawn of history."[28] As Johnson knew well, the vindicationist view of history turned the discourse of the Germanic folk on its head, using the same historical sources as did communal origins theorists to show, against the romanticized view of Anglo-Saxons, that Germanic cultures were barbaric and stunted compared to their African counterparts. For example, Alexander Crummell and Edward Wilmot Blyden—two figures Johnson mentions admiringly in editorials throughout the run of *The Champion*—both turned to the same passages in Tacitus that inspired Anglo-Saxonists, but Crummell and Blyden read these passages against the grain to find proof of the barbarity of Europeans. As Moses notes, Crummell and Blyden saw in Tacitus evidence "that pristine African villages were in some ways more healthy than European cities," and Crummell in particular "graft[ed] the myth of the virile Germanic barbarian onto the virile barbarian of the West African forest" in order to valorize the premodern vigor of African societies and to denigrate the relative backwardness of European tribes.[29] What Monroe promoted as Aryan vigor and vitality became, in the vindicationist tradition, evidence of the imitative, inferior cultural development of Europeans.[30]

Articles like Ellis's and Ferris's also signal Johnson's engagement with a tradition of Black bibliography reaching back to the nineteenth century, which "focused on ancient African and Egyptian history to prove the greatness of Black peoples and civilizations prior to enslavement."[31] As Jacqueline Goldsby and Meredith McGill note, "these 'grand narrative' bibliographies (to recall scholar-activist Abdul Alkalimat's rubric) aimed to collect materials printed across the Black diaspora . . . to knit together global networks of Black print communities."[32] In part because, as Elizabeth McHenry argues, the early twentieth-century "literary landscape was, for Black writers, still very much under construction," "lists and bibliographies" like those *The Champion* provided to its readers "were a crucial mode of African intellectual practice" that generated "structures through which their creators worked to assemble and sort elements of Black print culture to make it both visible and useable."[33] Against essentializing discourses like those about Anglo-Saxon and "primitive" rhythms, which worked to stabilize ideas about racial identity as biological fact, such bibliographic projects helped to present diasporic Black cultures as textually and historically mediated and as multifarious and ever-changing instead of static.

Johnson's interest in making Black literature "visible and useable" for diasporic readers and authors is readily apparent in every issue of *The Champion*. In the column "The Editors' Blue Pencil" in the second issue (October 1916), for instance, Johnson begins by listing a familiar litany of Black cultural accomplishments — "the early culture of Babylon and Nineveh was the culture of the Negro. . . . Negroes fought under Hannibal in the Punic wars. Jugurtha was a Negro. Negro soldiers helped to establish the supremacy of Islam in North Africa and early Spain. Great leaders of Mohammedan civilization were Negroes" — and ends by celebrating Pushkin, Dumas, W. S. Braithwaite, and Booker T. Washington, who, in this telling, take up the mantle of Black greatness from their Egyptian and Babylonian forebears.[34] George Ellis's article "The Outlook of the Negro in Literature," quoted earlier, also stressed the continued vibrancy of Black literature, drawing links between the early modern writings of African authors including Ahmed Baba and Abderrahman Sadi; the linguistic prowess of early modern scholars and writers including Juan Latino, Anthony William Amo, and James Eliza John Capitein; and the literary accomplishments of more well-known figures such as Olaudah Equiano, Phillis Wheatley, Edward Wilmot

Blyden, Alexander Pushkin, Alexandre Dumas *pére*, Alexander Crummell, W. E. B. Du Bois, Charles Chesnutt, Paul Laurence Dunbar, Alice Ruth Dunbar, William Stanley Braithwaite, and, of course, Fenton Johnson. According to Ellis, just as it seemed to *Poetry*'s editors that white free versifiers were returning to the glories of their Anglo-Saxon ancestors in the 1910s, "the Negro in the very highest forms of life and literature is reclaiming the lost prestige of his ancient glory."[35]

The Champion was especially interested in the contributions of Black women to American life, particularly in the realm of literature. Here too, *The Champion* provided much-needed counterprogramming to *Poetry*, which, as I discussed in chapter 2, published and reviewed no work by Black women during Monroe's tenure as editor. The February 1917 issue of *The Champion*, for instance, featured a long review by William Ferris of a new edition of Phillis Wheatley's poems, published by Arturo Schomburg and Charles Fred Heartman. The layout of the article, spread across two pages and followed by the poem "Pilgrims" by Georgia Douglas Johnson, implicitly establishes a lineage running from Wheatley to Douglas Johnson, emphasizing the ongoing, intertextual, collaborative project of Black literary creation.

The content of the review of the Wheatley volume echoes the content of Douglas Johnson's poem as well. Ferris weighs various assessments of Wheatley's writing and ultimately sides with Schomburg, who argues that "there was no great American poetry in the eighteenth century and Phillis Wheatley's poetry was as good as the best American poetry of her age."[36] Ferris argues that there could be no great poetry then because "when the clearing of forests, the blazing of trails, the building of roads, the tilling of fields, the development of agricultural resources, the warring with the Indians and the French, the settling of political differences with the Mother Country, were the things of main import in American life, . . . there was little time for day dreaming, musing and meditation."[37] The settlers mentioned in the review morph into the titular pilgrims of Georgia Douglas Johnson's poem, countering the common whitewashing of national history to remind readers that the work of settler colonial nation building was done in large part by enslaved laborers. In full, Douglas Johnson's poem reads,

> Winding a steep and rugged trail,
> Up from a sunless, sullen vale,
> A weary band of pilgrims grope,
> Out of its shadowings, to hope.

The scaling chromatique of woe,
Their viol-throated voices know,
And yet they lift to grief's caress,
A smile, unmixed with bitterness.

Within their wake, an oozing stain,
Is vocal, of a voiceless pain,
When smiling eye a desert keeps,
The bleeding heart in silence, weeps![38]

The invocation of sorrow songs and spirituals ("The scaling chromatique of woe") suggests that the pilgrims coming out of a dark valley into hope are formerly enslaved people, forever marked by the "oozing stain" of the institution of slavery but also rising out of this past into a new future. (While the poem is abstract enough that it could be argued that it is not specifically about living in the wake of enslavement, it is notable that Douglas Johnson's poem "The Passing of the Ex-Slave," published in *Bronze* in 1922, refers to ex-slaves as "These uncrowned Pilgrims of the Night.")[39] *The Champion*'s careful page design, then, does double historiographical work. It establishes a network of Black women's poetry reaching at least as far back as Wheatley and up through Georgia Douglas Johnson, and it corrects the frequent whitewashing of historical accounts of the eighteenth-century United States, reminding readers that the labor of enslaved and free African Americans was crucial to the growth of the nation, materially, politically, spiritually, and literarily.

The Champion's forging of links between authors whose lives were temporally separated by centuries speaks to Brigitte Fielder's argument that the metaphors of genealogy we use to envision Black modernity can best be understood "not as a progressive, biological lineage, but as a complex network of kinship."[40] The genealogies *The Champion* presented its readers encouraged them to develop a sense of cross-generational memory and continuity that was not necessarily oriented in a straight line of influence from past to future. The difference between the kind of kinship network of Black poets Johnson advanced and the stadial metrical histories put for by *Poetry* cannot be overstated. Against historical accounts that would render figures like Wheatley and Frances Ellen Watkins Harper relics of a distant past, whose couplets and tetrameters had been superseded by the organic rhythms of Anglo-Saxon free verse, *The Champion* stressed the ongoing resonance of those figures in the present moment. The same February 1917 issue that established the link between Wheatley and Douglas Johnson, for instance, was the "Douglass Centennial Number," which also featured articles by

Richard T. Greener and by Archibald Grimké offering personal stories of Greener's acquaintance with Frederick Douglass and exhorting young readers to remember the lessons offered by this great man's life, respectively, along with a reprint of part of Douglass's "Bloody Shirt" speech of 1888. The issue reminded readers that there were still living memories of Douglass and other prominent Black nineteenth-century figures, resisting the cordoning off of a monolithic, outdated past from the modern twentieth century. The March 1917 issue similarly included a section on the Colored Old Settler's Club of Chicago, titled "Prominent Chicago Negroes of Early Days," as well as a cartoon by Fon Holly of "The First Settler of Chicago," which reminded readers that this founding figure was "a fugitive slave from San Domingo, named Point De Sable."[41]

To Johnson, creating this sense of cross-generational continuity was not simply a matter of looking backward; it was a fundamental way of ensuring vibrant Black futures.[42] In this way, we can understand Johnson's historicizing project in *The Champion* as being in line with Frances Smith Foster's theorization of Sankofa, an "Akan concept" that "translates, more or less, as the following imperative: 'We must go back and reclaim our past so we can move forward; so we can understand why and how we came to be who we are today.'"[43] This connection between historical consciousness and future-oriented thinking is perhaps most evident in *The Champion*'s untimely review of a bound edition of *The Anglo-African Magazine* (1859). *The Anglo-African Magazine*, edited by Thomas Hamilton, was a landmark in African American publishing. *The Anglo-African* is, "according to all available evidence, the first black literary magazine," created at a time when the Black publishing world revolved around newspapers.[44] Johnson's choice to review this bound edition in 1916 was curious, since there were no reprints of the volume until 1968.[45] But it is not difficult to see why Johnson, as the editor of a Black magazine with literary ambitions, would have been interested in *The Anglo-African Magazine*. As Ivy Wilson notes, *Anglo-African* editor Thomas Hamilton's target audience was "the nation's small but growing free black middle class," just as Johnson's target audience was the Black middle and upper classes of Chicago.[46] Too, as Mary Fair Burks notes, *The Anglo-African* had great literary ambitions, expressed concisely in Frances Ellen Watkins Harper's article "Our Greatest Want," published in the November 1859 issue. In this piece, Watkins Harper "sounded the clarion call to blacks to leave propaganda for *belles lettres*" and to "prove [themselves] in the field of imaginative literature."[47] Hamilton's advertisements for his magazine also stressed Black literary self-determination, arguing that "[Negroes], in order to assert and maintain their rank among men must speak for themselves. No outside tongue, however gifted with eloquence, can tell their story; no outside organization, however benevolently intended, however cunningly contrived, can develop the energies and aspirations which make up their mission."[48] As the Black editor of a literary magazine who believed that the expansion of the Black middle class and Black literary success were crucial to Black life in the United States, Johnson recognized the importance of *The Anglo-African* as a forerunner to his own editorial venture. Indeed, Johnson makes explicit Wilson's observation that "the *Anglo-African* is a precursor to later periodicals like the 1924 special issue of *Survey Graphic* and the single 1926 issue of *Fire!!*"[49] While *The Champion* does not have the stature of *Survey Graphic* or *Fire!!* within periodical studies, Johnson's ambitions for his magazine can be seen in his alignment of *The Champion* with *The Anglo-African*. Like Hamilton, Johnson sought to make a space for Black literary endeavors and to create a sense of Black historical excellence as the basis of future achievement.

Tellingly, Johnson's review of *The Anglo-African Magazine* focused on William J. Wilson's short story "Afric-American Picture Gallery," which was printed in seven installments in 1859. Given that the bound edition under review is four hundred pages long, it matters that "Afric-American Picture Gallery" is the only piece in the volume Johnson chooses to comment on extensively, particularly because the story is fascinated with temporality and historiography. The episodic story is narrated by Ethiop (Wilson's pen name for his work in *Frederick Douglass' Paper*), who, in the first installment, responds to the lack of "'distinguished *black*' figures in [New York art] galleries, and in American visual culture more broadly," by "tak[ing] readers through a virtual tour of a completely imagined gallery of art comprising sketches, paintings, and works of sculpture that represent black life in the United States and across the diaspora."[50] While this first installment "takes its normative form from the periodical genre of the urban sketch," subsequent installments get generically stranger, running from gothic to fairy tale to slave narrative.[51] Johnson's review focuses on the third installment, the plot of which he explains thusly: "The author purports to find a manuscript written in the year 4000 A.D., during the era of Negro supremacy, in which the passing of the white race is described. This extract will best give you an idea of what was in the Negro mind before the Civil War."[52] The plot is a bit more involved and intriguing than what Johnson here suggests. Ethiop is the guest of Bernice, a Black artist who lives in a house at the top of Black Forest Mountain. Bernice gives Ethiop a tour of his studio, where Ethiop finds paintings, sculptures, and drawings that rival Italian Renaissance masters. Bernice assures Ethiop that his work "will yet not only see the light, but command the just approbation of even the enemies of [his] race."[53] Curiously, as he surveys Bernice's work, Ethiop also finds a stone tablet that Bernice explains he dug out of the mountain. Ethiop describes the words on the tablet as "curiously spelt by the aid of 41 singular, new and beautiful characters, or letters, each representing a distinct sound; and so many only are employed as are necessary to make up each word": "I have by dint of hard study, been enabled to make out its contents; but of its history or origin, or aught else of it, I leave for the learned in such matters. It certainly challenges the attention of the Historian, the Ethnologist, and the Antiquarian. Is it fiction, is it history, is it prophecy? Who can tell?"[54] The tablet, bearing the title "Year 4,000. The Amecans, or Milk White Race," is addressed to "ye who dwell in this age of pure light and perfect liberty."[55] It tells the story of a forgotten people who enslaved the ancestors of those reading the tablet—a people who built a great civilization but who grew decadent and gradually weakened and disappeared. After reading the tablet, Ethiop is taken to an inner chamber of Bernice's studio, where he is shocked to find a white man in chains. Bernice explains that the man had once enslaved him and had destroyed his family and hence is doomed to live imprisoned in the cave until his death. Bernice tells Ethiop that he once "had a son, a son dear to [him]," who "despite oppression . . . [had] grown to beautiful manhood," until the enslaver "blew out the brains of [his] child without provocation and without warning; and would not so much as allow his body burial."[56]

I dwell on the details of Wilson's story because of how insistently they align Black artistry with futurity and white culture with a civilizational dead end. Not only does Bernice create stunning art that he is confident will bring him future fame, not only does he possess a mysterious tablet that seems to be from the distant future and that prophecies the extinction of the white race entirely, not only does that tablet show yet another instance of Black ingenuity in building a civilization (the creation of a new alphabet, the "age of pure light and perfect liberty"), but his studio also becomes the place where a white enslaver—and his family line—goes to die as punishment for his murder of the next generation of Black artists. As Eckstrom and Rusert note, Wilson's speculative piece was meant "to hail a radical black futurity that antebellum readers and writers might describe but not quite glimpse," and Johnson seizes on this vision of a historical power reversal as part of a larger vision of eventual Black liberation, even as he downplays the radical nature of the story.[57] ("This extract will best give you an idea of what was in the Negro mind before the Civil War.")

Johnson's interest in "Afric-American Picture Gallery" as a historical document that contained an enduringly radical vision of the future sheds light on why Romantic poetry—particularly the poetry of what Matt Sandler calls the "Black Romantic revolution"—continued to matter to Johnson in the twentieth century. Sandler argues that Black Romanticism was "an independent and distinct form of Romanticism" that "took shape among the Black writers of the US abolition movement and radical Reconstruction."[58] Black Romantic poets such as Frances Ellen Watkins Harper, Albery Allson Whitman, George Moses Horton, George Boyer Vashon, and James Monroe Whitfield "borrowed and transformed the techniques and theories of Romanticism in an effort to bring about the end of slavery and the self-conscious regeneration of Black community . . . and imagined their liberation as part of an ongoing, total cultural and political transformation."[59] As so many scholars of nineteenth-century American poetry have shown, antislavery and abolitionist poetry had a great deal of both "commercial success and . . . political force," as Meredith McGill puts it.[60] Johnson understood Black Romantic poetry to have ongoing revolutionary and prophetic force for twentieth-century Black poets, who faced a radically changed publishing environment and radically dashed hopes for post-Emancipation liberation. As Sandler notes, Black Romantic poets "did not seek the meager citizenship rights they were ultimately afforded; their visions of freedom remain unfulfilled today."[61] Johnson's use of this poetry in his own twentieth-century work highlights the ongoing project of Black liberation and reminds readers of the radical, disruptive force of supposedly outmoded nineteenth-century poetic conventions.

Looking back to the fiery prophetic poetry published by the *Anglo-African* contributor Frances Ellen Watkins Harper (1825–1911), one might well ask, as Ethiop does of the mysterious tablet, "Is it fiction, is it history, is it prophecy?" To Johnson, the answer to all of these questions was a resounding "yes." That is, Johnson presents linear, teleological conceptions of history as inadequate to the task of understanding past, present, and future struggles for Black freedom; only a palimpsestic return to past poetic, prophetic visions could capture the fullness of Black diasporic experience and the longed-for vision of a Black future. Johnson's review of *The Anglo-African*, along with specific references in his poetry, suggest that he was especially attuned to the Romantic poetic vision of Watkins Harper, whom Johnson called one of the "immortals" who helped to make *The Anglo-African* such a success and who had died only five years before *The Champion* began publishing.[62] What, specifically, did Johnson learn from Watkins Harper and her contemporaries? I turn now to Johnson's poem "Ethiopia," published in his second book, *Visions of the Dusk*, in 1915. This epic historical poem invokes Watkins Harper's poem of the same name (ca. 1846), along with Black interpellations of Byron, Albery Allson Whitman's "The Lute of Afric's Tribe" (1877), and Paul Laurence Dunbar's "Ode to Ethiopia" (1893), in order to construct a link between Black Romantic visionary prophecy, early twentieth-century Black diasporic life, and an unrealized future-tense freedom. Johnson's "Ethiopia" helps to show why nineteenth-century poetry remained a vital political and literary force for an author writing amid the polemical calls for poetic newness and formal experimentation in the 1910s.

Twentieth-Century Black Romanticism

Johnson found in Watkins Harper's poetry a resource for questioning narratives of historical progress and for imagining future Black liberation as a collective endeavor, mediated in part through poetry. As Magdalena Zapędowska has argued, Watkins Harper created in her poetry "a complex affective dynamic of protest and affirmation, rejection of injustice and anticipation of 'genuine freedom'" that acknowledged past and present injustices while keeping an eye on a future that could be created through collective action.[63] Crucially, Watkins Harper saw "intergenerational dialogue" as a key way to contest progressive narratives of history, creating "a racial sense of revolutionary time, in which ancestors and descendants work together to transform the future."[64] Johnson's "Ethiopia" picks up these ideas of intergenerational dialogue and of revolutionary time via its poetic allusions. The poem is a historical epic in blank verse that narrates Black history from its African origins to the present moment. The choice to write in the epic mode underscores Johnson's appreciation of Black Romantic poetic innovation, as African American epic poetry was a Black Romantic invention.[65] It also underscores the way Johnson's early poetry works against the kind of stadial metrical histories that Monroe and Henderson wanted to popularize. Because "Ethiopia" is a historical epic, with distinct sections narrating distinct moments in world history, it would have easily lent itself to such a vision of metrical progress. Johnson could have modeled the poem on metrical histories like Thomas Dibdin's *A Metrical History of England*, which attempted to narrate the history of distinct eras through representative meters, meaning that "the shifting style of meter" between historical episodes in the poem would "signa[l] a historical shift."[66] Rather than reinforce the sense of progressive, teleological metrical history through such shifting meters, however, Johnson narrates every episode in the same blank verse. At the same time, while the content of the poem moves chronologically, the poetic allusions do not, subtly suggesting, along with the steady metrical pattern, that progressive models of history are inadequate for understanding Black diasporic life. Instead, a concatenation of poetic styles, voices, and citations muddies the sense of linear temporality, creating a palimpsestic, choral model of history that can also function as a mode of prophecy. Against the romantic racialism of the Anglo-Saxon throng, Johnson marshals a dialogic poetics of citation and collaboration.

The muddying of linear temporality and the creation of intergenerational dialogue via citation begins immediately. Although the title of the poem echoes Watkins Harper's 1846 poem, Johnson's "Ethiopia" begins where Paul Laurence Dunbar's 1893 "Ode to Ethiopia" ends: with the invocation of the bard who will sing the past triumphs and future glories of Black history. The final stanza of Dunbar's ode, addressed to "Proud Ethiope's swarthy children," reads,

> Go on and up! Our souls and eyes
> Shall follow thy continuous rise;
> Our ears shall list thy story
> From bards who from thy root shall spring,
> and proudly tune their lyres to sing
> Of Ethiopia's glory.[67]

Dunbar's closing vision is of linear progress; he predicts a "continuous rise" for Black diasporic subjects as "Proud Ethiope's swarthy children" "go on and up." The predominating iambic pattern of Dunbar's lines mimics the rising motion of Ethiope's children, underscoring the inevitable glory of future freedom.

Johnson's poem begins by taking up the bardic mantle from Dunbar:

> O minstrel lyre of ancient Ethiop,
> Whose flaming song awoke the Orient,
> O long forgotten harp, whose mouldering strings
> Hath once enthralled the hearts of warriors,
> I pray thee let my burning fingers press
> Thee once again that I may sing my song
>
> . . . .
> I touch the ancient lyre, and burning sing
> The song of Ethiopia the Queen,

The song of her who sits among the gates,
Her eye upon the dawn of liberty and hope.[68]

Johnson references and redirects Dunbar's opening apostrophe ("O Mother Race! to thee I bring/This pledge of faith unwavering, this tribute to thy glory") from the figure of Ethiopia to the poet who can sing her song. Like Dunbar, Johnson calls up a long tradition of using "Ethiopia as an abstraction, as a metaphoric nationalizing of racial union" within African American literature.[69] Dunbar's abstraction of Ethiopia as the "Mother Race" primarily functions to celebrate Black achievement in the present tense; though it begins by casting a backward glance to the time "When Slavery crushed thee with its heel," the bulk of Dunbar's poem applauds the contemporary actions of Black diasporic peoples. Johnson's poem, by contrast, addresses "Ethiopia the Queen" in order to tell a more sweeping epic that imagines history as a cyclical, recursive, iterative project rather than as a progressive narrative. The resistance to narrating historical progress as inevitable or regular is mirrored in Johnson's meter; his iambs are less markedly regular than Dunbar's, in part because they lack the reinforcement of end rhyme and in part because of his pyrrhic substitutions at the end of lines ("Ethiop," "Orient," "warriors"). Unlike the "continuous rise" of Dunbar's metrical pattern, Johnson's meter stalls and restarts, the pyrrhic endings reinforcing the sense of the high costs of the nominal freedom of Emancipation.

Johnson's intergenerational dialogue perhaps also includes Albery Allson Whitman (1851–1901)—specifically, Whitman's poem "The Lute of Afric's Tribe" (1877). In Whitman's poem, as in Johnson's, the lute of the tribe is silenced ("O long forgotten harp") by oppression:

When Israel sate by Babel's stream and wept,
The heathen said, "Sing one of Zion's songs;"
But tuneless lay the lyre of those who slept

. . . .
So, when her iron clutch the Slave power reached,
And sable generations captive held;
When Wrong the gospel of endurance preached;
The lute of Afric's tribe, tho' oft beseeched,
In all its wild, sweet warblings never swelled.[70]

In Allson Whitman's poem, the lute is revivified by abolitionist revolution:

And yet when Freedom's lispings o'er it stole,
Soft as the breath of undefiled morn,

A wand'ring accent from its strings would stroll—
Thus was our Simpson, man of song and soul,
And stalwart energies to bless us born.

. . . .

He sang exultant: "Let her banner wave!"
And cheering senates, fired by his zeal,
Helped snatch their country from rebellion's grave.[71]

Allson Whitman's poem causally links poetry and revolution, making the poet who could play "the lute of Afric's tribe" the figure who could "fire" soldiers and politicians to revolutionary action. As Sandler notes, "The titular 'lute of Afric's tribe' functions like the Aeolian harp of Romantic thought, a medium for the enactment of Black liberation. . . . Whitman imagines [fellow abolitionist poet Joshua McCarter] Simpson's rise as a correspondent breeze, 'Freedom's lispings' across the strings of that lute, and his music thus performing the self-realization of Black peoplehood."[72] Johnson revives this image of the bardic poet as revolutionary. At the moment that the singer of "Ethiopia" declares, "I touch the ancient lyre, and burning sing/The song of Ethiopia the Queen," Ethiopia keeps "Her eye upon the dawn of liberty and hope," once again linking poetry and revolution. Too, Johnson's meter revivifies Whitman's, as "Freedom's lispings" once again play across the lute of Afric's tribe to create iambic pentameter lines that keep the hope of more than nominal freedom alive.

While the figure of the bard is of course highly conventional and found across a wide range of poetry, the concatenation of Watkins Harper, Dunbar, and Allson Whitman in the title and opening of Johnson's "Ethiopia" signals an investment in a specifically African American literary tradition and in Black imaginings of bardic nationalism. As Sandler notes, Allson Whitman's poem in particular is "unique in the period for its address to another Black poet" and is "a crucial document in establishing the internal coherence of Black Romantic aesthetics, and in connecting Black Romantic lyrics to longer-term conceptions of African-American culture."[73] In playing on Whitman's lute, building a new song out of the poems of Dunbar and Watkins Harper, Johnson creates a chorus of Black poets singing revolutions accomplished and revolutions yet to come. In this way, Johnson crafts what Brigitte Fielder calls "a polyphonic vocality that speaks to modernity from multiple vantage points."[74]

The particular utility of Black Romanticism to Johnson's poetic chorus can perhaps best be seen in section 3 of "Ethiopia," which connects the Haitian

Revolution to Nat Turner's rebellion and to future, as yet unplanned rebellions. The first two sections of the poem are somewhat fatalistic; section 1 narrates the decline of a mythical ancient Ethiopia as part of the eternal rise and fall of all human civilizations ("So the will of God/Removes the nations, races, and the tribes,/Lest man should be the peer of God himself"), while section 2 is a diasporic lamentation about the rise of the European slave trade ("The haughty race that built the pyramids . . . / With bleeding wounds are prostrate to the west;/In bondage to the priest of Christ and love/Exiled the men of dusk must dwell a day"). Section 3 turns to narrate a temporary dawning of hope in the long struggle for freedom:

> The chains that man hath forged the heavens break,
> Divine is liberty the slaves achieve;
> And Hayti smoulders with the flames of dusk,
> Her saviour loving Toussaint, prince of men.[75]

The poem emphasizes the temporary nature of hard-won liberties, noting that "the renaissance of Ethiop" brought about by Louverture, "like other fires, was quenched awhile" amid "The cruel splendour Christophe embraced." But, importantly, the Haitian Revolution kindled another fire: "Thy message came to old Virginia's woods,/'Ah! Freemen shall we be,' gaunt Turner cries." This section ends with a pair of linked allusions to two of the most famous lines in Black Romantic poetry: "Each blow for freedom struck is freedom's gain,/And Ethiop shall yet stretch forth her hand."[76] The first line is a reference to Byron's *Childe Harold's Pilgrimage*—specifically, to the lines "Hereditary bondsmen! know ye not/Who would be free, themselves must strike the blow?" As Sandler notes, "this little bit of British Romantic poetry . . . appears in most of the major early texts of the Black radical tradition," from Henry Highland Garnet's 1843 address to the National Convention of Colored Citizens to Martin Delany's newspaper *The Mystery* to Frederick Douglass's *My Bondage and My Freedom* to W. E. B. Du Bois's *The Souls of Black Folk*, making these lines "a kind of shibboleth for the movement." Sandler shows that "the citation became a refrain of Black radical intellection, and in its rhythmic repetition through the nineteenth century, Black writers signaled their belonging within a world-historical struggle for emancipation."[77] Johnson's invocation of Byron's lines thus indicates his world-historical ambitions in this poem—he seeks nothing less than an account of an ongoing, unfinished project of Black liberation and of Black diasporic life. Importantly, Johnson's citation of Byron also resists world-historical accounts of poetry that trace a line from Anglo-Saxon alliterative verse to contemporary free verse poetry. Unlike Byron's contemporary Samuel Taylor Coleridge, who was influenced by Friedrich Klopstock's accentualist account of the German language, Byron could not be retrospectively conscripted into the Anglo-Saxonist metrical histories that started to appear in the late 1830s, as he was not interested in the project of creating accentualist accounts of English poetry.

Johnson's citation also subtly shifts the impact of early Black Romantic uses of Byron. As Sandler argues, "the fundamental impacts [of "Byron's call for violence"] were epistemological. . . . With each citation, abolitionists reflected on the conditional dimensions of Byron's point: the enslaved may or may not know that violence would set them free; violence may or may not in fact set them free; and they may or may not commit violent acts in prospective service to their freedom."[78] In Johnson's citation, the conditional tense is gone, and instead he asserts the necessity of revolutionary violence. A blow is a gain, always, and cumulatively; each moment of revolutionary violence, from Louverture to Turner and beyond, leads to the future liberation Watkins Harper prophesied.

Indeed, Johnson's use of the conjunction "and" ("Each blow for freedom struck is freedom's gain/And Ethiop shall yet stretch forth her hand") links Byron's call for violence with Watkins Harper's vision. Though the title of Johnson's poem echoes Watkins Harper's, this is the first line of hers he explicitly quotes. Watkins Harper's "Ethiopia" rephrases the prophecy of Psalms 68:31 ("Princes shall come forth out of Egypt; Ethiopia shall soon stretch forth her hands unto God") in its opening and closing stanzas:

> Yes! Ethiopia yet shall stretch
> Her bleeding hands abroad;
> Her cry of agony shall reach
> The burning throne of God.
>
> . . . .
> Then, Ethiopia! stretch, oh! stretch
> Thy bleeding hands abroad;
> Thy cry of agony shall reach
> And find redress from God.[79]

The "yet" in Johnson's citation both preserves the prophetic mode of Watkins Harper's original and underscores the political disappointment that remained after Emancipation and Reconstruction. The extra beat in Johnson's blank verse lines (compared to the tetrameter and trimeter lines in Watkins Harper's hymnal meter) stretches Ethiopia's reach one foot longer, suggesting the need to extend the Black Romantic poetic project into the early twentieth century. Johnson thus shows, in these two allusive lines, that Black Romanticism as generic, conventional, and radical aesthetic project remains relevant because Black liberation as a political project remains incomplete, only ever partially and temporarily realized.

While in Watkins Harper's poem justice will eventually come from God, who will hear the ongoing "cry of agony" of his people, in Johnson's, justice will come from the work of the Black diasporic community, united together symbolically by the poet's dialogic poetics. The final section of the poem shifts from addressing the abstraction of Ethiopia to addressing the Black diasporic community; it promises the "sons of Libya," "Thy faith, they deeds, thy love for fellow men" will bring about "another dawn." Not divine intervention but collective work becomes the redemptive force that could bring about a more just future. Central to maintaining that vision is the heroic poet, whose citational, dialogic song helps to unite a scattered, diasporic people:

> And thus I sing the song of Ethiop
> Though I am dwelling in a stranger's land,
> A lonely minstrel, born to serve and love
> Throughout the world his fellows of the dusk.[80]

The poet serves as a unifying figure—the singer whose song can symbolically bring together the dispersed "fellows of the dusk" who continue to work for "another dawn." In "Ethiopia," Johnson thus shows how the "conventional" forms and genres of Black Romantic poetry continued to give shape to political disappointment, rage, hope, and revolutionary, abolitionist politics—at least for those who knew how to listen for the sounds of Ethiop's lyre coming back to life once again.

The Enclosure of Free Verse

The world-historical ambition registered in generic poems like "Ethiopia" is crucial to understanding how free verse functioned as a form of enclosure for Johnson. Johnson was deeply committed to the idea that literature could play a role in securing Black liberation ("A lonely minstrel, born to serve and love/Throughout the world his fellows of the dusk"), though, as Courage and Hall note, the exact details of how literature might change social life were never systematically spelled out in any of Johnson's work.[81] Instead, Johnson fervently and frequently connected generic mobility with cultural, social, and political mobility for Black diasporic subjects. The much-commented-on irony and sardonic tone of Johnson's free verse is, I contend, directed specifically at what he perceived as the loss of generic mobility, and the consequent loss of social mobility, that resulted from the reductive racialized reading practices of white editors and critics.

Johnson's frequent focus on metaphors of mobility and spatiality is illuminated by Katherine McKittrick's argument that "Black matters are spatial matters."[82] McKittrick argues that material, metaphorical, and imagined geographies are central to understanding how "space and place give black lives meaning in a world that has . . . deemed black populations and their attendant geographies as 'ungeographic' and/or philosophically underdeveloped."[83] As I discussed earlier, in Johnson's citation of Black Romantic poetry, he created a dialogic, collaborative poetics that imagined Black diasporic subjects united by shared textual practices and shared political goals. This poetry intentionally underscores both the globalized geography of the Black diaspora, connecting Ethiopia to Haiti to Virginia, and the philosophical and historical weight of Black intellectual and political traditions. Too, Johnson's pre-free-verse books of poetry—those "conventional" and "insipid" works— are ambitiously generically and formally mobile, connecting textual forms of mobility to desired political freedoms. In these books, Johnson moves across and between the orthographies, meters, subjects, and genres associated with "high" literature, those associated with Black folk art, and those associated with European folk art, deliberately blurring the boundary lines between Black and white literary and generic traditions.[84] *A Little Dreaming* (1913) contains elegies for Dunbar, Swinburne, and victims of the *Titanic*; homages to Tennyson, Blake, and Poe; dialect poems in the plantation tradition; Yiddish, Scottish, and Irish dialect poems; and a Miltonic epic, among other genres and forms. *Visions of the Dusk* (1915) brings together rewritings of Tennyson, Watkins Harper, Dunbar, Longfellow, and Burns with spirituals in "standard" English, dialect poems in the plantation tradition, hymns, and love lyrics. Even *Songs of the Soil* (1916), in which Johnson claims to "cast aside the English of the Victorians and assume the language of the plantation and levee," contains multiple poems in "standard" English about topics other than "Negro life in the rural districts of the South" and specifically continues the project of rewriting Poe and Tennyson begun in his earlier books.[85] The purpose of this deliberate and virtuosic generic and formal intermixing was to show that African American folk art (in Johnson's conception, primarily dialect poetry and spirituals) was as useful a literary resource as the art of various European folk—no more or less "authentic"—and to claim white genres and forms as the rightful property of Black poets. Generic mobility, in Johnson's view, was a key to cultural and political mobility—a way of creating a "diasporic analytical opening, which advances creative acts that influence and undermine existing [segregated] spatial arrangements," in McKittrick's terms.[86]

Johnson made this argument about the connection between generic mobility and cultural and political mobility perhaps most clearly in his introduction to *Songs of the Soil*. He explained that "the Negro . . . is the most misunderstood creature in our latter day civilization" because the historic "wealth" of Black culture had been "buried." Even though he was "builder of empires that have crumbled, . . . he has taken his place in the greatest of republics as a peasant and menial," while "add[ing] to what we call Americanism his droll racial instincts."[87] To Johnson, one crucial way to challenge that degraded "place in the greatest of republics" was through literature— that written both in Black dialect and in the dialect of "standard" English. Although *Songs of the Soil* contains a higher percentage of dialect poems than any of his other work (thirty out of forty-one poems, compared to ten out of fifty-nine in *A Little Dreaming* and nineteen out of sixty-one in *Visions of the Dusk*), Johnson ends his introduction by explaining, "I do not hope to complete my career as merely a singer of the plantation. As I said in the beginning of this introduction there is a wealth of buried Negro tradition. I hope that it shall be my fortune to unearth it and give it to the world in some attractive form so that men may realize that the Negro has a history and is something more than a peasant."[88] In other words, giving poetic expression, in varied forms and genres, to Black history would lead to increased social status for Black Americans living in an illogically racist society.

This claim for a generically and formally mobile literature as a means of social change was one Johnson returned to often. For instance, in the April 1917 issue of *The Champion*, in "The Editor's Blue Pencil" column, Johnson argued,

To the Negro race, at this time, Easter is pregnant with a meaning of particular and peculiar import. We who have long been sleeping have heard the resounding trumpet of the resurrection. Rousing from our deep and deathly rest, we came forth, and found that Faith and Imagination were rolling the stone form the door of our tomb. We saw them at work. We saw them in the twinkle of an eye liberate the souls of those who had lain captive for centuries. And, we have not been disobedient unto the heavenly vision and unto the demonstration of the heavenly agents—Faith and Imagination.

These are still with us and it is well that they are, for there are many stones still to be rolled away. Among these are the stones that hinder our way to health, to shelter and sustenance, the training of our children, and the preservation of our rights as citizens of the world's greatest republic. . . .

In the near future, we must at least enter the portals that swing before the palace of our own Art and Literature. To do this, we must encourage the producers of art and literature by learning who they are and by purchasing and pondering their works. In these we shall see ourselves, as we are, as we should be, and as we may become. Thus we shall be reborn to the beauty and sanctity of black, brown and sallow manhood and womanhood, and, in time, we shall realize again the heights to which we had attained long, long ago before we fell asleep. For this is the time of trumpet and thunder. This is the resurrection and the renaissance. This is Easter.[89]

Here too, Johnson uses spatialized metaphors to imagine a nonracist social order. In Johnson's telling, the enclosure of the metaphorical tomb bars the way from "the portals that swing before the palace of our own Art and Literature." Johnson positions a generically mobile Black literature as one force that can counter white supremacist oppression by reflecting "ourselves, as we are, as we should be, and as we may become." According to Johnson, self-representation in literature carves a path back to the greatness of those lost African empires Johnson references in this passage and in the introduction to *Songs of the Soil*, again connecting an imagined, textualized geography to Black liberation. To Johnson, restoring this spatialized, textualized greatness to view would help change Black Americans' access "to health, to shelter and sustenance, [to] the training of our children, and [to] the preservation of our rights as citizens."[90] Johnson's spatial metaphors work to understand the "'imbrication of material and metaphorical space' . . . so that black lives and black histories can be conceptualized and talked about in new ways," making it possible to "envision[n] an interpretive alterable world, rather than a transparent and knowable world."[91] Spatializing and textualizing Black diasporic histories and lives was, to Johnson, a potential key to "the resurrection and the renaissance" that might create a more just world.

Johnson's free verse poetry—particularly the poetry published in *Others*—reflects the disappointment of these hopes for generically mobile literature as an agent of social and political change. The status of Black folk art and the ability of the Black artist to move across genres, forms, and registers remain key concerns in Johnson's free verse; but here generic and geographic mobility are constricted, and that constriction gives rise to a bitter sense of irony. Johnson's free verse poems are remarkably geographically, formally, and culturally contained, reflecting the way that the spatialized racial dominations of modernity are "upheld by . . . [a] language of insides and outsides, borders and belongings, and inclusions and exclusions."[92] This is particularly visible in the sequence "African Nights," published in the anthology *Others for 1919: An Anthology of the New Verse*, which includes most of the poems Johnson published in *Others* ("Tired," "Aunt Hannah Jackson," "Aunt Jane Allen," "The Gambler," "The Barber," "The Drunkard," "The Artist," "Dreams"), plus "The Banjo Player," "The Minister," and "The Scarlet Woman." The specific place names mentioned in the poems—State Street, Wabash Avenue, the Last Chance Saloon, and Big Lizzie's "house for white men"—indicate that all of these poems are set in the small area of the South Loop, known locally as the Levee. The geographic constraints placed on the subjects of the poems, who move only around this small area of Chicago, are mirrored by the formal constraints of the poems. Each is written in free verse, with the sentence constituting the line length. The syntax is simple and straightforward, consisting largely of declarative statements. Each poem is roughly a short paragraph. They tend to be sardonic and to suggest an audience outside of the scene who knows more than the speakers. They are very much in the style of Edgar Lee Masters's most biting portraits of midwestern life and of Carl Sandburg's grittiest poems in *Chicago Poems*. The sameness of the syntax lends a sameness to the voices of the speakers, creating a sense of repetition rather than the sense of formal openness and wide-ranging generic experimentation that characterized Johnson's earlier poetic works.

Culturally too, these poems are marked by the forced stasis and the diminished life chances of their speakers. Aunt Hannah Jackson is a washerwoman who spends her days talking to herself about her lost love and who, "For rubbing on other people's clothes . . . gets a dollar and fifty cents a day and a worn out dress on Christmas." Aunt Jane Allen is remembered as someone who "hobbled along" "up and down State Street trying to sell" her "basket of aprons" until her death. The subject of "The Drunkard" has replaced his lost wife with "a gallon jug of the reddest liquor that ever burned the throat of man" and now stays "in the rear of Mike's saloon." "The Minister" is the only figure in the sequence who seemed to have had the possibility of cultural and social mobility. He "mastered pastoral theology, the Greek of the Apostles, and all the difficult subjects in a minister's curriculum." But all this cultural mastery proves to be for naught, as he ends up "los[ing] [his] charge to Sam Jenkins, who has not been to school four years in his life" simply because "[he] could not make [his] congregations shout./And my dollar money was small, very small. . . . /Sam Jenkins leads in the gift of raising dollar money./Such is religion." "The Scarlet Woman" explains that even though her "father worked for Mr. Pullman and white people's tips," "he died two days after his insurance expired." She "had nothing, so [she] had to go to work./All the stock [she] had was a white girl's education and a face that enchanted the men of both races." Facing "starvation," the scarlet woman goes to work for "Big Lizzie, who kept a house for white men," and ends up a drunk who drinks to forget ("Gin is better than all the water in Lethe"). Every possibility of social mobility is foreclosed, and consequently the characters are confined to the South Loop and to the textual boxes of the free verse poems.[93]

The multiple constraints of Johnson's free verse poems point to an underappreciated aspect of this work: the way Johnson connects the forced stasis caused by systemic oppression to racialized reading practices that abstracted genres of poems into genres of persons. Johnson portrays racialized reading practices as one of the mechanisms that produce what Jodi Melamed calls "trapping fictions of blackness."[94] In particular, Johnson singles out ballad reading as a violently reductive mode of racialized reading.[95] As I discussed in chapters 1 and 2, scholars and critics like Gummere and his peers had understood Scottish and English ballads to be the paradigmatic forms of folk art that indexed bygone premodern modes of life, and later scholars were quick to present any form of folk poetry as performing the same kinds of cultural preservation work as ballads. Ballad readings of folk poetry depended on what Caroline Gelmi calls the "double fantasy of loss and preservation."[96] That is, because the "authentic" folk always seemed to be a receding figure, whether because print capitalism had ruined their pristine oral culture, as Gummere believed, or because the end of slavery meant the end of Black folk life on plantations, as Dunbar's editors argued, many cultural workers believed it was imperative to write down the vestiges of folk song and folk poetry before it disappeared forever. In practice, this meant reading the work of Black authors (especially the work of authors of dialect poetry) as if that work "ha[d] a deeper author in the folk" rather than accepting it as imaginative literature consciously produced by an individual.[97] Though in a Gummerian framework such poetry could never exactly capture the authentic folk that was passing away, it could at least make "vanishing folk voices accessible as literature" so that it could be appreciated by educated, literate white audiences.[98]

What mattered in ballad readings of folk poetry, in other words, was the genre of person represented in the poem rather than the genre of the poem itself.[99]

By the early twentieth century, ballad reading thus meant approaching anything perceived to be folk poetry as the authentic expression of a vanishing genre of people that was somehow outside of or adjacent to modernity. As Gelmi notes, Paul Laurence Dunbar's *Poems of Cabin and Field*—a text that Johnson specifically references in his free verse poetry, as I discuss in more detail shortly—helps to make visible the "instrumentalizing logic" of ballad reading that allowed white editors and critics to imagine that Dunbar's highly crafted literary dialect poetry represented the authentic voices of a vanishing Black folk.[100] In ballad readings of poetry conceived to be folk poetry, what matters is not the person of the poet or the speaker but the ability of both of these figures to function typologically, "as representative[s] of the Black folk" that was understood to be vanishing.[101] As Gelmi puts it, practices of ballad reading turn Black individuals, both fictional and actual, speakers and authors, "into absent objects, figures whose negation supports their aesthetic production."[102]

In many of Johnson's poems, but especially in "The Banjo Player," published in Kreymborg's *Others for 1919*, he pointed out and contested such reductive, instrumentalizing reading practices. The poem reads,

> There is music in me, the music of a peasant people.
>   I wander through the levee, picking my banjo and singing my songs of the cabin and the field. At the Last Chance Saloon I am as welcome as the violets in March; there is always food and drink for me there, and the dimes of those who love honest music. Behind the railroad tracks the little children clap their hands and love me as they love Kris Kringle.
>   But I fear that I am a failure. Last night a woman called me a troubadour. What is a troubadour?[103]

Johnson's banjo player reflects the double edge of ballad reading for Black artists. On the one hand, such racialized reading practices confirmed that Black cultures existed and were valuable; on the other, that value was abstracted and extracted by white audiences, who continued to position Black artists as mediums for folk voices rather than as artists. Indeed, Johnson's invocation of Dunbar's 1899 *Poems of Cabin and Field* ("singing my songs of the cabin and the field") points to perhaps the most famous case of reductive ballad reading in African American literary history. Johnson's "The Banjo Player" creates a dialogue with Dunbar's "A Banjo Song" to ironize ballad logic and the racialized reading practices it encouraged. In the illustrated edition of *Poems of Cabin and Field* produced in conjunction with the Hampton Institute's Camera Club, "A Banjo Song" is illustrated with a portrait of a banjo that structurally mirrors earlier portraits of human figures meant to represent members of the antebellum Black folk, as Gelmi's reading of the volume shows. Gelmi argues that the portrait sequence in the book makes visible the instrumentalizing logic of ballad reading by turning the images of people, who represent the "speakers" of individual poems, into the image of an object. This transformation presents the idea that the banjo is the "truer version" of the speaker, because, "as a banjo, the speaker purveys lost voices," functioning as "a sign of the imagined orality that holds the hearts and minds of the Black folk largely beyond literary representation."[104] Johnson's poem pointedly reverses this objectification, returning to the player of the banjo to think about what it means for him to be presented as a medium for a lost folk culture.

The poem begins with the idea that the folk, as a particular genre of persons and not individual authors or artists, are indeed the true source of folk art: The banjo player plays because he has "the music of a peasant people" inside of him. But Johnson quickly shifts focus from the fantasy of the disappearing folk represented by the banjo player to the reality of the persistence of that folk in enclosed, constrained spaces, both geographical and cultural. The banjo player's music makes available the fantasy of authentic Black American culture as the product of Southern plantations: He "wander[s] through the levee, picking [his] banjo and singing [his] songs of the cabin and the field." But the Last Chance Saloon, the railroad tracks, and the dimes of auditors puncture this fantasy of bygone Southern folk life. The transmutation of the levees of the Mississippi River into a red-light district in Chicago—the South Loop Levee—reminds readers that the Black folk did not in fact disappear into the past when slavery ended; many migrated north and continued to find ways to live and thrive. Like Johnson's rewriting of nineteenth-century historical epics and odes, his free verse insists on the importance of historical continuity over the ruptures that structured ballad reading. These poems also insist on understanding how "practices of domination . . . naturalize both identity and place, repetitively spatializing where nondominant groups 'naturally' belong."[105] The repetition of the same form—the same enclosures of the box of free verse—underscores the real spatial enclosures of a segregated city located in a segregated country.

"The Banjo Player" also highlights the fact that ballad reading is meant to preserve and immortalize the folk, which means locating them firmly in the past. The presence of the unmarked but presumably white woman observer in the poem points to the way ballad reading disenfranchises the folk through this backward-looking focus. Just as the banjo player cannot seem to travel beyond the South Loop, he cannot travel through cultural space, and a good measure of the poem's potent irony comes from the player's inability to forge connections with other poetic traditions. That is, the player does not recognize how his "songs of the cabin and the field" are related to other "authentic," supposedly premodern traditions like those of the European troubadours the woman compares him to. The player is blocked from understanding how his songs related to the songs of European singers as part of a world literature—he has no chance of becoming a syncretic, cosmopolitan artist like Ezra Pound or T. S. Eliot. And so the Dunbar songs that the poem conjures are not the springboard into greater cultural mobility and achievement that Johnson imagined they could be in his earlier poems and essays. Instead, they provide the player's entire cultural geography. The banjo player is the proper untutored folk musician, but this very fact bars him from cultural and social mobility, condemning him to stasis and making him vulnerable to misinterpretation by white audiences who see him as the medium of bygone folk voices rather than as an artist in his own right. At the same time, the banjo player has greater knowledge of specific folk genres—the songs of cabin and field—than does the woman performing the racialized ballad reading of the player, who can only understand the songs through a European framework. Johnson thus punctures the fantasy that, if a "pure orality" could be "properly represented in literary terms," it would "make the minds and lives of a people legible."[106] The actual lives of Black people supposedly represented in folk poetry are clearly not legible to the woman who calls the banjo player a troubadour, and the woman's ballad framing of the player is not legible to him. Rather than a scene of transmission and recognition, we have a scene of mutual unintelligibility, in which it seems that no knowledge is transmitted or received.

Notably, "The Banjo Player" withholds the player's songs from the poem's audience. We are given no lyrics and no description of what the player's songs sound like. Johnson refuses to reproduce the supposedly authentic folk art of the player so as to better foreground the conflict over racialized modes of literary interpretation raised by the woman who calls the player a troubadour. To the Black folk artist, to be called a troubadour is to be read as premodern and thus to be consigned to a static place in the kinds of fantasies of poetic evolution that were so prevalent in *Poetry* and in other predominantly white poetic spaces—fantasies that imagined that transhistorical legacies of whiteness could be encoded in poetic meter. Because ballad readings of folk poetry depend on the fantasy that the receding folk would fade away with the rise of modernity but would be preserved in printed poetry, ballad reading turns the Black artist into an equally fantasmatic figure—a fiction like "Kris Kringle" rather than a literary craftsperson. In Johnson's telling, ballad reading—the white abstraction and valuation of Black folk culture—can only result in a feeling of "failure" for the Black artist.

The final poem Johnson published in *Others*, "The Artist," also registers his frustration with white racialized readings of Black poetry and the generic constraints they brought to bear on Black poets. The poem reads,

> It is a wonderful world that greets me.
> I can hear the music of a wild rose in June, riotous with the joy of living.
> I can hear the soft music of snowflakes falling November.
> I remember the wind singing through the pines in Georgia, singing the
>   songs my fathers chanted in the days of slavery.
> I remember magnolias dropping upon the grave of my grandmother,
>   a pathetic melody.
> Sunlight, moonlight, dawn and dusk walk with me and talk with me,
>   telling me strange tales of the jungle and the desert, of wild beasts
>   and slave gangs, of kings and mighty warriors.
> In the dewdrop I see the eyes of a Pharaoh, angry at the desolation
>   of his land by the hordes of Ethiopian warriors.
> In the mist I see the rise of a new Ethiopia, liberator of a world long
>   stagnant.
> Who cares to hear my song of this wonderful world?
> Who cares?[107]

"The Artist" offers a condensed description of Johnson's earlier poems. The "wild rose in June, riotous with the joy of living" is a frequent metaphor in poems in *A Little Dreaming*.[108] The "wind singing through the pines in Georgia, singing the songs my fathers chanted in the days of slavery" recalls "A Georgia Lullaby" in *Visions of the Dusk*, along with the spirituals and dialect poems of all three of Johnson's books. The "strange tales of the jungle and the desert" and "the rise of a new Ethiopia" recall the many poems about Ethiopia in *A Little Dreaming* and *Visions of the Dusk*.[109] But the progression implied in the poem, from poetic inspiration derived from nature to that derived from tradition to a poetic prophecy of Black liberation ("I see the rise of a new Ethiopia"), is checked by the closing lines. The repetition of "Who cares?" suggests that this is the question of an embittered artist who cannot find the audience he seeks to hear his "song of this wonderful world." "Who cares" about these overlooked poetic genres when it is the much bleaker songs of State Street that fired the imaginations of white editors and tastemakers? Who cares, when these bleak songs of enclosure continue to be the only poems from Johnson's dense oeuvre that critics return to as significant? *Others* wanted his free verse and *Poetry* wanted his spirituals, but it seemed that no one wanted the generic poetry—twentieth-century Black Romantic epics and odes—that he thought could help to bring about a broad racial reconciliation through its polyphonic, intergenerational voicing of global Black history and imagined Black futures.[110]

Johnson's ironic stance in these free verse poems is thus directed at the changing valuation of genre within modernist poetics. If, in the nineteenth century, poetry was "popular literature addressed to print publics that crossed genres and media and nations and genders and races and educations and classes"—literature that organized particular reading publics around shared political causes through shared reading practices of recognized genres—by the twentieth century, this was no longer the case.[111] Publics began to "recogniz[e] poems [not] as particular genres" but "rather . . . as representative expressions of particular persons," so that "genres of poems became less important than the genres of persons represented in and by them"—genres of persons like the imagined Black folk.[112] I have been arguing that Johnson saw this abstraction of genre as integral to racialized reading practices and that he attempted to restore to view nineteenth-century Black engagements with genres like the historical epic and the ode to envision Black American history as something other than the story of the vanished Black folk. Johnson's free verse, by contrast, registers the diminishment of the world-historical ambition he displayed in his early work and the loss of what he had experienced as a joyous generic and formal mobility that would help to "influence and undermine existing spatial arrangements."[113]

Staking a claim to literary convention as a Black author was thus a radical act for Johnson—one that resisted the narrow generic and formal confines white readers insisted on. To Johnson, a poetics of Black liberation was a generically mobile poetics: one in which all traditions are open for Black poets to interpret, shape, add to, and change to better represent the fullness of Black life and the world-spanning reach of Black diasporic geographies, material and metaphorical. It is my hope that my reading of Johnson's interest in "conventional" nineteenth-century poetry will encourage modernist scholars to finally read his poetry—not just his free verse—as deeply engaged with the process of social transformation through acts of reading and writing against hegemonic white imaginaries. As Brigitte Fielder argues of Black literary genealogies, "readers may have to develop new ways of reading . . . once new [genealogical] paths are forged or uncovered."[114] Johnson's multidirectional, global genealogies of Black poetry ask scholars of poetic modernism to reconsider what it might have meant for Black poets writing in the modernist era to find a usable past and what it might mean for contemporary scholars to acknowledge our own still-racialized reading practices.

CHAPTER FOUR

Mary Austin's Time Machine and
E. Pauline Johnson's Canoe

Thus far, my account of the racialization of free verse has focused on the construction of a Black and white color line in early twentieth-century American prosodic discourse. As I have briefly suggested in chapters 1 and 2, the anti-Blackness of many theories of free verse was inextricable from a settler colonial viewpoint. In this chapter, I take up the construction of North American Indigeneity in debates about the nature of free verse rhythms in greater detail. My focus is the influential modernist anthology *The Path on the Rainbow: The Book of Indian Poems*, first published in 1918 and reprinted in 1934, 1970, 1991, and 1997. The significance of *The Path on the Rainbow* to the development of both modernist and Native American literature has been well documented.[1] Though the anthology has garnered scholarly attention, there remains an important lacuna in accounts of *The Path on the Rainbow*. There is only one Indigenous author in the anthology: E. Pauline Johnson (the bulk of the anthology consists of ethnographic texts, transcribed by non-Native ethnologists and anthropologists). And since Louis Untermeyer argued in his 1919 review of *The Path on the Rainbow* for *The Dial* that it was "a disappointment to come across jingles like Pauline Johnson's 'The Song My Paddle Sings,' which is neither original nor aboriginal," critics have consistently failed or declined to read Johnson's poems when they talk about the anthology as a whole.[2] Untermeyer's assessment that Johnson's verse was "time-dusty" has thus gone unchallenged within modernist studies.[3] As Margery Fee notes, "the rise of modernist tastes meant [Johnson's] work was rarely anthologized between 1940 and 1990," and the generative recovery work that has been done on Johnson since 1990 has been firmly located in nineteenth-century and Victorian studies.[4] But as I will show, the poems of Johnson's that were included in *The Path on the Rainbow* are worth the attention of modernist scholars, as they productively trouble the settler colonial project of the anthology by resisting its pathologization of Indigenous sexuality and its equally relentless racialization of poetic form.

This chapter proceeds through two sections. The first explores how Austin's introduction to *The Path on the Rainbow* produced a mode of dispossessive reading that tied together free verse forms, settler temporality, and heteropatriarchal modes of social organization. *The Path on the Rainbow* was published during the era when heteronormative marriage was legally codified as a tool of Indigenous dispossession through the Dawes Act in the United States and the Indian Act in Canada—a context that has not often been considered in scholarship on this anthology. I show that Austin's theory of free verse and the organization of the anthology as a whole utilized the heteropatriarchal settler colonial logic exemplified in the Dawes and Indian Acts as they made the case for why white readers should attend to what they called Native American poetry, highlighting how the dispossessive reading practices the anthology encouraged went hand in hand with more overt forms of dispossession. The second section reassesses Johnson's contributions to *The Path on the Rainbow* to unpack how her supposedly outmoded nineteenth-century verse works against what Audra Simpson calls "the snaking, dividing, and yet organizing logic of raced and gendered heteropatriarchy."[5] By misrecognizing Johnson's mastery of poetic conventions as a simplistic reproduction of outmoded poetic forms or as a sign of her successful colonization, modernist studies assessments of *The Path on the Rainbow* have continued to engage in dispossessive reading practices that strip Johnson's work of its nuance and complexity and that privilege settler narratives of progressive literary history.

I use the term "dispossessive reading" to signal the ways that modernist reading practices work hand in hand with other forms of colonial dispossession to render Indigenous texts and textualized songs and ceremonies the property of white authors and readers. Dispossessive reading involves many of the same tactics as modes of material dispossession; as Simpson argues, there are "a whole host of . . . self-authorizing techniques and frameworks that *sustain* dispossession and occupation," including but not limited to "occupying, treating, forceful elimination, containment, assimilation, the coterminous logics and practices and languages of race and civilization, the practice of immigration, . . . the legal notion of natal right, and presumptions of just occupancy."[6] These techniques are used to pursue what Simpson calls the "colonial dream" of "Indigenous pacification, containment, and demobilization."[7] Although dispossessive reading involves claiming texts and cultural practices as the rightful inheritance of settlers rather than claiming land or other material resources, the two modes of dispossession are intertwined, and they work in tandem as part of the "logics and practices and languages of race and civilization" that subtend the larger project of settler colonialism.

Dispossessive reading is a particular form of racialized reading that is connected to other modes of cultural appropriation in literature. While figures like Harriet Monroe and Alice Corbin Henderson were interested in claiming Black folk materials as the property of white poets, they did still occasionally acknowledge the future potential of Black poets to use those same folk materials to create modern art. By contrast, Monroe, Henderson, and like-minded critics were quick to position Indigenous peoples as already vanished into a distant past. Dispossessive readings of ethnographic materials thus helped to promulgate the ideas that there could be no future for modern Indigenous peoples other than assimilation and also, paradoxically, that vanished Indigenous cultures were the foundation of American culture.[8] While modernist studies as a field has paid a great deal of attention to the way modernist primitivism produced modes of dispossessive reading, less recognized is the way that approaches to poetic form continue to operate as such.[9] This chapter brings to the fore the argument that runs throughout this book: that learning how to read poetic form differently, in a way that does not dismiss convention out of hand or automatically valorize formal "experiment," is one way modernist studies can grapple with the settler colonial logics that continue to structure the field.

Nowhere, perhaps, is this argument more salient than in recent attempts to understand early twentieth-century poetry by Native American and Indigenous authors. The few notable attempts to credit early twentieth-century Native poets with doing vital cultural work have still naturalized a division between complex, experimental poetry and simplified conventional poetry. In Michael Taylor's reading of the effects of modernist poetic primitivism on the reputations of early twentieth-century Indigenous poets, for instance, he opposes "experiment[s] with meter, rhyme, or syntax" to "straightforward iambic tetrameter and rhyme," arguing that "marginalized poets" often "chose clarity over artistic obscurity" in order to attain political ends.[10] Veronica Strong-Boag and Carole Gerson similarly read E. Pauline Johnson's decision to use "popular narrative forms" of poetry as a bid for "accessibility."[11] But the suggestion that poetic convention is straightforward or automatically accessible is misleading, particularly since modernist tastes have calcified into critical dogma. The choice to write in rhymed iambic tetrameter did not necessarily signal an interest in clarity; it signaled participation in other poetic traditions than a narrow high modernist tradition. As Alexandra Socarides argues, learning to read "how conventions work necessarily inverts the significance that has long been placed on the poetic qualities of originality and experimentation" and "allows us to see anew that which we thought we knew and could discard."[12] I propose that learning to leave behind dispossessive reading—which means leaving behind received ideas about the values of different poetic forms—can help us to see how Johnson's seemingly forgettable, conventional verse worked against the modernist settler colonial framing of poetic form within the pages of *The Path on the Rainbow*.

Mary Austin's Time Machine

Mary Austin is a vexing figure. Austin created a position for herself in the 1910s through the 1930s as one of the foremost "interpreters" of Native American poetry and cultural traditions. She was appointed to the School of American Research in Native American Literature in 1918, authored the "Aboriginal Literature" entry for the *Cambridge History of American Literature* in 1921,[13] and published widely on Native American literatures and cultures in popular magazines like *The Nation* and *Atlantic Monthly*.[14] She managed to attain this stature in spite of the fact that she spoke no Native languages and generally worked from the ethnographic reports of non-Indigenous ethnographers rather than with Indigenous collaborators.[15] She also engaged in effective forms of political activism and lobbying with Indigenous peoples, and she did have some knowledge of the cultural practices of specific tribal groups, gathered during her interactions with Native communities.[16] But, in attempting to advocate for the importance of Native American poetry, which she presented as the earliest known form of free verse, Austin also turned free verse into a tool of cultural domination.[17]

Austin shared an interest with contemporaries like Harriet Monroe in finding ways to cut through what she saw as unnecessary academic jargon in discussions of poetic form. Throughout her career, she argued that terms like "meter" obscured the essential bodily basis of poetic rhythm and that the term "rhythm" also obscured what actually mattered about poetry: its ability to coordinate diverse individuals into a coherent community. Austin, as an adherent of the communal origins theory of poetry, believed that groups of people began to conceive of themselves as a community only when they sang and danced together, harmonizing their unruly bodies in the shared rhythms of what she called the "poetic orgy."[18] She advocated for a return to "primitive" modes of poetry, in which there was supposedly no distinction between song, dance, and verse, so that modern poets and readers could access the community-building function of poetic rhythm.[19]

Austin was particularly interested in contemporaneous scholarship that tried to measure the rhythms of poetry in laboratories, which seemed to be pinning down fundamental truths about poetic rhythm and meter. Austin was keyed in to the work of one of Monroe's favorite prosodic theorists,

William Morrison Patterson (discussed in chapter 2), who collaborated with Amy Lowell on a series of experiments at Columbia University in the 1910s. (It is worth noting that Patterson and Lowell pursued their imaging of speech patterns on the same campus where Franz Boas was remaking anthropology during this era.) In their published findings, Patterson and Lowell argued that poetic rhythms were fundamentally made up of units of time and that a good sense of rhythm was nothing more than the ability to group those units of time into coherent sequences. Patterson and Lowell argued that this insight was crucial to any understanding of free verse rhythms, which seemed at first to be haphazard and unsystematizable but which were in fact effectively coordinated units of time.[20]

Austin combined this understanding of free verse as a kind of time-management tool—a technology that could make unequal units of time into equal units—with the communal origins theory of poetry to posit not only that Native American poetry was the oldest available form of poetry and that it was also the foundation for a new form of free verse destined to be developed in the United States by non-Native poets. As Jeremy Braddock puts it, "Austin summoned an alternative past and future for free verse" that seemed to make the form quintessentially American rather than transnational, as it had seemed to be when critics focused on Imagist poets as exemplary free versifiers.[21] Austin argued that scholars were correct in positing that poetry was originally used to create social cohesion out of a group of diverse individuals—it coordinated them into a "throng"—but that scholars had missed opportunities to study such primitive poetry in situ. Austin explained that while scholars fixated on "degraded" European ballads that had fallen far from their original oral forms, Native American cultures remained, "for the most part of the type called neolithic."[22] Native Americans were, in other words, the primal throng, living, breathing, and dancing in the United States and just waiting to be studied by scholars of poetics. Austin argued that in this seemingly most ancient form of poetry, "the combination of voice and drum . . . is *never for any other purpose than that of producing and sustaining collective states*. Among primitives there is no other distinction between prose and poetry than this. Prose is the medium of communication, but Poetry is the mode of communion."[23] Poetic rhythm became for Austin not just an abstraction of meter—a term more general and unspecific that could encompass a wide range of phenomena—but also an abstraction of social relations: an ideal of communality that could only be achieved through poetry. Austin believed that unlocking the secrets of how this "Neolithic" verse linked together the rhythms of individual bodies into a cohesive group was especially crucial for non-Native Americans, who had lost the practice of communal dancing and singing. For non-Native poets, getting back to primal rhythms would also mean strengthening a sense of national identity. In this way, Austin proposed, collections like *The Path on the Rainbow* could "act as a historical archive for the nourishment of contemporary writing."[24]

Of course, as Mark Rifkin's work reminds us, theories of temporality were hotly debated in the modernist era and had serious consequences for Native communities. Rifkin takes up the problems of what he calls "settler time" and "Indigenous temporal sovereignty," explaining that, in response to discourses that position Indigenous peoples as eternally ancient, locked into the past, there has been a scholarly tendency to insist on the temporal copresence of Native peoples and settlers. Rifkin argues that this approach, though it has political uses, risks normalizing and reifying settler time. Settler time orients events according to the trajectories of the nation-state and modernity and conscripts Native lives and stories into histories determined by those settler trajectories. As Rifkin argues,

> Settler superintendence of Native peoples imposes a particular account of how time works—a normative language or framework of temporality that serves as the basis for forms of temporal inclusion and recognition. Settler time reduces the unfolding and adaptive expressions of Indigenous peoplehood to a set of points—the supposedly shared now of the present, modernity, and national history— within a configuration that is positioned as the commonsensical frame in ways that deny the immanent motion of indigeneity. Native people get plotted in ways that deny the movement inherent in its ongoing emergence.[25]

The tendency to think in terms of temporal copresence, in other words, has the effect of foreclosing possibilities for thinking about temporality beyond settler time. Rifkin argues for an approach to temporality that thinks through the lens of relativity instead. He reads Henri Bergson's idea of duration as an important move away from the concept of time as homogeneous, empty, and divisible into equal units that can then be spatially plotted, as along a timeline. Rifkin shows how Bergson's theories can work against the settler colonial spatialization of time, explaining that,

> against this uniformity of division, Bergson presents *duration* as the transition among qualitatively differentiable sensations such that they permeate each other in ways that defy enumeration. . . . Rather than

seeking to divide time into discrete, homogeneous units, Bergson conceptualizes it as "a continuous or qualitative multiplicity with no resemblance to number." . . . From within Bergson's analysis, an insistence on "natural" time—that everyone occupies a singular present—looks like a mathematizing abstraction that effaces the experience of duration.[26]

Bergson's concept of duration helps us to see how modernist conceptions of free verse rhythms as made up of "discrete, homogeneous units" of time fit neatly into settler colonial conceptions of national history. According to prosodic theorists like Patterson, Lowell, and Austin, free verse was the balancing of unlike units of time into new and equal units, as in bars of music. As Austin argued, "even in the freest free verse there is a subjective disposition to set up temporal equivalence between a single strong and many weak syllables."[27] Free verse rhythms were, in other words, ways to make sense of time by dividing it into units that could be made equivalent to each other and plotted on a graph, making such rhythms useful tools for the implementation of settler time on Native cultural expressions. It is thus especially important to attend to Austin's linkage of free verse with Native American poetry. This move has been read as an attempt to gain greater recognition for Native American art and as a sign that free verse did indeed open poetry to a greater range of poets and readers. But viewed in another light, it is also possible to see the ways in which it was an imposition of a normative framework of temporality that became the basis for forms of recognition, to borrow Rifkin's phrasing, and to see how recognition as a paradigm has continuously failed Native communities.[28]

In what at first might appear to be a move toward a Bergsonian or Einsteinian understanding of temporality as relative and nonlinear, Austin argued that Native poetry had rhythms that seemed to be unsystematizable or that at least were unsystematizable according to the rules of English-language prosody. According to Austin, the units of Native American rhythms could not be weighed out into equal units, as the rhythms of English-language poetry could be. She explained that "the Amerind has no system, of which he can give an account, of coördinating rhythmic impressions" and that Native American poetry was composed of "rhythms which the white man cannot always perceive and not easily resolve into mathematical indices."[29] Rather than theorizing what might be unique and interesting about an approach to rhythm that was not based on temporal units, however, Austin constructed systematizable, spatializable rhythms as a technology that could manage time and integrate histories that seemed violently incompatible at first glance. She explained that accent in poetry was "a device for establishing temporal coincidences" and that, unlike in English-language poetry, "accent does not appear to have any place in Amerind poetry."[30] This meant that, while unaccented Native poetries were firmly rooted in their "Neolithic" moment, accented English-language poetry would be able to bring that Neolithic form into the future, making English-language translations and "interpretations" of Native verbal arts privileged forms. Non-Natives (and only non-Natives) could create a "temporal coincidence" between the beginnings and the ends of poetry, according to Austin, through their use of accented poetic rhythms in "aboriginal" free verse forms. It had been the technology of poetic accent that had allowed Vachel Lindsay to create "points of simultaneity" between "the Mississippi and the Congo" in his free verse poetry, and it would be the technology of accent that would lead non-Native poets to nurture "the common root of aboriginal and modern Americanness" into what she called "the rise of a new verse form in America."[31] The right poetic rhythms, in other words, wielded by white poets, could create material connections between the past and the future, making history visualizable and graphically representable as the rhythms of modern poetry. Rhythm was a time machine that moved between the "unaccented dub dub, dub dub, dub dub, dub dub in the plazas of Zuñi and Oraibi" and the accented "*chuff chuff* of a steam engine."[32] This translation across time would make those primal unaccented rhythms intelligible to the non-Natives on board the forward-moving train.

Austin's analysis of ethnographic translations of Indigenous oral performances led her to argue that there was an economy of form inherent to Native American poetry. As she put it, "the Amerind excels in the art of occupying space without filling it."[33] The claim that Native Americans left plenty of space open for non-Natives to occupy was echoed in the design of *The Path on the Rainbow*. The anthology first presents literal translations of Native American songs and oral expressions, made by non-Native ethnographers and divided into "Songs from the Eastern Woodlands," "Songs from the Southeast," "Songs from the Great Plains," "Songs from the Southwest," "Songs from California," "Songs from the Northwest Coast," and "Songs from the Far North."[34] These ethnographic translations are followed by "Interpretations" by Constance Lindsay Skinner, Mary Austin, Frank Gordon, Alice Corbin Henderson, and E. Pauline Johnson. Whereas the ethnographic translations are marked by the names of their collectors and the tribal groups from which they were collected, the "interpretations" do not have consistent textual apparatuses to explain which sources, if any, the poets were interpreting, indicating that the cultural specificity of the oral arts of different Native nations mattered less to the anthology's editors than the ways those oral cultural productions were interpreted by non-Native authors.

This textual presentation of Native American verbal expressions operates according to the logic of allotment employed by the US government, showing how containment (in certain poetic forms) and assimilation (into a national literary tradition) work as "techniques . . . that sustain dispossession and occupation" in the literary realm no less than in the political.[35] Allotment affected different Native nations unevenly, but many found their "surplus" allotments sold to white settlers, whose presence on reservation land was meant to hasten the dissolution of tribal communities. The aim of allotment was to do away with tribal identities entirely and to make "use" of the land that was, to borrow Austin's words, "occupied but not filled" by Native Americans. *The Path on the Rainbow* and the many anthologies it spawned applied the same sort of logic to Native American oral expressions, enacting a type of poetic allotment through the spatial organization of poems on the page (containment). By first presenting translations of Native art, which "occup[ied] space without filling it," followed by "reinterpretations" of that art by white poets, which filled the white space left "open" by the economical originals, these anthologies suggested that the logical "evolution" of Native American poetry was its incorporation into the bodies and texts of white poets (assimilation). The seemingly unsystematizable, unaccented rhythms of Native American song would be incorporated into the system of English-language poetic rhythm, meaning that "neolithic" Native cultures would be brought into the modern world on settler terms. Austin's introduction ends with a call to action for non-Native poets: "the long divided Muses of poetry, music and dance must come together again for the absolute rendering." The translators of Native American poetry had done their job, according to Austin, but "the interpreter's work is all before him."[36]

Very little scholarly attention has been paid to the kinds of work done by those non-Native interpreters in *The Path on the Rainbow*, but reading the "interpretations" helps to illuminate what made Johnson's poems so unsettling to early readers of the anthology. The "interpretations" of unidentified Native songs in *The Path on the Rainbow* participate in the doubled project of pathologizing Indigenous sexualities while also folding Native cultures into a "naturalize[d] . . . heteropatriarchy of nationhood."[37] As Jennifer Nez Denetdale has shown through a study of the uprising at Beautiful Mountain in 1913 (an act of resistance following the arrest of a Diné family for practicing polygamy), early twentieth-century US federal policy focused on

Indigenous marriage practices and family formations as part of the attempt to transform Native nations into "heterosexual patriarch[ies], even as [nations such as] the Navajo remain matrilineal and LGBTQ people assert k'é [a Navajo concept of relationality and kinship] as the foundation by which they belong to their people and the land."[38] That is to say that, in the early twentieth century, Indigenous sexualities and kinship practices were often positioned as primitive and pathological (oversexed and/or nonheteronormative), at the same time as emerging narratives of the United States as a liberal multicultural nation positioned Native nations "as always heterosexual and monogamous."[39]

This doubled pathologization and naturalization is everywhere evident in *The Path on the Rainbow*. Because the texts collected in the anthology are ethnographic texts, there were already colonial categories at work in the selection of "genuine" or "authentic" Native materials. It is thus unsurprising that many of the texts in the anthology reflect an idealization of monogamous, patriarchal heterosexuality. The anthology begins, in fact, with a linked set of poems titled "The Parted Lovers." The first section of the poem is split into stanzas separated by gender: "The Man Sings" and "The Woman Sings." The poem portrays the masculine lover as active and the feminine lover as passive; the man states, "my parents think they can separate me from the girl I love . . . /Their commands are in vain: we shall see each other while the world lasts." This statement of willful defiance stands in marked contrast to the woman in the pair, who begins by stating, "here I sit on this point, whence I can see the man that I love. . . . /Here shall I remain, in sight of the one I love."[40] Other sections in the poem are also explicitly gendered, as in "The Girl Deserted by Her Jealous Companions Sings," in which the titular heroine is "left on this lonely island to die" while her masculine lover is described as active, "swift as the deer," steering a canoe that "shoot[s] through the water."[41] The passive woman and the active man form a recurring pair throughout the anthology, reinforcing the sense that Native cultures share patriarchal, heterosexual gender roles with settler cultures, making assimilation seem to be an attainable goal.

The poetic "interpretations" in the anthology reinforce the idea of the essential binary nature of sex and gender in Native cultures. In "Summer Dawn (Tem-Eyos-Kyi)" by Constance Lindsay Skinner, women are addressed as "women, maidens and wives" and are separated from the men, who are "sons, lovers, young chiefs, hunters with arrows."[42] The poem emphasizes the beauty rituals of the women and the more practical activities of the men, describing the men's hunting with active verbs. Sex is also described as something that happens between an active man and a passive woman; the poem metaphorizes the woods in springtime as "in the warm sudden grasp of Spring;/Like a woman when her lover has suddenly, swiftly taken her." The poem ends when "two by two, they come up from the forest—the men and the women," and the men "firmly . . . hold the hands of the women,/Who have given peace to their strength, and a meaning./Together, together, the race-makers enter the lodges."[43] The idea of sex as a "race-making" activity returns in Mary Austin's interpretation "Song for the Passing of Beautiful Women (from the Paiute)," in which a male speaker exclaims, "great races in my loins to thee that cry!/My blood is redder for thy loveliness."[44]

At the same time that the anthology presents Native nations as traditionally heteropatriarchal, it also codes premodern Native sexualities as violently primitive and hence as located in a distinctly unmodern past. The violence of "authentic" or precontact Native sexuality becomes a sign of the lack of modernity of Indigenous cultures and justifies the need for those cultures to disappear into a multicultural modern American nation, illustrating Joanne Barker's argument that "imperialism and colonialism require Indigenous people to fit within the heteronormative archetypes of an Indigeneity that was authentic in the past but is culturally and legally vacated in the present."[45] This is most evident in Skinner's "Song of the Young Mother," which presents an Orientalized rape fantasy as an example of "traditional" Native culture. The titular young mother sings to her male infant about the pains of being a woman. She remembers giving birth to her son and muses, "Strange, that pain came with love; / I knew it not until thy father sought me. / Yet—what woman would cast love out?"[46] The specific kinds of pain women experience because of heterosexual love become more explicit as the young mother describes her first experience of sex as a violent encounter. She remembers of her partner,

> He circled my house with the arms of strength,
> And took me with weapons . . . Joy?
> Ay. Yet I cried from the depths with a sudden deep cry,
> And in grieving earth was the torch quenched.
> . . . Darkness . . . and his, his utterly, in that dark . . .
> None had told me . . .
> Nor that his strength would leap, rejoicing at my cry.[47]

The man's pleasure in sex is specifically pleasure in the woman's pain. The poem presents this violence as traditionally Indigenous through the repetition of the phrase "it is our custom," connecting a primitivizing idea of sexual violence as part of "authentic" Native cultures. Indeed, the poem goes on to portray a ceremony consecrating patriarchal violence as the foundation of marriage. The young mother remembers,

My tears fell, shining among the earth's bright drops;
For now I knew
Why the maiden plaits a whip of cedar-fibre,
To give into her husband's hand on her marriage-day.
Once I asked my father—it seemed so strange
A maid should weave and weave a rod for her own sorrow.
He laughed and said: "It is our custom; ay, an old custom. . ."
. . . .
My mother sat near. Ay, I have remembered that she spoke not;
But, silently, in the shadow of his body, drooped her head.

      Ay, 'tis old, the custom,
Old as earth is old;
Ancient as passion[48]

This "interpretation" works to pathologize a caricature of Indigenous sexuality at the same time that it naturalizes patriarchal heterosexuality as part of Indigenous cultural practices. Because the poem does not mark the ethnographic sources it is interpreting, it makes this form of violent patriarchal control appear to be broadly Indigenous rather than specific to particular Native nations. And because the emphasis is on a supposedly authentic tradition, it also appears timeless, part of the premodern temporality to which Indigenous cultures were assigned by settler cultures. Skinner's interpretation thus works as what Joanne Barker calls "a racially gendered and sexed snapshot, a still image of a movingly malleable narrative of Indigenous womanhood/femininity and manhood/masculinity that reenacts Indigenous peoples' lack of knowledge and power over their own culture and identity in an inherently imperialist and colonialist world."[49]

This insistence on both the violence of "primitive" Indigenous sexualities and the naturalness and enduringness of heteropatriarchal gender roles within Indigenous societies is not incidental in the era, when, in Mishuana Goeman's words, Canada and the United States "were attempting to construct Native women in the image of European contemporaries or exile and expunge them from the nation's 'proper' territory."[50] Because the Dawes Act in the United States and the Indian Act in Canada imbued marriage with the ability to define the citizenship status of Indigenous women, the representation of Indigenous sexualities and gender roles was especially fraught in this moment. By connecting *The Path on the Rainbow*'s insistence that Native poetry is an ancient form of free verse with its insistence that Indigenous societies are traditionally heteropatriarchal, I have been attending to an instantiation of what Simpson calls the "systemic relationship to gender in particular" that shapes "the structure of settler colonialism."[51] Literary anthologies obviously do not have the force of law, but *The Path on the Rainbow* echoes the gendered "bounding of space and people" evident in the reservation systems of the United States and Canada by seeking to limit Indigenous peoples to certain literary forms (only "ancient" free verse forms count as authentic Native poetry) and to certain temporalities (the rapidly receding past).[52] The anthology imposes heteropatriarchy on Native nations as part of its drive to assimilate Native cultural materials into settler literary cultures. *The Path on the Rainbow* textualizes, spatializes, and temporally orients oral expressions in ways that emphasize that Native forms would naturally give way to white free verse "reinterpretations" of those forms, so that Native poetry would eventually become the product of white American poets. The path on the rainbow, in this view, led directly to a renewed settler nation.

E. Pauline Johnson's Canoe

Given this context, it is perhaps no wonder that contemporaneous readers experienced E. Pauline Johnson's poems as disruptive or as not belonging to *The Path on the Rainbow*. Both "The Lost Lagoon" and "The Song My Paddle Sings" belong to Johnson's body of queer erotic canoe poetry, challenging the essentializing, primitivist heteropatriarchal orientation of the other texts in the anthology. They also make use of rhyme and tetrameter, working against the idea that authentic Native poetries could only be textualized as free verse. As I have shown, *The Path on the Rainbow* primed its readers to think that there was an absolute difference at the level of rhythm between English and Indigenous poetries—a critical move that automatically positioned poetry written in English by Indigenous authors as ersatz. The fact that Johnson's poems are included in the "Interpretations" section of the anthology underscores their supposedly ersatz status; as Austin's framing of the texts in *The Path on the Rainbow* makes clear, the texts that truly mattered were "authentic," ancient (meaning pre-nineteenth century), and supposedly culturally pure Indigenous expressions that could be textualized as free verse.[53] In editor George Cronyn's words, Johnson's poetry "show[s] how far the Indian poet strays from her own primitive tribal songs, when attempting the White Man's mode."[54]

The irony of critics arguing that Johnson was too much of the nineteenth century was immense, as the majority of the ethnographic texts collected in the anthology and presented as "ancient" examples of free verse were produced during the nineteenth century. Nevertheless, reviews by T. S. Eliot and Louis Untermeyer insisted that the anthology's failings were the result of allowing in too much mannered nineteenth-century verse. Eliot's review argued that truly "primitive poetry" was to be welcomed "because it has more significance, in relation to its own age or culture, than 'Kehama' and 'Aurora Leigh' have for theirs."[55] Nineteenth-century poetry, whether by Robert Southey or Elizabeth Barrett Browning or E. Pauline Johnson, would, in this view, always remain too artificial to play any role in serious art and contemporary life. According to Eliot, Cronyn and his collaborators had failed in their project by including too much of such nineteenth-century treacle. Eliot specifically singled out "Maple Sugar Song" as a poor example of primitive poetry: "suddenly, egged on by New York and Chicago *intelligentsia*, the romantic Chippaway [*sic*] bursts into the drawing-room, and among murmurs of approval declaims his 'Maple Sugar Song.' . . . The Red Man is here: what are we to do with him, except to feed him on maple sugar?"[56] Louis Untermeyer too condemned what he portrayed as the sugary elements of the anthology—what he called E. Pauline Johnson's "rhymed sweetmeats," which stood in contrast to the "sharp flavour" that white interpreters had supposedly managed to put into their contributions.[57]

In these misreadings of Johnson and of nineteenth-century poetry generally, bad poetry is coded as sickly sweet—it is the overly refined, feminized drawing-room entertainment that is too simplistic to provide intellectual nourishment. But if Johnson's engagement with poetic conventions seems so simplistic as to require no unpacking, that is only because we have forgotten the complexity of nineteenth-century verse cultures and of the cultural work poetic conventions performed. Johnson was especially attuned to the complicated functions of poetic convention because her ability to support herself financially depended on her ability to appeal to the expectations of specific audiences—both those who came to see her perform and those who only encountered her work in print. Johnson was a master of multiple generic and formal conventions who used that mastery to navigate the wide variety of generic expectations different audiences brought to her poetry. This was no small feat, given that her paying audiences included white men who overtly sexualized her political poetry, white women who feared that Johnson's expressions of sexuality would corrupt white men, and First Nations and Native American communities who were actively fighting for survival and who sometimes viewed Johnson's work with deep skepticism and disapproval.[58]

Johnson was the child of an English mother and a Kanien'kehá:ka father, meaning that she was often positioned as both "insider and outsider," a position that, Strong-Boag and Gerson argue, allowed her to "ac[t] as a highly visible bicultural mediator."[59] Johnson was proud of her Six Nations heritage and family but did not speak any Iroquoian languages and seems to have had fairly limited knowledge of Haudenosaunee culture.[60] As Rick Monture notes, Johnson grew up listening to the stories of her grandfather John "Smoke" Johnson, who "told stories of Iroquois history and their prowess on the battlefield, as well as their great skills at diplomacy," and she incorporated some of these stories in her work; but she also "employed creative license in her later approaches to Six Nations subject matter, . . . [relying] on literary and fictionalized accounts rather than historical or traditional representations of important cultural information."[61] In 1894, after she had already achieved some literary fame, Johnson appended her great-grandfather's name, Tekahionwake, to her own in many of her publications, but "no evidence survives as to whether she followed proper Mohawk custom to obtain legitimate use of the name."[62]

Critics spilled a great deal of ink in the attempt to adjudicate Johnson's level of Indigeneity. Johnson's first major publication, for instance, framed her as a Canadian, rather than a First Nations, author. The anthology *Songs of the Great Dominion* (1889) featured a few of Johnson's poems in sections titled "Sports and Free Life" and "Places" rather than in the section titled "The Indian." As Strong-Boag and Gerson note, this went against Johnson's desires; she had selected the poems "A Cry from an Indian Wife" and "The Indian Death Cry" as "her 'best' verse, that was 'most Canadian in tone and color.'"[63] When Johnson published *The White Wampum* in 1895—a text that clearly positions her as an Indigenous woman—Johnson's family friend the anthropologist Horatio Hale again tried to downplay her self-presentation as a First Nations woman. He argued that "her compositions will be judged as those of a 'wild Indian girl,' and not as those of a well-bred and accomplished young Canadian lady with a dash of Indian blood, such as she really is."[64] According to most non-Indigenous reviewers, Johnson was either not Indigenous enough or was, conversely, "the erotic Other, the passionate poetess whose non-European heritage accounts for the unabashed sexuality of poems which are not, in themselves, explicitly Indian."[65] Johnson's promotional materials for her recitals, by contrast, referred to her as "the Mohawk Indian Poet-Reciter," an "Indian Poet-Reciter," an "Iroquois Indian Poet-Entertainer," and a "Mohawk Author-Entertainer."[66]

Johnson's "hybrid" identity was probably especially troubling to non-Indigenous critics who would have understood Iroquoian peoples to be culturally conservative. Within nineteenth-century American anthropology, Iroquois nations, including the Six Nations, were understood to be fundamentally traditional and unchanging in their cultural practices and thus were often held up as exemplary "authentic" Native peoples. Simpson has shown that the "authenticating discourse" within American anthropological writings about the Iroquois has relied on "an unproblematized and narrow model of 'tradition'" because it seems to offer "an instance of cultural stability and cultural difference, two preconditions of anthropological inquiry of the time." But of course this supposedly pure tradition was "one that grew as a result of acculturative and colonial forces."[67] For readers who understood Iroquoian peoples to be particularly culturally "authentic," Johnson's generic hybridity in her person and in her art may have seemed especially troubling (Johnson consistently defied ideas of authenticity, deliberately mixing signifiers of Indigeneity with signifiers of Canadian nationalism and British imperialism). Johnson's insistence on hybridity and cultural inter-mixing was one strategy for insisting on the modernity of First Nations peoples, as critics including Kristen Brown and Colleen Kim Daniher have argued. Johnson stood as living proof that the idea of the Iroquois as static and unchanging was false and that it made little sense to talk about First Nations peoples as fundamentally separated from other cultures. As Simpson argues of contemporary Kanien'kehá:ka individuals, Johnson had "a command of the theater in which [she was] being apprehended, the space of recognition that [she was] flipping back, questioning, not signing on to."[68] Johnson's complex engagements with Anglo North American poetic and performance cultures and with Six Nations history and contemporaneous politics reflect this command.

Though Johnson passed away in 1913, five years before *The Path on the Rainbow* was published, her poems in the anthology continue her project of asserting that First Nations peoples were active shapers of contemporary life, operating well outside the boundaries that settler nations attempted to impose on them — including the boundaries imposed by formal expectations for Indigenous poetry. "The Lost Lagoon" and "The Song My Paddle Sings" belong to Johnson's body of queer erotic canoe poetry, identified as such by scholars including Strong-Boag and Gerson, Kristen Brown, and Linda Revie.[69]

If contemporaneous and contemporary critics have understood these poems to be politically neutral pastoral idylls, it is only because critics have failed to think about the fact that "the structure of settler colonialism" has a "systemic relationship to gender in particular" that has to be accounted for in reading these poems.[70] Too, the form of "The Lost Lagoon" would have called to mind Tennyson's *In Memoriam* (both employ envelope rhymes; *In Memoriam* is *abba*, while "The Lost Lagoon" is *abbba*), which to modernist readers would have signaled an outmoded Victorianism as often as it would have signaled queerness. It also would have been easy for contemporaneous readers to see these poems as of a piece with patriotic canoe poems by Johnson's peers. For readers who knew how to read "The Lost Lagoon" and "The Song My Paddle Sings" through their intertexts, however, a different picture emerges. "The Lost Lagoon" (1910) in particular requires careful unpacking, as it is the least overtly erotic of Johnson's sexy canoe poems and is thus easily misread as a sentimental, nostalgic poem about lost love. Read against Johnson's other canoe poems, however—especially "The Idlers" (1890), "Re-Voyage" (1891), and "Wave-Won" (1892)—it becomes clear that "The Lost Lagoon" is a poem about nonheteronormative sex. Further, in both "The Lost Lagoon" and "The Song My Paddle Sings," Johnson links queered sexuality to Indigenous mobility and land claims, making these poems unsettling indeed within the framework of *The Path on the Rainbow*.

Each of the erotic canoe poems in the set just identified begins by establishing an atmosphere of luxurious, amorous idleness during a canoe trip taken by a speaker and their lover, progresses through a barely coded sexual encounter (though "The Lost Lagoon" omits an explicit description of such an encounter), and ends with a lament for love lost after the canoe trip. Across these four poems, similar forms, vocabulary, and phrasing recur, as does a consistent color imagery, wherein blue and yellow signify eroticism and gray signifies danger and loss. Although the memory of lost love that the speaker reminisces about in "The Lost Lagoon" is hazy and unclear, the shared formal elements across these canoe poems signal that the dreamy, hazy memories that make up "The Lost Lagoon" are sexual.

Color imagery operates consistently in Johnson's erotic canoe poetry. In "The Idlers," scenes of sexual activity take place under "The sun's red pulses" on a "yellow beach"; in "Re-Voyage," they take place under a blue sky in a "warm and yellow afternoon," and in "Wave-Won," they take place in "The dusky summer night" on a "path of gold and white" cast by the moon on the water. The "golden moon" and the "haunting blue" of the water in "The Lost Lagoon" call back to these images, and the "twilight gray" over the Lost

Lagoon mirrors the lover's "cloud-grey eyes" in "The Idlers." "The Idlers" and "Re-Voyage" both end with the loss of the speaker's lover to some unnamed force ("The Idlers" ends with the statement, "you and I have lost/More than the homeward blowing wind that died an hour ago"; "Re-Voyage" ends with the speaker steering their "long canoe" through the same waters they had shared with their lover in the past), and this is perhaps the loss that gives the Lost Lagoon its name.[71]

The wistful, seemingly nonerotic "dreaming" that happens in "The Lost Lagoon" is thus in fact a reference to the explicit eroticism of the other canoe poems. And the sexuality of these poems is transgressive in multiple ways. First, because the gender of both speaker and lover are unmarked, even as the speaker describes their lover's body in detail, these poems invite queer readings, as Kristen Brown has argued. And while explicit poems about queer sex in the 1890s were of course already transgressive, as Brown notes, in the context of Canada's Indian Act and the United States' Dawes Act, these scenes of nonreproductive, nonmarital sex become all the more charged. Brown argues that Johnson's "erotic gestures . . . challenge settler colonial constructions of desire as something to be pragmatically contained within the heteronormative boundaries of marriage" and hence challenge the imposition of heteronormative marriage as a tool of dispossession.[72]

We can see this challenge in the way "The Idlers" glories in the lover's physical form and the pleasures of sex. The poem spends multiple stanzas describing the allure of the lover's body:

Against the *thwart*, near by,
Inactively you lie,
And all too near my arm your temple bends.
Your *indolently* crude,
Abandoned attitude,
Is one of ease and art, in which a perfect languor blends.

Your costume, loose and light,
Leaves unconcealed your might
Of muscle, half suspected, half defined;
And falling well aside,
Your vesture opens wide,
Above your splendid sunburnt throat that *pulses* unconfined

With easy unreserve,
Across the gunwale's curve,

Your arm superb is lying, brown and bare;
Your hand just touches mine
With import firm and fine,
(I kiss the very wind that blows about your tumbled hair.)[73]

The description of the lover's "muscle" and "puls[ing]" "sunburnt throat" caused contemporaneous reviewers to code the lover as male. But Johnson reveled in describing the swell of her own arm muscles in her journalism about recreational canoeing and was an advocate of clothing reform for women, making the image of loose, light "costume" (the word she used to describe her own dress for performances) falling open to reveal an alluringly muscled body a potentially queer image.[74] As Gerson notes, "flexing one's muscles was not a common trait of Victorian femininity, yet Johnson explicitly relishes the physical work of handling a canoe" in many of her poems.[75] Indeed, in "Wave-Won," the speaker refers to "my arm as strong as steel."[76]

The form of "The Idlers" also signals its queerness: It is written in the Swinburne sestet (*aabccb*). Swinburne was of course the poster boy for the linkage of poetic meter with nonnormative sexuality. In Johnson's hands, the Swinburne sestet works to imbue the watery landscape she describes with erotic power. The stress patterns in each stanza of "The Idlers" are 4, 4, 4, 3, 3, 5. Along with the *aabccb* rhyme scheme, the ebb and flow of the poem's form echoes the ebb and flow of the waters that lap against the lovers' canoe, which in turn mirrors the lovers' caresses. "The Lost Lagoon" too uses its form to mimic the motion of the canoe and the seclusion of the lovers. "The Lost Lagoon" consists of three stanzas of five lines each, rhymed *abbba*. The middle tercet is closed in by the rhyme of the first and last lines, just as the lagoon forms a natural enclosure. The first and last lines of each stanza contain three stresses, and the middle three lines contain four. This creates a feeling of a gentle wave-like motion, as the middles of the stanzas expand and then contract. The middle tercet adds to the feeling of suspension or stasis, as there is no progression in the rhyme but only repetition and return, idling in the middle. "The Lost Lagoon" thus harnesses the association of Tennysonian envelope forms with nostalgia for lost love (this is the *In Memoriam* form, after all) but also foregrounds the queerness of that Tennysonian form.

The queerness encoded in the forms of the erotic canoe poems is made much more explicit in the later "Re-Voyage," which recalls the scene described in "The Idlers." "The Idlers" takes place on a hot July afternoon, and "Re-Voyage" recalls a canoe trip taken on a hot July afternoon. Both poems share key words that suggest that these describe the same canoe trip and the same sexual experience. In "Re-Voyage," the speaker addresses the lover:

Have you no longing to relive the dreaming,
Adrift in my canoe?
To watch my paddle blade all wet and gleaming
Cleaving the waters through?
To lie wind-blown and wave-caressed, until
Your restless *pulse* grows still?

Do you not long to listen to the purling
Of foam *athwart* the keel?
To hear the nearing rapids softly swirling
Among their stones, to feel
The boat's unsteady tremor as it braves
The wild and snarling waves?

What need of question, what of your replying?
Oh! well I know that you
Would toss the world away to be but lying
Again in my canoe,
In listless *indolence* entranced and lost,
Wave-rocked, and passion-tossed.[77]

"Re-Voyage" employs the nearly pornographic image of the "paddle blade all wet and gleaming / Cleaving the waters through" until the lover, "wind-blow and wave-caressed," finally is able to have their "restless pulse gro[w] still." The repetition of "pulse," "[a]thwart," and "indolence" across these poems ties them together, as does the title of "Re-Voyage," signaling the speaker's desire to revisit the memory of a sexual encounter in a canoe on a hot July afternoon.

I want to draw attention to the way that these poems work together as intertexts. By employing the same vocabulary and imagery, Johnson has created her own subgenre of queer erotic canoe poems, highlighting the subversive potential of nineteenth-century metrical forms to work against settler impositions of heterosexuality on Indigenous peoples. Although "The Lost Lagoon" is less explicitly erotic than the other poems discussed here, it is connected to that overt eroticism through the shared elements of all of these poems. Far from being a simple romantic pastoral poem, "The Lost Lagoon" is about the memory of a queered sexual encounter. Within the context of the hyperheterosexual *The Path on the Rainbow*, "The Lost

Lagoon" thus works to denaturalize heterosexual sex—still a radical move in 1918, as settler governments turned heterosexual marriage into yet another avenue of legal dispossession.

In addition to offering a portrait of queer sexuality, "The Lost Lagoon" is linked to inter-Indigenous collaboration through its connection to Johnson's friend Su-á-pu-luck, also known as Chief Joe Capilano (Squamish). This move—connecting nonheteronormative sexuality with Indigenous stories, histories, and land claims—is one that Johnson makes repeatedly, as we will see. As Steve Dickinson notes, "The Lost Lagoon" was initially published as part of the story "The True Legend of Deadman's Island" in the *Vancouver Daily Magazine* and was later printed in *Legends of Vancouver*, a collection of Squamish stories that Capilano and his wife, Líxwelut, told to Johnson.[78] Dickinson argues that Johnson's poem elegizes both Capilano, who died shortly before "The Lost Lagoon" was published, and Johnson's "favourite canoeing spot in the Burrard Inlet," which was known by the far more prosaic name "Coal Harbour" until Johnson renamed it. Toward the end of Johnson's life, a proposal to construct a lake and causeway in Coal Harbour/The Lost Lagoon was hotly debated, meaning that "Johnson must have been aware that her 'pet idling-place' would be permanently changed" by the proposed construction.[79] In "The True Legend of Deadman's Island," Johnson recalls standing with Capilano at sunset "looking over Coal Harbour."[80] Dickinson thus argues that "The Lost Lagoon" serves as an "eco-elegy" for Johnson's beloved canoeing spot and as an elegy for Chief Capilano, with whom she enjoyed the Lost Lagoon.[81] Read alone, out of context, it certainly could seem that "The Lost Lagoon" is a nostalgic, elegiac, outmoded poem of sentiment. But read through its intertexts, it is clear that "The Lost Lagoon" ties a queer erotics together with Indigenous presence and movement through the Canadian landscape.

"The Song My Paddle Sings" (1892) also connects queer eroticism with Indigenous presence and mobility, but it does so by explicitly thinking through the relationship between Anglo poetics and Indigenous practices. Johnson performed this poem both in her Anglo-Canadian canoeing costume and in her infamous Native dress, signaling to her audience that this poem attempted to bridge the seeming impenetrable divide between settler and Indigenous cultures.[82] Once again, the intertexts Johnson references and creates for this poem are key to its interpretation—particularly the poem's reworking of Shelley's "Ode to the West Wind."

Crucial to Johnson's cultural mediation in this poem is, as Monture has argued, the "Iroquoian cultural metaphor" of the Two Row Wampum. Monture explains,

> The Two Row Wampum is a treaty agreement that the Haudenosaunee made with the European nations in the seventeenth century, which established and affirmed a separate-but-equal status between them, meaning that these nations were not to interfere with each other's affairs but to recognize the sovereignty of each. This was affirmed by using the metaphor of two vessels, the Haudenosaunee canoe and the European sailing ship, moving along side by side, each containing the "contents" (language, culture, customs) of its respective nation. It is also said that one cannot straddle the two vessels, or live in both worlds, without the risk of falling between them and being lost.[83]

Monture argues that "such an image would be almost impossible to ignore" for Johnson as the daughter of a Kanien'kehá:ka father and an English mother.[84] Monture reads "The Song My Paddle Sings" as an extended meditation on her position between two cultures, making the poem work against audience expectations that Johnson "'perform' her identity" by "employ[ing] the canoe as a cultural metaphor about herself as a mixed-race Iroquois person" in a poem that otherwise does not employ the expected tropes related to Indian identity.[85] Monture notes that in some ways the poem almost immediately departs from the image of the Two Row Wampum, however, since in the Two Row Wampum, "all Haundenosaunee are understood to be aboard," while in Johnson's poem, the speaker is alone in her canoe.[86] But the poem is perhaps more invested in the metaphor of the Two Row Wampum than Monture notices. The poem begins with the speaker tucking away a sail after the west wind refuses to blow. It is significant that it is a sail the speaker discards, since in the Two Row Wampum, European nations are signified by a sailing ship, and it is also significant that it is specifically the west wind that refuses to blow, because this signals the poem's rewriting of Shelley's "Ode to the West Wind." In "The Song My Paddle Sings," both the European sailing ship of the Two Row Wampum and the personified west wind of Romantic poetic tradition are set aside as the speaker glories in her own abilities to steer her canoe through Six Nations territory, making this poem a joyful celebration of modern Indigenous womanhood, outside the narrow gender and racial categories of settler culture.

"The Song My Paddle Sings" opens by apostrophizing the west wind. In Barbara Johnson's classic reading of Shelley's "Ode to the West Wind," she highlights the poem's agonistic framing of apostrophe. Johnson notes that Shelley "addresses, gives animation, gives the capacity of responsiveness, to the wind, not in order to make it speak but in order to make it listen to him—in order to make it listen to him doing nothing but address *it*"—and that the poem elaborates a "power struggle" and "rivalry" between the speaker and the apostrophized west wind.[87] Johnson ultimately reads apostrophe as a trope as "structured like demand"—particularly the "demand [that] is the originary vocative" of the infant in a Lacanian developmental framework.[88] E. Pauline Johnson, in stark contrast to the history of apostrophe as demand that Barbara Johnson traces, imagines what happens when a demand is refused. More specifically, she imagines accepting the refusal of the apostrophized other as a precondition for her own song, which forms part of a larger sonic landscape. E. Pauline Johnson, in other words, uses apostrophe as a way of navigating a reciprocal relationship that acknowledges and accepts alterity, versus Shelley's agonistic framing of apostrophe. In this way, "The Song My Paddle Sings" functions as one of the poems that reconfigures Anglo-Canadian nature poetry not as a matter of "conquest" and domination but rather as a matter of elucidating a "harmonious relationship with the outdoor setting."[89]

The first two stanzas of "The Song My Paddle Sings" invoke the animating powers of Shelleyean apostrophe only to put them to bed.[90] The poem begins by calling to the west wind: "West wind, blow from your prairie nest,/Blow from the mountains, blow from the west." But the wind refuses the poet's demand:

Blow, blow!
I have wooed you so,
But never a favor you bestow.
You rock your cradle the hills between,
But scorn to notice my white lateen.[91]

The demand of apostrophic address is unanswered here, as the wind has its own agency and its own cares, rocking its cradle rather than attending to the speaker who would demand its attention. Instead of continuing the demand, the speaker accepts the wind's competing desires: "I stow the sail, unship the mast:/I wooed you long but my wooing's past;/My paddle will lull you into rest."[92] The speaker's song becomes a lullaby ("soft is the song my paddle sings") that rocks the wind to sleep, and the poem then turns to the song of the speaker's paddle, which is answered by the song of the river and of the trees on the shore. The third through sixth stanzas describe canoeing through

rapids as a pulse-quickening sexual encounter, in which the speaker, her canoe, and her paddle "slip" "over [the] breast" of the river's waters, causing the
river to "ru[n] swifter," circling and swirling "about [the speaker's] bow." The
keel of the canoe "trembl[es]" in response to the rushing waters, until these mutual vibrations give way to a postcoital peace, as "the river slips through its silent
bed," joining the west wind that slumbers in the hills around them. The poem
ends with the song of the speaker's paddle being echoed and amplified by the
entities that make up the natural landscape:

> Sway, sway,
> As bubbles spray
> And fall in tinkling tunes away.
> And up on the hills against the sky,
> A fir tree rocking its lullaby,
> Swings, swings,
> Its emerald wings,
> Swelling the song that my paddle sings.[93]

The trees "swell" the speaker's paddle's song, which is counterpointed by the
"tinkling tunes" of the river waters. Personified natural entities here are not
locked in an embattled set of apostrophic demands but rather form a chorus with the speaker, creating musical harmony out of elements that could
have been framed as a contest between human and nature (the wind that will
not power the sail; the river that seeks to dash the canoe on the rocks within
it). As Strong-Boag and Gerson argue in their reading of the poem, "The Song
My Paddle Sings" "celebrates the physical prowess of a solo woman canoeist
fearlessly making her way through a sensual, wild landscape that hums with
its own vitality, but whose challenges invite collaboration (the paddler and
her canoe become 'we') rather than the confrontation that colours the rhetoric of conquest typical of men's poetry."[94] In this way, the poem endorses
what Jodi Melamed calls, in reference to other texts, "a conceptual paradigm
that signifies land in terms of its cultural relations with human beings rather
than one that conceives of land as primarily property."[95]

This move to portray a relationship with nature that is reciprocal rather
than colonizing is not inherently reflective of an Iroquoian sensibility, but
another of Johnson's intertexts does explicitly link the sensual pleasures of
movement by canoe with Six Nations land claims. The year after she published the poem "The Song My Paddle Sings," Johnson published an article
of the same name in the *Detroit Free Press*. The fact that the article carries the
same title as one of her most famous poems may have been a calculated

choice on the part of the newspaper publisher, but it also establishes a tie between the two texts. The article details a multiday canoe trip down O:se Kenhionhata:tie (the Grand River) in Ontario. Notably, the article celebrates Johnson's ability to engage in gender role reversals, and it also connects mobility across a landscape to Indigenous land claims. Johnson mentions with pleasure the fact that the women of the group were addressed as men, noting, "we were all 'boys' on that cruise." The end of the article emphasizes the upending of normative gender roles, as a group of men on land who predicted that the trip would be a disaster greet the fleet's return: "The men cheer and hurrah us, call us 'some of the boys,' and shake hands heartily as we beach the last time." The article begins by noting that the three canoes on the trip were "manned at the stern, maidened at the bow," in accordance with expected gender roles, but when a group member announces that they are approaching the famed Eleven Link rapids, Johnson takes charge. She explains, "The very name of it went to my head like wine. Full often had I heard of this famous stretch of seven miles, wherein eleven wildcats followed one another like the links in a chain," and she tells the man then steering in the stern of the canoe to move to the bow. He willingly obliges, and Johnson steers the canoe through the rapids. Her description of running the rapids is ecstatic, and the language mirrors the sensual, erotic language of her canoe poems: "There is nothing in life that sends me as crazy as a rapid. My brain goes aflame when I see the distant whitecaps, my heart pulses wildly with the first faint music of waters galloping madly over their rocky obstructions, singing, surging, laughing their needless, restless poetry—the world holds no such music for me as the cool calling of waters that my bow will kiss and conquer before the hour is over." And indeed, the women on the trip are portrayed as the most active, adventurous members of the group. Following a run through a difficult rapid, Johnson reports that one of the women of the group, Jeannie, "demanded . . . 'What's next?'" According to Johnson, Jeannie "is the greatest dare-devil alive (for her size)."[96]

Johnson thus shows how canoeing provides women with opportunities to be active adventure seekers. She also connects canoeing with First Nations practices in this article in a way she often does not in her canoe poems. In describing a run of rapids, Johnson writes, "we made our first plunge, our sturdy basswood shivering like an aspen, but darting ahead like an arrow leaving an Indian bowstring." Here Johnson reminds readers that, although the canoe was often used as a symbol of Canadian nationalism, it was an Indigenous invention. Even more explicitly, she reminds readers that the Grand River was central to Six Nations peoples and that the territory around the river had been forcefully taken from them. In the middle of the rapturous descriptions of running rapids, Johnson explains,

> Few people that see this gem river of Ontario know how importantly the name of the Grand figured in the early treaties between Britain and the Indians. After the war of independence, when the Iroquois adhered to England and signalized their intention to settle in her domain, the royal grant of land to "The Six Nations" comprised "the territory lying within six miles on both sides of the Grand River, from its source up to its mouth," a tract that included a larger portion of the present Counties of Wellington, Waterloo, Brant and Haldimand. That was 100 years ago; and what have the Six Nations now? A scrap of reserve embracing 53,000 acres of uninteresting, timberless and in many places marshy land, while the garden lands of the river are again in the white man's possession. To be sure, the Six Nations have deposited $800,000 with the Dominion Government. It is the sale price of only some of their lands, but not nearly the value thereof.[97]

This history of land theft is presented as a crucial part of what it means to enjoy canoeing down the Grand River in Johnson's moment. Johnson celebrates her delight in moving freely on the river, but she notes that this delight has been hard-won as the Six Nations were pushed into smaller and smaller reserves. Johnson's joy in moving through this landscape is thus politicized in this article, and the pleasures of the woman canoeist celebrated in the poem "The Song My Paddle Sings" are connected to the free movement of Six Nations peoples in part of their homelands.[98] Against Austin's framing claim that Indigenous peoples "occupy space without filling it," Johnson's poetry presents an Indigenous erotics of place, where occupying space is a relational act that establishes kinship with the land and accompanying claims to Indigenous sovereignty and self-determination. If, as Joanne Barker argues, "the core place of gender and sexuality in Indigenous sovereignty and self-determination has been minimized and deflected" in much scholarship, Johnson's erotics of place return us to the connections between free movement, racialized sexuality and gender identities, and Indigenous sovereignty.[99]

Johnson's poetry also returns us to Jodi Byrd's reminder that "interpretation is an act of sovereignty."[100] Johnson's reinterpretation of "Ode to the West Wind" and of various metrical forms can be thought of as "act[s] of . . . interpretive agency" that work through "a dialogical process of exchange and negotiation" to Indigenize particular poetic conventions, to use Adam Spry's formulation.[101] *The Path on the Rainbow* worked hard to contain and reframe such acts of interpretive agency; a concluding essay by Constance Lindsay Skinner reiterated the introduction's insistence on the absolute difference between Native and English poetries. Skinner argued that when the Native poet enters "the Paleface lodges," the Native "Bard must listen sacredly to catch the pure rhythms of life across the false time-currents that seethe over him; for the true song, the arresting song, the clarion song, is still the song of kinship."[102] Johnson's work stands against this essentialist framing. She turns the supposedly "false time-currents" of English poetic meter to non-essentialist ends, pointing to the necessarily hybrid nature of any cultural identity. She shows that the Swinburne sestet, the Tennysonian envelope form, and the marching beat of tetrameter can all be used to represent the complexity of Indigenous modernity and the ongoing vitality, presence, and mobility of peoples who were supposed to be relegated to reserve lands and to a quickly receding past. In an era when free verse was explicitly framed as a tool of cultural dispossession, Johnson's poetry shows how poetic meter could become a tool of Indigenous survivance. Taking Johnson's poetry seriously within modernist studies necessarily challenges those of us working with the field to reconsider what kinds of formal and generic elements make a poem valuable or worth attending to. Such a reconsideration is integral to developing an antiracist modernist studies, in which the modernist measure of value is understood to be a racial formation of whiteness and in which there is room for aesthetics that imagine the world otherwise, in terms that resist the colonizing force of modernism and modernity.

Conclusion

Historical Poetics and Modernist Studies

I hope that the preceding chapters have begun to show the difference that historical poetics approaches can make to modernist studies of poetry and poetics. By way of conclusion, I want to think through the slow uptake and misapprehension of historical poetics arguments and methodologies in recent scholarship on modernist and contemporary poetry. As I argued in the introduction, it has been particularly difficult for historical poetics approaches to find purchase within modernist studies, due in part to the fact that historical poetics scholarship challenges the orienting idea within modernist studies that there was a coherent metrical tradition from which modernist poets could break free. In the realm of modernist poetics, this means that "experimental" or formally innovative poetry remains the default object of study, and the intellectual interest of "conventional" prosodies, forms, and genres—especially nineteenth-century prosodies, forms, and genres—is overlooked, along with the racial, national, and imperial ideologies that are part and parcel of much prosodic thinking. The slow uptake of historical poetics methodologies in modernist studies has been exacerbated by the mistaken and unfortunate conflation of historical poetics with the "new lyric studies." This conflation has made it difficult to understand the aims and outcomes of historical poetics scholarship, particularly when it comes to the ways such scholarship has dealt with race and racialization. I unpack the relation between the two here so as to underscore what historical poetics offers to scholars of twentieth- and twenty-first-century poetry and poetics.

The most obvious difference between historical poetics and the "new lyric studies" is that the former is a set of methodologies developed by a working group of fifteen scholars (give or take a few in any given year) of nineteenth-century transatlantic poetry, while the latter is a term used to describe a set of opposed theories of lyric poetry. Historical poetics is based on a shared understanding that the terms that we use to study poetry (including "lyric"), along with our reading practices and our preferred aesthetic modes, have (racialized, imperial, and decolonial) histories and that those histories have informed both poets' practices and critics' abilities to tell stories about poetry. The "new lyric studies," on the other hand, has not generated a shared understanding of the term "lyric" or a common set of methodologies. It refers instead to two overarching approaches to the study of poetry: that associated with Virginia Jackson and Yopie Prins, whose lyricization thesis has challenged the idea that lyric is a transhistorical term, and that associated with Jonathan Culler and others who make the diametrically opposed case that lyric is a transhistorical and transnational category.

Part of the confusion comes from the fact that Jackson and Prins are members of the historical poetics working group. But the reduction of historical poetics to Jackson and Prins's lyricization thesis does a disservice to the scholarship of others in the group and to the complexity and variety of approaches to the reading of poetry those scholars have developed. Most importantly, the reduction of historical poetics to the lyricization thesis (along with misunderstandings of that thesis, discussed more shortly) obscures the abiding interest of scholars of historical poetics in the ways that poetic forms and terms are racialized and imbricated in uneven systems of power. It has become common for scholars to point to the whiteness of the objects of the new lyric studies as evidence that historical poetics is uninterested in thinking about race and racialization. If one looks at the actual publications of historical poetics scholars, however, this claim becomes untenable. Meredith McGill has published extensively on nineteenth-century abolitionist poetry and on Black print cultures; Max Cavitch's research has explored how metrical discourse and printing and book trades in the nineteenth-century United States were intertwined with the institution of chattel slavery; Tricia Lootens's work theorizes the racialization of the poetess and the complex relationships between poetic and imperial discourses; Michael Cohen has helped us to understand how ballad reading is racialized; Yopie Prins and Jason Rudy have shown how seemingly apolitical metrical discourse has supported and challenged nationalist and imperial projects; Virginia Jackson has theorized "the racialization of the structure of American poetics."[1] As I hope is apparent from this very abridged list of some of the work that historical poetics scholars have done, historical poetics is a set of approaches to poetry that is fundamentally interested in how systems of metrical and poetic classification intersect with uneven, unjust systems of power and oppression.

Although this has been difficult for many scholars to see, thinking with the lyricization thesis also helps us read the ways that Anglo-American poetics has been racialized through processes of abstraction, such as the abstraction of genre into form I discussed in chapter 3 and the abstraction of meter into rhythm I discussed in chapters 1 and 4. For Jackson and Prins, lyricization is another such process of poetic abstraction that can eventuate in racialized modes of reading. At the heart of the lyricization thesis is the idea that lyricization happens over the course of multiple centuries because critics and poets and readers begin to engage in acts of "lyric reading"—reading all poems as if they are lyric poems, which is to say, as the utterances of individual speaking subjects. In other words, acts of lyric reading abstract more specific genres into the larger category of lyric. The argument of the lyricization thesis is not that it is wrong to read a poem as a lyric poem or that lyric poems do or do not exist or that New Critics are responsible for lyric reading or that every act of lyric reading produces racialized modes of reading or that only Anglophone poems are lyrics. Rather, the idea of the lyricization thesis is that many of us have come to expect, if we see something that looks like a poem, that it will in some way be the expression of an individual subject's experience, in part because of the New Critics but also in part because of the much longer, more complex history of poetics inside and outside the US academy. The lyricization thesis and the historical poetics scholarship behind it ask us to think about contemporary academic reading practices as part of that longer, more complex history. It prompts scholars to question when and why we are participating in the abstraction of specific poetic terms into broader categories and when and why we may not want to perform such abstractions in our readings. This is not to do away with acts of lyric reading or to insist that no one ever think about lyric poetry. It is to think carefully about where we might be making some textual evidence fit into our established ways of reading poems rather than developing ways of reading that work for that evidence.

For a concrete example of the difference between a lyric reading and a historical poetics reading of a text, I turn to Sonya Posmentier's account of what she calls Zora Neale Hurston's "lyric reading in the black ethnographic archive." Posmentier reads a grant proposal Hurston submitted to the Federal Writers' Project in 1939 for a "Recording Expedition into the Floridas" to collect folk songs and stories as Hurston's "lyric reading of Florida music." Posmentier argues that in this text, "Hurston was writing and thinking about *lyrics* and *poetry*."[2] But there is something funny about this assertion; Hurston never uses the word "lyric" in her grant proposal. Indeed, Hurston does not use the word "lyric" in any of the textual evidence Posmentier reads to make the case that Hurston is performing a lyric reading. So why does Posmentier understand Hurston to be a lyric reader?

Posmentier's reading turns on the ending of Hurston's proposal, which closes with a quotation from a performance of a hymn based on Psalm 19:14. The entirety of that quotation reads,

(Sanctified Anthem)

O Lord, O Lord,
Let the words of my mouth, O Lord
Let the words of my mouth, meditations of my heart
Be accepted in Thy sight, O Lord
(Sung by Mrs. Orrie Jones, Palm Beach, Florida)

Respectfully Submitted,
Zora Neale Hurston[3]

Posmentier argues that this quotation of a "Sanctified Anthem" sung by Mrs. Orrie Jones of Palm Beach, Florida, is proof that Hurston is engaging in an act of lyric reading because the quotation becomes words "emanating from the writing subject, Zora Neale Hurston." Indeed, for Posmentier, all of the songs Hurston quotes throughout her proposal become "the words of *my* [Hurston's] mouth" through her quotation of these lines of this "Sanctified Anthem."[4] What, then, is Mrs. Orrie Jones doing in between the quotation and Hurston's signature? How can we attribute the written words of Hurston's proposal to Hurston's mouth alone if those textualized words are also giving voice to Mrs. Orrie Jones's voicing of a song that has been voiced and textualized by many others? Mrs. Orrie Jones's words are "submitted" by Hurston as evidence of the kinds of "plentiful" materials she will be able to record as audio and as text if her project is funded, which suggests that Mrs. Orrie Jones's voice is as important to Hurston's in this proposal as her own.[5] For Posmentier, however, Hurston's closing has to be "a meditative secular prayer in her [Hurston's] own voice" in order for Hurston to be performing a lyric reading of an ethnographic collection of songs.[6]

Because Posmentier sees Hurston "transform[ing] . . . multiple folk materials into a singular poetic voice," she argues that "some might" see Hurston engaging in "*lyricization*, a critical process of abstracting poems from their material, historical, generic, and bibliographic contexts in support of a stand-alone, universally available poem called 'lyric.'"[7] But this is pointedly what Hurston does not do. The lyricization thesis equips us to see that, ironically, Posmentier's lyric reading of Hurston's grant proposal provides ample evidence of Hurston's *unlyric* reading of the Black ethnographic archive. Posmentier notes that Hurston's is "a contextual account of poetry in relationship to its particular geographies, cultures, languages, and social functions," since the proposal is organized by "geographic region, . . . linking each type of *lyric* to a specific location, cultural group, and/or social purpose."[8] It is impossible, however, for Hurston to link each type of *lyric* to those specificities because she does not call them "lyrics." She instead calls them by other, more granular genre names: "sermons and prayers," "folk poems," "religious and secular songs," "railroad songs," "chants," "songs of road and camp," "spirituals," "anthems," "Cuban songs," and "games."[9] As Posmentier's evidence shows, rather than thinking about lyric poetry, Hurston is thinking about how the songs and poems she wants to collect are constantly performed and remediated in particular "material, historical, [and] generic . . . contexts," producing the kinds of complicated voicings and textualized representations of song we see when Hurston ends her proposal by quoting Mrs. Orrie Jones singing a "Sanctified Anthem" based on a psalm.[10] To put the case bluntly, Hurston cannot both be "abstracting poems from their material, historical, [and] generic . . . contexts" in an act of lyric reading and also providing "a contextual account of poetry in relationship to its particular geographies, cultures, languages, and social functions," to say nothing of the specific genres Hurston is careful to enumerate throughout the proposal.[11]

Lyric reading thus seems to be particularly ill suited as a framework for understanding Hurston's project in this grant proposal. Historical poetics, on the other hand, is built in part from Prins's work on the ways ideas of voice are mediated in print in the Victorian era and has thus developed a complex vocabulary and methodological framework for thinking about something like Hurston's textual representation of Mrs. Orrie Jones's performance of a "sanctified anthem," which of course has a long history of textual and aural remediation prior to Mrs. Orrie Jones's performance of it and Hurston's transcription of the words sung in that performance. As Prins has argued, "the sound of poetry is never heard without mediation," and "a turn to historical poetics is one way to theorize as well as historicize alternatives to the assumption of voice in lyric reading."[12] That is to say that rather than attempting to isolate Hurston's voice in an act of lyric reading, making her inclusion of Mrs. Orrie Jones in the text drop out of view, we might ask how Hurston textualizes multiply voiced songs that have been shaped by looping, recursive processes of textual and aural remediation. To think through the multiple voicings collected in Hurston's proposal would be to do the kind of work historical poetics attempts to do; to elide the multiple voices in Hurston's proposal into Hurston's singular voice is to engage in an act of lyric reading.

Historical poetics is of course not the only approach germane to understanding Hurston's grant proposal, as Posmentier's engagement with sound studies and with Fred Moten's theorization of "the lyricism of the surplus" makes clear.[13] However, historical poetics can help us see that to lyricize

Hurston's grant proposal is to miss the import of the fact that Hurston attempts to unlyricize the "sermons and prayers," "folk poems," "religious and secular songs," "railroad songs," "chants," "songs of road and camp," "spirituals," "anthems," "Cuban songs," and "games" that she seeks to collect from particular communities at particular times. That is to say that she enumerates these genres multiple times, never once using the term "lyric" to describe the objects she wants to collect. This enumeration of multiple genres and of specific performers in the context of ethnographic approaches to folk culture in the 1930s was not pedantic; it was a rejection of a mode of racialized reading that came from the abstraction of particular folk genres into textualized lyric poems through acts of ballad reading. As I discussed in chapter 3, ideas of folk song and folk poetry were deeply intertwined with ballad reading, which was meant to make "vanishing folk voices accessible as literature."[14] What mattered in ballad readings of folk poetry was the genre of person represented in the poem—the vanishing folk—rather than the genre of the poem itself. Thus, ethnographic collections of folk materials often engaged in a mode of lyric reading, abstracting transmedial cultural artifacts from their "material, historical, generic, . . . bibliographic," and social contexts in order to produce the unitary voice of a folk that could be preserved in print, generally for white literary consumption.[15]

Hurston's unlyric reading in the Black ethnographic archive—her refusal to group specific, place-based performances of transmedial songs under the label of lyric poetry—is thus aligned with Fenton Johnson's skewering of the racializing, extractive logic of ballad reading in "The Banjo Player." As Posmentier notes, throughout the proposal, Hurston is careful to "collec[t] not the existence of a 'folk' song in general, but a particular instance of its performance."[16] To collect "'folk' song in general" would be to ignore the subjectivity and artistry of performers like Mrs. Orrie Jones; to insist on the importance of Mrs. Orrie Jones's performance of a hymn that has been sung in many other contexts would be to refuse to lyricize her text as the utterance of a singular lyric speaker. Hurston shows us not the racialized abstraction of the Black folk into a textualized lyric poem but particular people engaged in creative acts of invention and collaborative remediation. Thus, while I agree with Posmentier that "to read Hurston . . . is to continue the project of historical poetics," I would argue that the project of historical poetics is not to "defamiliariz[e] the 'normativity' of lyric subjectivity," as Posmentier has it, but to defamiliarize acts of lyric reading.[17] Why do we want to hear Hurston's singular voice when Hurston is directing our attention to the voices of Mrs. Orrie Jones, Waldo Wishart, Willie Joe Roberts, Fred James

Watson, Richard Jenkins, Lias Strawn, and "Stew Beef" in her proposal?[18] Why, in other words, do we continue to try to perform lyric readings of texts that frustrate our attempts to create a singular poetic voice when we look at them more closely?

This is what I have always found exciting and valuable about historical poetics and the lyricization thesis that grows out of this scholarship. Caricatures of both would have it that historical poetics scholars want to dissolve the lyric or to return us to the study of only odes and elegies or to abandon transnational comparative work or to focus only on the historical context of poetry and not poems themselves. But the project of historical poetics is neither so grand nor so limiting. Historical poetics scholarship asks us to think about poems and interpretive acts that do not fit well into our normative reading practices and to consider some of the reasons why those normative reading practices cannot account for those texts. It is not a coincidence that the historical poetics working group began as a reading group devoted to nineteenth-century Anglo-American poetry and poetics, because much of the poetry and poetics of the nineteenth-century Anglophone world has seemed to modern readers to be of merely historical interest. (It is also not an indication that historical poetics is limited to Anglo-American poetry and poetics.) By learning other models of reading from that seemingly irrelevant body of poetry and poetics, historical poetics defamiliarizes acts of lyric reading and the regimes of aesthetic value that those acts can uphold.

I have brought historical poetics approaches to bear on the modernist history of free verse in part because they help to open up the infrequently crossed border between studies of nineteenth- and twentieth-century poetry, and that opening changes what we are able to see about the politics of modernist prosodic discourse. Such a reorientation helps us understand how the ballad reading of folk culture (a mode of lyric reading) was intertwined with the racialization of a free verse as a white form and how some poets worked against racializing abstractions of poetic terms by thinking with the poetic conventions many modernists wanted to discard.[19] This understanding of how prosodic discourse was racialized can help us to reconfigure our genealogies of literary influence, so that we can understand a figure like Frances Ellen Watkins Harper, who lived until 1911, as relevant to the modernist period rather than as important only to discussions of nineteenth-century poetry. As Brigitte Fielder has argued, the kind of nonlinear Black genealogy that Fenton Johnson created in his poems in the 1910s with Watkins Harper at the center of a network of Black activist poets should push us "to develop new ways of reading genealogies"—and new ways of reading early twentieth-century poetry.[20] These readings would not always rush forward to the Harlem Renaissance or to the Black Arts Movement but would understand progress narratives to be one possible aesthetic path among many. (This would also be a chance to reconsider an oft-returned-to visual object in modernist studies: the network map of modernist authors in Bonnie Kime Scott's *The Gender of Modernism* that traces lateral connections among contemporaries.[21] What would a map with Watkins Harper at the center allow us to see?) As Derrick Spires has argued, "despite decades of recovery and literary historical work, we are still in the early stages of fleshing out nineteenth-century literary histories and critical frameworks to account for the wide range of forms, genres, and aesthetic sensibilities in play."[22] A modernist studies that is more deeply informed by the vital archival work of scholars of nineteenth-century Black poetry would be a fundamentally altered and expanded modernist studies—one that would not remake the nineteenth century in its own image but that would instead allow itself to be changed by new understandings of Black aesthetic projects that predate the Harlem Renaissance. This reorientation might help us to better understand figures like Fenton Johnson not as failed or minor modernists but as poets who were failed by white modernism and who found other ways to theorize and create aesthetic value within a "total climate" of anti-Blackness.[23] Johnson's writing does not offer a "romance of resistance" to white modernism or modernity, to use Anthony Reed's phrase, but rather shows us a project of poetic and aesthetic world-building that works against the partitioning force of categories like modernism and modernity, avant-garde and rearguard.[24] Johnson was certainly not the only Black author to undertake such a project, as Posmentier's reading of Hurston's grant proposal indicates, and modernist studies stands to be productively transformed by the unsettling possibilities of such "failed" Black literature.

The case of writing by Indigenous authors in the modernist era requires special care in a field that has often operated on a colonial model of expansion, claiming more and more objects as modernist. Like postcolonial studies and Black studies, Native American and Indigenous studies raises foundational challenges to modernist studies, particularly in the realm of poetics. I have offered my reading of E. Pauline Johnson in *The Path on the Rainbow* in the hopes of enlarging the dialogue between modernist studies and Native American and Indigenous studies through the mediation of historical poetics. Historical poetics approaches have not been part of recent conversations about the place of Indigenous authors within modernist studies like those sparked by Kirby Brown's (Cherokee) 2017 article "American

Indian Modernities and New Modernist Studies' 'Indian Problem,'" but historical poetics has much to contribute to these conversations. In this article, Brown pointed to the fact that, in spite of the increasing attention to transnational and planetary approaches within modernist studies, Indigenous authors remain largely overlooked by most scholars working in the field.[25] Two years after Brown's article, the annual conference of the Modernist Studies Association (MSA) featured a special stream and a keynote roundtable on "Indigenous Modernisms" (spurred in part by the response to a panel on "Indigenous Modernisms" at the 2018 meeting in Columbus, Ohio), and these MSA presentations resulted in the publication of a cluster on "Indigenous Modernities," edited by Brown, in the *Modernism/modernity Print Plus* platform and the 2022 publication of *The Routledge Handbook of North American Indigenous Modernisms*, edited by Brown, Stephen Ross, and Alana Sayers. These works center the question of what modernist studies can offer to scholars of Indigenous studies.[26] As Brown notes, the question of "what this work might look like and how the two fields might productively speak to/with one another theoretically, methodologically, politically, and ethically" is a live one, particularly given the propensity for "ever-wider, ever-expansive critical frameworks" like those that have been critical to the new modernist studies to crowd into the "institutional and disciplinary space for Indigenous studies as a field in its own right."[27] Brown also points to the potential for "concepts like mod*ern* or modern*ist* . . . [to] reinforce dominant expectations about Indigenous culture, identity, and authenticity in opposition to modernity, rather than productively troubling both sets of terms."[28] As Robert Dale Parker puts the issue, a modernist studies more attuned to Native literatures "risks recovering an indigeneity that reproduces the modernism we already know."[29]

I am proposing that historical poetics offers tools to help modernist studies scholars avoid that risk. Because historical poetics does not take it for granted that there is such a thing as a singular Anglo poetic or metrical tradition or that poetic conventions are transparent or that early twentieth-century poetry was simply either modernist or antimodernist, a historical poetics approach can help us to understand the fact that so many Indigenous poets writing at the turn of the twentieth century utilized "conventional" forms and genres. Historical poetics methodologies can help us to better understand the kinds of generic knowledge early twentieth-century Native poets had and the ways they deployed that knowledge as tools of "survivance and continuance."[30] Rather than searching for Indigenous poets who wrote in "experimental" forms or whose work accords with white modernist aesthetics or discounting the "conventional" forms Indigenous poets worked in as transparent, in other words, modernist scholars might think about "the imaginative and dynamic ways in which Indigenous peoples engage with settler colonialism," as Jonathan Radocay (Cherokee) puts it—including its myriad aesthetic forms—in ways that upend the narrow categories of modernism and modernist poetics.[31] For an author like E. Pauline Johnson, writing in recognized metrical forms was not simply a Romantic or decadent or antimodernist move; it was a practice of Indigenizing settler literary forms and categories in ways that challenged settler historiography and periodization. Such seemingly conventional works thus "disrupt and exceed a progressive 'settler time' or colonial time,'" putting pressure on standard narratives of poetic evolution from "conventional" meters to free rhythms and challenging modernist scholars to find other ways to understand poetic value at the turn of the twentieth century.[32]

I have used a historical poetics approach to free verse prosodies to tell an unsettling story about modernist poetics in these pages in the hopes that it will contribute to structural changes in our literary historical accounts of early twentieth-century Anglophone poetry. Restoring to view the fact that free verse was racialized as a white form from the outset can help us to better understand the white supremacist colonial foundations of modernist studies in the United States and can make it easier to see why, "in historical and theoretical terms, experimentation and race seem opposed" in so much twentieth-century scholarship on poetry and poetics.[33] Such a reorientation to the politics of free verse might lead to a modernist studies that understands itself to be part of a much longer history of white supremacy within the academy and that thinks of "modernism" and "modernity" as organizing terms but not as valorized or valued terms, following the paradigm-shifting scholarship of thinkers working in postcolonial studies, Black studies, and Native American and Indigenous studies. This reorientation can help us to formulate reading practices that do justice to the interpretive density of poetic conventions, taking seriously early twentieth-century poetic projects whose seemingly outmoded aesthetics were in fact a refusal of racialized modernist aesthetic hierarchies. Fenton Johnson's revival of abolitionist poetic genres and E. Pauline Johnson's Indigenization of received metrical forms are a very small part of this story, and I hope to have opened the door to other explorations of modernist-era engagements with nineteenth-century poetic cultures and practices. At the very least, it is my hope that the story I have told about the racialization of free verse as a white form will make it impossible to hear the term "free verse" without thinking of the histories of enslavement and colonization that have shaped the concept of freedom in poetics as much as in politics and social life.

Notes

Introduction

1. See Beyers, *History of Free Verse*; Finch, *Ghost of Meter*; Hartman, *Free Verse*; Kirby-Smith, *Origins of Free Verse*; Steele, *Missing Measures*; Sutton, *American Free Verse*. For more recent studies, see Andrews, *Prosody of Free Verse*; and Glaser, *Modernism's Metronome*.

2. Steele, *Missing Measures*; Sutton, *American Free Verse*.

3. Cavitch, "Stephen Crane's Refrain," 33.

4. See Hall, *Meter Matters*; Hart, *Nations of Nothing*; Martin, "Imperfectly Civilized"; Martin, *Rise and Fall*; Prins, "Metrical Translation"; Prins, "Victorian Meters."

5. Martin, *Rise and Fall*, 10.

6. Lowes, *Convention and Revolt*, 237.

7. See Beyers, *History of Free Verse*; Cushman, *Fictions of Form*; Hartman, *Free Verse*.

8. For instance, Yopie Prins has shown how debates about translating classical quantitative meters into English were used to support varying ideals of English national identity. Prins, "Metrical Translation"; Prins, "Victorian Meters." Jason Rudy has traced how Sidney Lanier's metrical theories created an imagined continuity between Anglo-Saxon England and the post–Civil War United States. Rudy, "Manifest Prosody."

9. Ehlers, *Left of Poetry*, 6.

10. Ehlers, *Left of Poetry*, 9, 6.

11. Goldstone, "Modernist Studies," 21. Goldstone notes the "distinct[iveness]" of this situation: "in modernist studies, unlike Victorian studies or American studies, there is an unusually close correspondence between the norms of scholars in the subfield and the norms propounded by the writers they tend to study," so that modernists remain "commit[ted] . . . to a necessarily partial understanding of the cultural field of [their] historical period." Goldstone, "Modernist Studies," 1, 23.

12. Ehlers, *Left of Poetry*, 19.

13. Melamed, *Represent and Destroy*, 14.

14. Goldstone, "Modernist Studies," 24.

15. Chatterjee et al., "Introduction," 380.

16. Baker, *Modernism and the Harlem Renaissance*, 101 (italics in original).

17. Chaterjee et al., "Introduction," 377.

18. Scholarship on American free verse does occasionally look back to Walt Whitman or Stephen Crane, but it generally does so to position them as anomalies or as proto-modernists. For notable exceptions to this tendency to disavow nineteenth-century poetry and poetics in scholarship on modern poetry, see Ehlers, *Left of Poetry*; V. Jackson, *Before Modernism*; Martin, *Rise and Fall*.

19. Cecire, *Experimental*, 33–34. Free verse is often studied under the rubric of experimental or avant-garde writing, precisely because it has so often been understood as antimetrical and hence as standing against tradition and convention. In studies of later twentieth- and twenty-first-century experimental or avant-garde poetry, modernist free verse is presented as an origin point for later experimental poetic movements. This genealogy is a retroprojection that took hold after the 1970s, in part thanks to the work of poetic theorists associated with the Language movement (Ron Silliman, Charles Bernstein, Bruce Andrews, Barrett Watten, Lyn Hejinian). Marjorie Perloff's literary histories have also been hugely influential in arguing for a "two traditions" model of twentieth- and twenty-first-century poetics, in which different modes of free verse are positioned as leading either to an avant-garde poetics (language focused, "experimental," antimetrical) or to "establishment poetry" (expressive lyric poetry that may use received or "traditional" forms). Perloff, *21st-Century Modernism*, 4.

20. As Reed and Yu emphasize, scholarship on poetic avant-gardes tends to read "experimental" writing by white poets, including early twentieth-century free verse, as being primarily about form or aesthetics and "experimental" writing by nonwhite poets, also including free verse, as being primarily about identity or autobiography. As Reed notes, "in historical and theoretical terms, experimentation and race seem opposed." Reed, *Freedom Time*, 3. Thus, recent scholarship on race and experimental poetry is interested in developing reading practices that counter this false dichotomy, highlighting the formal experimentalism of Black, Indigenous, and other people of color (BIPOC) poets. This work is important and generative, but it also has the effect of continuing to privilege "experimental" or modernist or avant-garde aesthetics, giving short shrift to poets whose aesthetic projects challenge the hegemony of those aesthetic paradigms.

21. Kelley, *Freedom Dreams*.

22. Posmentier, "Lyric Reading," 78.

23. Hines, *Outside Literary Studies*, 7–8.

24. Pound, *Lustra*, 21.

25. Kabir, "Anglo-Saxon Textual Attitudes," 310.

26. Schuller and Gill-Peterson, "Introduction," 4.

27. Matthiessen, *American Renaissance*, 564.

28. Newcomb, *How Did Poetry Survive?*, 26.

29. Wang, *Thinking Its Presence*, xx.

30. Timothy Yu's careful reception history of Theresa Hak Kyung Cha's *Dictee* is illustrative of this point. Yu tracks a persistent critical tendency to read this formally experimental work as a form of autobiography, in spite of all the ways the text explicitly rejects such a reading. Yu, *Race and the Avant-Garde*. I am also indebted to Natalia Cecire for pointing out that the University of California Press reprint of *Dictee* (2022) classifies it as autobiography, further entrenching the division between "experimental" and "identity-based" poetries.

31. McHenry, *To Make Negro Literature*, 4.

32. McHenry, *To Make Negro Literature*, 6.

33. It may be objected that Cary Nelson's *Repression and Recovery* and the work it helped to inspire revalued "conventional" forms. But Nelson and like-minded critics working within modernist studies do not actually revalue poetic convention; they po-

sition conventional forms as transparent and easy to read. In such accounts, "traditional" poetic forms are portrayed as forms that poets turn to when they want to be easily understandable to a mass audience, maintaining a binary between radical politics and conventional form. See, for instance, Nelson's evaluation of Max Eastman, who "remained trapped in a genteel, idealized notion of the poetic . . . despite his revolutionary politics." Nelson, *Repression and Recovery*, 55. I am arguing for an approach informed by scholarship in nineteenth-century poetics, which has shown how interpretively dense "traditional" poetic conventions are. Rather than valuing "traditional" or "conventional" poetic forms in spite of themselves, because they served political or social aims, I am attempting to show that "traditional" poetic forms provided unique resources for poets who understood the political and social work those forms had done in nineteenth-century contexts.

34. Melamed, *Represent and Destroy*, 89.

35. Taylor, "Not Primitive Enough," 67, 53–54.

36. Socarides, *In Plain Sight*, 27.

37. Socarides, *In Plain Sight*, 4, 30. There has been much generative work on poetic convention within nineteenth-century American studies and Victorian studies, but this scholarship often does not overlap with Native American and Indigenous studies (NAIS). Much work in NAIS has focused on novels, essays, plays, and oratory rather than on poetry, so that "conventional" or generic poetry by Indigenous authors tends to fall between the cracks of various disciplinary formations. I am interested in how bringing together scholarship on poetic convention with work on the Indigenization of various literary forms can help to illuminate poetry that would otherwise go unread within the academy.

38. Braddock, *Collecting as Modernist Practice*, 160.

39. Louis Untermeyer, "The Indian as Poet," *Dial* 8 (1919): 241, Internet Archive.

40. Untermeyer, "Indian as Poet," 241; Taylor, "Not Primitive Enough," 47.

41. Fielder, "Recovery," 20.

Chapter One

1. Stokes, *Writers in Retrospect*, 8–9.

2. Beissinger, "Oral Poetry."

3. Gummere, *Beginnings of Poetry*, 69.

4. Gummere, *Beginnings of Poetry*, 92.

5. Mufti, *Forget English*, 19–20 (italics in original).

6. Mufti, *Forget English*, 11 (italics in original).

7. This version of world literature as a set of comparable practices, Mufti argues, "was from its inception a concept and practice, in a strong sense, of bourgeois society, that is to say, a concept of exchange," making it "part and parcel of the bourgeoisie's continuous attempt to create a 'world market,' which entailed (and continues to entail) the almost continuous and massive destruction of lived social and cultural forms across the world's diverse societies." Mufti, *Forget English*, 36. That is to say, the concept of literature as a universal category that develops through similar stages across

societies is part of larger processes of globalization that are destructive of the local and the particular. Mufti's account obviously builds on Said's *Orientalism*; as Said noted of Sir William Jones's (and others) philological work on the origins of language, the goal was "the grounding of the European languages in a distant, and harmless, Oriental source," so that the "Orient" became "a sort of surrogate and even underground self." Mufti, *Forget English*, 78, 3. In this chapter, I track how the mediating figure of a premodern throng helped philologically trained scholars of English to imagine a continuous history of Western poetry and poetics that stretched back to the beginnings of humanity, so that all national literatures were imagined to develop through the same phases, even as "Aryan" cultures were imagined to be superior to other racialized cultures. For another account of the coloniality of philology, see Wynter, "Ceremony."

8. Horsman, *Race and Manifest Destiny*, 30.

9. Martin, *Rise and Fall*, 36.

10. Martin, *Rise and Fall*, 36. As Martin notes, these arguments about the history of English prosody were also about "competing histories of Englishness." Walter Skeat, who had reissued the Anglo-Saxonist Edwin Guest's account of the Germanic roots of English prosody, helped to popularize the idea that the history of English prosody was the history of the "steady beating Anglo-Saxon rhythms" holding out "against the foreignness of classical verse forms." Martin, *Rise and Fall*, 96.

11. Warner, "Professionalization," 20; Renker, *Origins of American Literature Studies*, 20.

12. Gerald Graff, for instance, notes that theories of race were hugely important "in the formation of language and literature departments in the 1880s," but he argues that serious literary critics quickly moved away from the "nationalist idiom" of departmental founders and that the romantic nationalism of historians like Taine and philologists like Herder and the brothers Grimm had become "embarrassing" to serious scholars by the 1880s. Graff, *Professing Literature*, 70, 72, 76. Similarly, although John Guillory notes that "philology was able to defend its claim to scientificity through the end of the nineteenth century and beyond, and even to erect its theories alongside the powerful monument of Darwinian biology (as in the work of Max Müller)," his account of the discipline also downplays the effects of romanticized theories of racial evolution on the construction of English literature in the US university system. Guillory claims that, "in the later decades of the nineteenth century, philology began to move away from the biological analogy popularized by Müller, or the alternative Hegelian version of evolutionist philology espoused by August Schleicher," so that philologists were no longer invested in "any overarching destiny of humankind, or a mission of Bildung." Guillory, "Literary Study," 29–30.

13. As Sylvia Wynter argues, "the Indo-European mode of being was canonized through the discourse of philologists and literary scholars, such as Schlegel and his pupil Lassen, as the expression of the most perfect 'organic' realization of the biogenetic elan vital that was the superior will being of its peoples." Wynter, "Ceremony," 36. Philology and the disciplinary field of English literature that emerged from it were thus both from the outset part of what David Lloyd, building on Wynter, calls "a regulative discourse of the human." Lloyd, *Under Representation*, 3.

14. Lloyd, *Under Representation*, 3.

15. Providing a glimpse of a lost (or perhaps always fantasmatic) academic world, Gummere told John Matthews Manly that "he believed the ideal life of the productive scholar was more nearly attainable in a small college with a well-equipped library than in a great university, that he had at Haverford all the books he needed, that his college work was thoroughly familiar to him, and that he had greater leisure for research than he could ever hope for elsewhere." Manly, "Francis Barton Gummere," 62.

16. Newman, *Ballad Collection*, 201.

17. Newman, *Ballad Collection*, 205.

18. Gayley and Scott, *Introduction*, vi.

19. Gayley and Scott, *Introduction*, 266.

20. Gayley and Scott, *Introduction*, 270.

21. Glazener, *Literature in the Making*, 163.

22. Moulton, *Modern Study*, 49–50.

23. Foundational disciplinary histories tended to focus on the conflicts between philologists and generalists or belletrists in order to explain current disciplinary divides between literature and composition. The details of romantic racialism in constructing modern literary theory thus tend to be glossed over as typical of a moment that did not last. Graff, for instance, argues that "the winds shifted from philology to literature in the [eighteen-]nineties," as professors of English began to focus much more on literary works as pieces of art than on linguistic and cultural histories. Graff, *Professing Literature*, 65. But the shift from philology to literature was not as abrupt or as complete as such accounts imply, and the failure to account for the lasting influence of nineteenth-century philology on twentieth-century literary theory leads to the failure to understand the discipline of English as a colonial, racial formation of whiteness.

24. Schuller, *Biopolitics of Feeling*, 31. Of course, the push and pull between theories of development that privilege genetics and those that privilege epigenetics is ongoing and irresolvable, and I do not mean to suggest that either framework has ever decisively won out over the other.

25. Schuller and Gill-Peterson, "Introduction," 1.

26. Schuller, *Biopolitics of Feeling*, 55.

27. J. A. Symonds quoted in Alden, *English Verse*, 214–15.

28. Gollancz, *Middle Ages*, 18 (italics added).

29. Gollancz, *Middle Ages*, 18. The evidence of the importance of plasticity to studies of English poetry in this moment is abundant. To cite just a few other examples, Egerton Smith's *The Principles of English Metre* (1923) explained that "English words are evidently more plastic than Latin." Smith, *Principles of English Metre*, 157. Donald Lemen Clark, a professor at Columbia University, traced "plasticity" as a key term back to Aristotle, arguing that Aristotle understood imitation to be "a conscious selection and plastic mastery of the sense impressions stored as images by the image-forming faculty of the author, whose writings are addressed to the imagination of the reader or auditor." Clark, *Rhetoric and Poetry*, 12. George Saintsbury's magisterial account of the development of English prosody likewise took "plasticity" as a key word, arguing that, between 1000 and 1300, there was "a plastic mass of decomposed or decomposing Anglo-Saxon verse-material, upon which are brought to bear . . . the influences of Latin, of French, and perhaps of other languages, together with that infinitely more

powerful though far more subtle and incalculable one of the race-spirit, which is forming and changing itself coincidentally." Saintsbury, *History of Prosody*, 79.

30. Schuller and Gill-Peterson, "Introduction," 6.

31. Hoskins, "Place and Function," 389.

32. Hoskins, "Biological Analogy," 415.

33. Hoskins, "Biological Analogy," 419–20.

34. Hoskins, "Biological Analogy," 423.

35. Manly, "Literary Forms," 582.

36. Matthews quoted in Glazener, *Literature in the Making*, 187.

37. Manly, "Literary Forms," 583.

38. Amos, *Linguistic Means*, 6.

39. Amos, *Linguistic Means*, 7.

40. Frantzen, *Desire for Origins*, 71. It is worth noting that while Frantzen's work on disciplinarity, cited here, and on Anglo-Saxonism, cited later, remains valuable, it also demonstrates the potential dangers of attempting to analyze racialization without understanding it as a gendering process—a topic I discuss in detail in chapter 2. Frantzen's participation in the so-called men's rights movement indicates his intellectual failure as a scholar of race and racialization.

41. Gummere, *Democracy and Poetry*, 61.

42. Gummere, *Germanic Origins*, 46, 65.

43. Schuller and Gill-Peterson, "Introduction," 6.

44. Jackson, *Dickinson's Misery*, 130–31.

45. Gummere, *Beginnings of Poetry*, 139.

46. Michael Cohen, "Paul Laurence Dunbar," 249. For more on the ballad, see Jackson, "Specters of the Ballad"; Martin, "Imperfectly Civilized"; McGill, "What Is a Ballad?"; Socarides, "What Happens"; Stewart, *Crimes of Writing*.

47. Brinton's name may be familiar to Whitman scholars; Whitman and Brinton had a long relationship and often discussed Brinton's attempt to categorize Indigenous languages. For more on Brinton and Whitman, see Matt Cohen, *Whitman's Drift*, 172–73.

48. Brinton, *Basis of Social Relations*, xv.

49. Gummere, *Beginnings of Poetry*, 314.

50. Gummere, *Beginnings of Poetry*, 67.

51. Brinton, *Basis of Social Relations*, xiii, 30–31.

52. Gummere, "Primitive Poetry," 201.

53. Ehrenreich quoted in Gummere, *Beginnings of Poetry*, 95–96.

54. Gummere, *Beginnings of Poetry*, 89.

55. Gummere, *Democracy and Poetry*, 234; Gummere, *Beginnings of Poetry*, 385.

56. Gummere, *Beginnings of Poetry*, 94. I combine sources here (*Democracy and Poetry* and *The Beginnings of Poetry*) because Gummere's argument about the communal function of poetry remained remarkably consistent throughout his career and was further elaborated in each of his published works rather than significantly changed. Although the two books are separated by a ten-year span, *Beginnings of Poetry* most clearly lays out the communal origins hypothesis, while *Democracy and Poetry* most clearly makes the connection between communal poetry and civic life.

57. Gummere, *Beginnings of Poetry*, 111–12.

58. Gummere, *Beginnings of Poetry*, 131.

59. Frantzen, *Desire for Origins*, xi.

60. Gummere argued that "survivals" of Anglo-Saxon cultural practices were everywhere and that "if we could only trace aright historical connections, we should find everywhere about us, imbedded in custom or tradition, the shards of our broken heathendom." Gummere, *Germanic Origins*, 471.

61. Gummere, *Beginnings of Poetry*, 110.

62. Gummere, *Beginnings of Poetry*, 111–12.

63. MacDougall, *Racial Myth*, 2.

64. Gummere, "English in Secondary Schools"; Gummere, "Old English Ballads"; Gummere, "What Place."

65. Gummere, "What Place," 171.

66. Gummere's project is thus primitivist in the sense theorized by Ben Etherington, in which "the transformative agency of aesthetic practice" is emphasized so that art is imagined to have the capacity "to reanimate the primitive remnant [in a fallen capitalist world] and reawaken the possibility of a social reconciliation with nature." Etherington, *Literary Primitivism*, xiii.

67. Sorby, *Schoolroom Poets*, 3.

68. Gummere, *Handbook of Poetics*, 144 (italics in original).

69. Gummere, *Handbook of Poetics*, 135–36.

70. Gummere, *Democracy and Poetry*, 17.

71. Gummere, *Democracy and Poetry*, 47.

72. Gummere, *Democracy and Poetry*, 38.

73. Gummere, *Democracy and Poetry*, 42–43.

74. Gummere, *Democracy and Poetry*, 44.

75. As Horsman shows, this was a cherished bit of Anglo-Saxonist mythology: "to the general innate superiority of the Caucasians, it was argued, the Anglo-Saxon branch of the Teutons added the inborn talent for political liberty. All the Germanic peoples had this innate sense of liberty, but only the Anglo-Saxons had shown the ability to transform the gift into effective political institutions." Horsman, *Race and Manifest Destiny*, 174.

76. Gummere, *Democracy and Poetry*, 61.

77. Horsman, *Race and Manifest Destiny*, 30.

78. Gummere, *Germanic Origins*, 30–31. The quotation at the end of this passage is Gummere's translation of a passage from an unidentified work by Victor Hehn.

79. Gummere, *Germanic Origins*, 33.

80. Gummere, *Germanic Origins*, 46.

81. Gummere, *Germanic Origins*, 128.

82. Gummere, *Germanic Origins*, 65. Such a view of the relationship between "primitive" societies and property was of course well established at this point and was also used to justify the colonization of Indigenous peoples globally. As Maureen Konkle notes, "Scottish historian William Robertson's *History of the Discovery and Settlement of North America*," published in 1777, "quickly became . . . the standard reference on Indians in North America in both Europe and the United States through the mid-nineteenth century." In Robertson's account, "because Indians do not appreciate the importance of

property, they are morally and intellectually incapable of perceiving the tenets of natural law and therefore incapable of forming governments administered by the rule of law and of being civilized, political subjects." Konkle, *Writing Indian Nations*, 9–10.

83. Pound, "Ballad and the Dance," 397n50, 400.

84. Pound, "High-School Ballad Composition," 496.

85. In many ways, Gummere's work was exceptionally well suited to the early twentieth-century elementary-school classroom. As Angela Sorby shows, it was commonly understood by pedagogues, including John Dewey, that "young children . . . recapitulate[ed] earlier stages of civilization," and seemingly "primitive" works like Longfellow's *The Song of Hiawatha* were "recruited to carry children 'back into a social past' where they could work at their own level." Sorby, *Schoolroom Poets*, 4–5. Ballads seemed to many educators to be the perfect tool to carry children back to this imagined past. If the rhythms of the ballads could be imagined to have come from thronging Anglo-Saxon bodies, so much the better for the education of white America's young. Sorby notes too the emphasis on "concrete" activities tied to the reading of such works, which, like the chanting, stomping, and clapping of ballads, was thought to help young readers "withdraw—temporarily—from the abstract realm of print, concretizing their experience of the text" and making their experience of reading "based not in analysis but in identification." Sorby, *Schoolroom Poets*, 7, 23.

86. Gummere, *Democracy and Poetry*, 115.

87. Kappeler, "Constructing Walt Whitman."

88. Csicsila, *Canons by Consensus*, 56.

89. See, for instance, "Review of *Leaves of Grass* (1891–92)," *Poet Lore*, 1892, https://whitmanarchive.org/criticism/reviews/lg1891/anc.00227.html; Edward P. Mitchell, "Walt Whitman and the Poetry of the Future," *New York Sun*, November 19, 1881, https://whitmanarchive.org/criticism/reviews/lg1881/anc.00082.html; Stedman, *Poets of America*.

90. F. Scott, "Most Fundamental Differentia," 254.

91. F. Scott, "Most Fundamental Differentia," 262, 263.

92. F. Scott, "Most Fundamental Differentia," 263.

93. F. Scott, "Note on Walt Whitman," 149 (italics added).

94. F. Scott, "Note on Walt Whitman," 149.

95. F. Scott, "Note on Walt Whitman," 137.

96. F. Scott, "Note on Walt Whitman," 149–50 (italics added).

97. Gummere, *Germanic Origins*, 57.

98. Gummere, *Germanic Origins*, 59.

99. Gummere, *Germanic Origins*, 281.

100. Lest there be any doubt that Scott was well versed in and in general accord with the Anglo-Saxonist ideas of his contemporaries, the edition of Sir Israel Gollancz's *The Middle Ages in the Lineage of English Poetry*, which I cited in the beginning of this chapter for its assertion that blank verse "became the plastic instrument able to bear the impress of varied human emotions, only when it had become, as it were, thoroughly Teutonised," was gifted to the University of Michigan's library by Fred Newton Scott. Gollancz, *Middle Ages*, 18. See the book plate in the digitized version housed at HathiTrust: https://babel.hathitrust.org/cgi/pt?id=mdp.39015031007514&view=1up&seq

=3&skin=2021. Evidence of Scott's investment in racialized reading practices can also be found in the fact that he published an edition of Herbert Spencer's *Philosophy of Style* in 1894—a text that Nancy Glazener, building on Christina Cogdell's work, shows was part of a eugenicist approach to "functionalist ideologies of design" across different art forms. Glazener, *Literature in the Making*, 180–81.

101. Renker, *Origins of American Literature Studies*, 35.

102. Weeks, "Phrasal Prosody," 14–15.

103. Weeks, "Phrasal Prosody," 17–18.

104. Weeks, "Phrasal Prosody," 19.

105. Weeks, "Phrasal Prosody," 13.

106. Weeks, "Phrasal Prosody," 19.

107. Erskine, "Note on Whitman's Prosody," 338–39.

108. Ware, "Poetic Convention," 49.

109. Bradley, "Fundamental Metrical Principle," 439.

110. Bradley, "Fundamental Metrical Principle," 441.

111. Bradley, "Fundamental Metrical Principle," 442–43.

112. Bradley, "Fundamental Metrical Principle," 444.

113. Matthiessen, *American Renaissance*, 564–65.

114. Matthiessen, *American Renaissance*, 567.

115. Matthiessen, *American Renaissance*, 586.

116. It is also beyond the scope of my project to offer an exhaustive account of Gummere's influence into the twenty-first century, but other scholars have undertaken such work. For a detailed account of Gummere's influence on Cleanth Brooks and Robert Penn Warren, see Newman, *Ballad Collection*. See also Jackson, "Cadence of Consent."

117. Brogan, "Foot"; Brogan, "Meter."

118. Genette, *Architext*, 5.

119. Robinson, *Black Marxism*, 3.

120. Wilton, "What Do We Mean," 439.

121. Wilton, "What Do We Mean," 442.

122. Wilton, "What Do We Mean," 452. Along with linguistic evidence like that cited by Wilton, archaeological evidence also highlights the ways that "Anglo-Saxon" covers over the complexities of societies in pre-Conquest England. As Catherine Hills, Barbara Yorke, and David Kirby, among others, note, the political units and cultural practices we now collect under the name "Anglo-Saxon" were varied and derived as much from Romano-British sociopolitical practices and institutions as they did from Germanic sources. Hills, in a study of archaeological approaches to the pre-Conquest era, explains that most of the people who are now called "Anglo-Saxon" would probably "not have thought of themselves as Anglo-Saxons at all, but as the people of a region or descendants of the followers of a leader, as preserved in the names of the Tribal Hidage." Hills, "Overview," 4. Yorke likewise emphasizes the provincial nature of the kingdoms we now collect under the name "Anglo-Saxon," noting that "the broader archaeological picture suggests that no one model will explain all the [pre-Conquest] Anglo-Saxon settlements in Britain and that there was considerable regional variation." Yorke also highlights the significant influence of Romano-British settlements,

political divisions, and cultural practices on these erstwhile Anglo-Saxons, giving the lie to the idea of Anglo-Saxon culture as a singular Germanic importation. Yorke, *Kings and Kingdoms*, 5, 7. Looking at historical records, Kirby notes that "the kingdoms of early England . . . were perceived as peoples (Northumbrians, East Angles, Mercians) but were rather units of government, in which royal power was exercised over territories on which were imposed fiscal and military obligations. . . . In socioeconomic terms these kingdoms can be characterized less as states than as chiefdoms." Kirby, *Earliest English Kings*, 2–3. John M. Hill notes that heroic poetry and mythicizing prose like the so-called *Anglo-Saxon Chronicle*, which may seem to bolster the idea of the coherence of Anglo-Saxon society, was "a kind of royalist, West Saxon propaganda." Hill, *Anglo-Saxon Warrior Ethic*, 2. Hill argues that this propaganda was connected to the "political needs of the Saxon rulers to create a unified kingdom by claiming a common Germanic heritage with a great past and ideals of loyalty to God and the king." Graham Caie quoted in Hill, *Anglo-Saxon Warrior Ethic*, 147. In short, what we refer to now as "Anglo-Saxon" literature and culture was as much Romano-British as it was Anglo or Saxon, and where continuity and coherence are implied, there was rather heterogeneity and provincialism. For some of the most trenchant analysis of contemporary usages of "Anglo-Saxon," see Rambaran-Olm, "Misnaming the Medieval."

123. Frantzen, *Desire for Origins*, 75.

124. Rambaran-Olm, "Misnaming the Medieval."

125. Amos, *Linguistic Means*, 2.

126. Lowes, *Convention and Revolt*, 312.

Chapter Two

1. See, for instance, Marek, *Women Editing Modernism*; Churchill, *Little Magazine*; Churchill and McKible, *Little Magazines and Modernism*; Newcomb, *How Did Poetry Survive*.

2. Snorton, *Black on Both Sides*, 66.

3. Marek's work is especially interested in recovering details about Monroe and Henderson's collaborative processes as a means to counter the narrative that Ezra Pound was truly the driving force behind *Poetry*'s success. Marek, *Women Editing Modernism*. Badaracco and Massa focus on Monroe's business acumen. Badaracco, "Writers and Their Public Appeal"; Massa, "Columbian Ode." Schulze explores how Monroe navigated the shift from Progressive-era ideals of "an American literary and cultural tradition based on widespread mythologies . . . of an American selfhood rooted in American nature" to an emerging interest in "scientific management, efficiency, scientific accuracy, expertise, precisionism, and professionalism." Schulze, *Degenerate Muse*, 50. Newcomb's account focuses on countering the caricature of Monroe as a Victorian spinster, highlighting what he sees as the avant-garde and progressive aspects of *Poetry*. Newcomb, *How Did Poetry Survive*.

4. Notable exceptions include Elizabeth Barnett, Sarah Ehlers, and Hester Furey. Barnett argues that the cultural position of the "little magazine" necessarily "leads directly to racial and cultural appropriation" on the part of white poets. Barnett,

"Destroyed by *Poetry*," 668. Ehlers critiques "the critical inclination, especially prevalent in studies of women's poetry, to recuperate late nineteenth- and early twentieth-century US poetry in the name of modernism" as one that reinforces "the derogatory terms in which American Victorian poetry—especially that of women—has been cast." Ehlers, "Making It Old," 42, 49. Furey challenges the standard account of *Poetry* ushering in and promoting a poetic renaissance centered on formal experimentation. Furey, "*Poetry* and the Rhetoric of Dissent."

5. Marek, *Women Editing Modernism*, 58. I want to underscore that my aim is in no way to downplay the importance of Marek's work or to overlook its very real value in countering reductive, misogynistic accounts of Henderson and Monroe's influence. As Marek so convincingly shows, literary historical accounts prior to feminist recovery efforts in the 1990s consistently gave almost all of the credit for *Poetry*'s successes to Ezra Pound rather than to Monroe and Henderson, and Henderson was often simply written out of the picture entirely. Marek is also attentive to the problem of cultural appropriation and minstrelsy within the pages of *Poetry*; as she notes with some understatement, "Henderson's interest in American racial and ethnic groups" was "problematic." Marek also notes that Henderson's actions were also sometimes blatantly racist, as in her dismissals of the Black critic William Stanley Braithwaite. Marek explains that "while *Poetry* went further than most such magazines in creating a forum in which different voices might be heard, it is clear that a 'gatekeeping' ideology was still in effect." Marek, *Women Editing Modernism*, 41. And yet Marek is still able to claim that the magazine "introduced and printed nearly every major figure in twentieth-century poetry," even though *Poetry* published only four Black poets during the entirety of Monroe's editorial career. Marek, *Women Editing Modernism*, 23. I point this out not to fault Marek but to show how the failure to understand *Poetry* as a project of whiteness keeps critics from reckoning seriously with the results of the "'gatekeeping' ideology" that Marek identifies but does not explore.

6. Newcomb, *How Did Poetry Survive*, 52.

7. Newcomb, *How Did Poetry Survive*, 26.

8. Carr, "*Poetry*," 41–42.

9. Biggs quoted in Newcomb, *How Did Poetry Survive*, 30.

10. Z. Jackson, *Becoming Human*, 9.

11. Z. Jackson, *Becoming Human*, 5.

12. Spillers, "Mama's Baby," 68.

13. To be clear, I do not wish to naturalize a connection between women and reproduction. I am arguing that in Monroe and Henderson's consistent turn to white women and children as the poets who could effectively give form to Black folk materials, they drew on the long figural association of women and children with reproductive futurity and on the Anglo-Saxonist argument that descendants of Anglo-Saxons were biologically more capable of generating new forms, both biological and cultural. In this way, Monroe and Henderson were able to position white women and children as the agents of cultural reproduction who could keep American poetry white in spite of its many nonwhite source materials. I am using "reproductive futurity" in the sense theorized by Lee Edelman in part because Edelman directs our attention to the figural force of the child, as opposed to actual historical children. Edelman, *No Future*. My

understanding of discourses of reproduction is also influenced by Alys Weinbaum's discussion of what she names "the race/reproduction bind," a "conceptual unit" that highlights how "the representation of women's reproductive capacity [has] been integral to the epistemological systems that are central to defining modernity," including racialized hierarchies of value. Weinbaum, *Wayward Reproductions*, 5, 4.

14. For more on racial hierarchies of plasticity, see Schuller, *Biopolitics of Feeling*; and Z. Jackson, *Becoming Human*. The ideas about plasticity that Monroe and Henderson were picking up from literary scholarship were not exactly the same set of ideas about plasticity that Schuller and Jackson take up. Instead, they were simplified distillations of the idea that white races were more capable of directing their own development than were nonwhite races, both culturally and biologically. This is the basic idea of literary plasticity discussed in chapter 1, in which Anglo-Saxons are understood to be more capable of inventing new literary and cultural forms because they are more evolutionarily "advanced" than other groups.

15. Newcomb notes Monroe's disciplinary ambitions: "Monroe and her editorial colleagues . . . sought to create a publishing format for verse that combined the aesthetic refinement and emotional complexity of 'high art,' the modernized marketing practices of mass culture, and the targeted audience and professionalized demeanor of the disciplinary journal." Newcomb, *How Did Poetry Survive*, 26.

16. Harriet Monroe, "The Audience: II," *Poetry* 5, no. 1 (1914): 32, JSTOR.

17. Harriet Monroe, "The Bigness of the World," *Atlantic Monthly* 108 (1911): 374, Internet Archive.

18. Stokes, *Writers in Retrospect*, 10.

19. Glazener, *Literature in the Making*, 9, 93.

20. "Readings in Modern Poetry," advertisement, box 12, folder 4, Harriet Monroe Papers, Hanna Holborn Gray Special Collections Research Center, University of Chicago Library, Chicago, IL; Harriet Monroe, "A Travel Tale," *Poetry* 28, no. 3 (1926), JSTOR.

21. Harriet Monroe to Edward C. Marsh, April 23, 1915, box 18, folder 1, Harriet Monroe Papers.

22. Alice Corbin Henderson, "Contemporary Poetry and the Universities," *Poetry* 5, no. 4 (1915): 177, JSTOR.

23. "The New Movement in Poetry," advertisement, box 12, folder 4, Harriet Monroe Papers.

24. Carr, "*Poetry*," 55.

25. This sense that metrical laws were at last about to be revealed is a recurring trope in prosodical discourse that dates at least as far back as the eighteenth century. As Meredith Martin notes, pedagogical imperatives to simplify the complexity of prosody for students eventually crystallized into the dogma that there were indeed clear laws of English prosody, even as scholars continued to disagree about exactly what those laws were. Martin, *Rise and Fall*, 42. That this is a trope has been consistently missed in scholarship about prosody in the modernist era; instead, scholars take at face value the claim that scientific investigations into poetic rhythms were indeed new.

26. Harriet Monroe, "Dr. Patterson on Rhythm," *Poetry* 12, no. 1 (1918): 31–32, JSTOR.

27. See, for instance, Monroe's argument in an article on prosody that "music and poetry seem to have been among the earliest and most direct human manifestations of the universal rhythmic impulse. At first they were united—lyric rapture instinctively fitted words to melody, as it does still in certain forms of spontaneous folk-song like keening over the dead or other primitive rhapsodies of prayer and praise. But as life became more complex, the two arts separated, developed each its own imaginative and technical expression of the rhythmic instinct. Literature began in the creation of poems too beautiful to be left to chance memories and tongues, and therefore committed to writing. After the passing centuries had heaped up an accumulation of these masterpieces, the analysts took hold of them; and out of the practice of dead poets grammarians began to make rules for poets yet to come." Harriet Monroe, "Prosody," *Poetry* 20, no. 3 (1922): 149, JSTOR.

28. See Monroe, "Prosody"; Harriet Monroe, "Rhythms of English Verse," *Poetry* 3, no. 2 (1913): 61–68, JSTOR; Harriet Monroe, "Rhythms of English Verse II," *Poetry* 3, no.3 (1913): 100–111, JSTOR.

29. Martin, *Rise and Fall*, 27.

30. Martin, *Rise and Fall*, 27.

31. Martin, *Rise and Fall*, 36.

32. Martin, *Rise and Fall*, 32. For more on the commitment to the imagined classical origins of England, see Martin, "Imperfectly Civilized"; Prins, "Metrical Translation"; Prins, "Victorian Meters."

33. This change can be seen in the reception of different editions of the prosodist and Anglo-Saxonist Edwin Guest's *History of English Rhythms*. The first edition, published in 1838, argued that "accent was 'the sole principle' that regulated English rhythm," because English was fundamentally derived from Anglo-Saxon, which was an accentual language. While this argument made a splash in prosodic circles in 1838, it was much more influential when it was reprinted in 1882. Martin, *Rise and Fall*, 43.

34. Martin, *Rise and Fall*, 39.

35. Martin, *Rise and Fall*, 41.

36. Martin, *Rise and Fall*, 45.

37. Harriet Monroe, "Chaucer and Langland," *Poetry* 6, no. 6 (1915): 298, JSTOR.

38. Monroe, "Chaucer and Langland," 300.

39. Monroe, "Chaucer and Langland," 301.

40. Monroe, "Chaucer and Langland," 302.

41. Monroe, "Chaucer and Langland," 298.

42. Monroe, "Chaucer and Langland," 300–301.

43. Monroe, "Chaucer and Langland," 297. The Anglo-Saxonist valence of the discussion of free verse as an inherently democratic form is consistently missed in scholarship on free verse. Suzanne Churchill and Ethan Jaffee, for instance, note that defenders of free verse "made extravagant claims about the vital functions and democratic roots of free verse," citing Monroe's claim that free verse "strives for a concrete and immediate realization of life" and John Gould Fletcher's claim that "never was the noble language which is ours surpassed either in richness or in concision." Churchill and Jaffee, "New Poetry," 309. That both of these claims emerged from Anglo-Saxonist

discourse is absent from discussion of these claims. The same can be seen in the discussion of how "American proponents of free verse emphasized its American roots," which does not get into the specifically Anglo-Saxonist ideas about American identity that drove such claims about the origins of free verse. Churchill and Jaffee, "New Poetry," 310.

44. Monroe and Henderson, introduction to *The New Poetry*, viii.

45. Monroe and Henderson, introduction to *The New Poetry*, xxxvi–xxxvii.

46. Harriet Monroe, "A Later Word from Dr. Patterson," *Poetry* 12, no. 3 (1918): 171, JSTOR.

47. Glenway Wescott, "Review, *Classics in English*," *Poetry* 18, no. 5 (1921): 287, JSTOR.

48. Baker Brownell, "Kinaesthetic Verse," *Poetry* 22, no. 1 (1923): 39, JSTOR.

49. Margery Swett, "Free Verse Again," *Poetry* 25, no. 3 (1924): 153–54, JSTOR.

50. Harriet Monroe, "A Word About Prosody," *Poetry* 27, no. 3 (1925): 149–50, JSTOR.

51. Monroe, "Word About Prosody," 152.

52. Horsman, *Race and Manifest Destiny*, 33.

53. Berenice Van Slyke, "Neihardt's Epic (Review of *The Song of the Indian Wars* by John G. Neihardt)," *Poetry* 27, no. 6 (1926): 329–30, JSTOR.

54. Margery Swett, "From Hawaii (Review of *Slants* by Clifford Gessler)," *Poetry* 26, no. 2 (1925): 107, JSTOR.

55. Newcomb, *How Did Poetry Survive*, 52.

56. Harriet Monroe, "Incarnations," *Poetry* 2, no. 3 (1913): 102, JSTOR.

57. Harriet Monroe, "To the Wilderness," *Poetry* 10, no. 5 (1917): 259, JSTOR. For more on what Robin G. Schulze calls Monroe's "pioneer modernism," see Schulze, "Harriet Monroe's Pioneer Modernism"; and Schulze, *Degenerate Muse*.

58. Monroe, "To the Wilderness," 260.

59. Monroe, "To the Wilderness," 262.

60. Monroe, "To the Wilderness," 263.

61. Monroe, "To the Wilderness," 260.

62. Monroe, "To the Wilderness," 263.

63. Monroe, "To the Wilderness," 263.

64. See especially Martin, "Imperfectly Civilized"; Prins, "Metrical Translation"; and Rudy, "Manifest Prosody."

65. Martin, *Rise and Fall*, 46.

66. Monroe and Henderson published many reviews of scholarly monographs on poetic origins and ethnographic and anthropological studies of folk poetry, including multiple poems and essays from the influential anthropologist Edward Sapir, and they also wrote frequently about the fate of the communal origins theory in the twentieth-century university. See, for instance, Alice Corbin Henderson, "Who Writes Folk-Songs? Review of *Poetic Origins and the Ballad* by Louise Pound," *Poetry* 18, no. 4 (1921), JSTOR.

67. Michael Bell quoted in Bendix, *In Search of Authenticity*, 89.

68. Bendix, *In Search of Authenticity*, 89.

69. Bendix, *In Search of Authenticity*, 144.

70. Sapir was an early reviewer of Robert Bridges's 1918 volume of the poetry of Gerard Manley Hopkins, and the uptake of Hopkins's work in this moment had much to do with Hopkins's investment in "Anglo-Saxon" rhythm.

71. Edward Sapir, "Civilization and Culture," *Dial* 67, no, 799, (1919): 233, Internet Archive.

72. Henderson quoted in Harriet Monroe, "Folk-Song Collections," *Poetry* 28, no. 6 (1926): 350, JSTOR.

73. For classic studies of modernist literary primitivism, see M. Bell, *Primitivism*; North, *Dialect of Modernism*; Torgovnick, *Gone Primitive*. For a foundational account of anthropological constructions of the primitive, see Kuper, *Invention of Primitive Society*. Ben Etherington has recently reassessed modernist-era literary primitivism as an aesthetic project, arguing that the scholarly consensus that primitivism was "a unidirectional ideological projection from the colonizer on to the colonized" is reductive and misses "the global nature of this aesthetic mode." Etherington, *Literary Primitivism*, xii. Etherington distinguishes between what he calls "philo-primitivism," or the fetishization of an imaginary primitive state of being or culture, and "emphatic primitivism," or "the urgent desire to become primitive, a condition whose fulfillment would require no less than an exit from the capitalist world-system." Etherington, *Literary Primitivism*, 33. Etherington's reevaluation of this romantic anticapitalist aesthetic project is generative, but as I discuss in more detail in chapters 3 and 4, there were many other aesthetic projects that rejected a white supremacist capitalist world order without relying on the imagined authenticity and immediacy of precapitalist life.

74. To Monroe and Henderson, as to many other white modernists interested in Black folk materials, what counted as an "authentic" folk artifact was essentially anything that appeared to be appropriatable because of the lack of a single author, such as spirituals, folk tales, and often, dialect poetry, which was misread as if it were authored by a group of untutored folk rather than by readily identifiable authors.

75. Alice Corbin Henderson, "Poetry of the American Negro (Review of *Songs of the Soil* by Fenton Johnson)," *Poetry* 10, no. 3 (1917): 158, JSTOR.

76. On Dunbar's supposed imitativeness, see Nurhussein, *Rhetorics of Literacy*. There are of course multiple centuries-long traditions of attributing imitativeness to Black individuals and Black cultures; perhaps most germane is Thomas Jefferson's dismissal of Phillis Wheatley. It was also common in the early twentieth century for scholars of folklore to attribute the origins of Black folk materials to European influence. As John W. Roberts notes, this view of Black folk materials as imitative dominated early twentieth-century folkloristics, which was founded on "a discursive tradition in which the European folk are still seen as the original folk and all other folk are mere imitators." Roberts, "African American Diversity," 160. Henderson echoed this argument in multiple essays in *Poetry*.

77. Henderson, "Poetry of the American Negro," 158–59.

78. Helen Hoyt, "Negro Poets," *Poetry* 16, no. 5 (1920): 287, JSTOR.

79. Hoyt, "Negro Poets," 287–88.

80. George Dillon, "Mr. Cullen's First Book (Review of *Color* by Countee Cullen)," *Poetry* 28, no. 1 (1926): 50, JSTOR.

81. For an account of *Palms*, see Thacker, "Poetry in Perspective."

82. "News Notes," *Poetry* 29, no. 2 (1926): 116, JSTOR.

83. "Brief Notices: *Southern Road* by Sterling Brown," *Poetry* 44, no. 2 (1934): 115, JSTOR.

84. Harold Rosenberg, "Truth and the Academic Style (Review of *Saint Peter Relates an Incident: Selected Poems* by James Weldon Johnson)," *Poetry* 49, no. 1 (1936): 51, JSTOR.

85. Harriet Monroe, "Negro Sermons (Review of *God's Trombones: Seven Negro Sermons in Verse* by James Weldon Johnson)," *Poetry* 30, no. 5 (1927): 293, JSTOR.

86. Eunice Tietjens, "Southern Songs (Review of *Plantation Songs and Other Verse* by Ruth McEnery Stuart)," *Poetry* 9, no. 1, (1916): 54–55, JSTOR.

87. Harriet Monroe, "The Old South (Review of *The Arrow of Lightning* by Beatrice Ravenel)," *Poetry* 30, no. 5 (1927): 289, JSTOR.

88. Julia Peterkin, "Negro Blue and Gold (Review of *Fine Clothes for the Jew* by Langston Hughes)," *Poetry* 31, no. 1 (1927): 45, JSTOR.

89. "News Notes," *Poetry* 23, no. 2 (1923): 114, JSTOR.

90. "News Notes," *Poetry* 23, no. 2 (1923): 114.

91. "News Notes," *Poetry* 23, no. 2 (1923): 114.

92. Alice Corbin Henderson, "The Folk Poetry of These States," *Poetry* 16, no. 5 (1920): 266–67, JSTOR.

93. Hervey Allen and DuBose Heyward, "Poetry South," *Poetry* 20, no. 1 (1922): 35–36, JSTOR.

94. Allen and Heyward, "Poetry South," 36–37.

95. Henderson, "Folk Poetry of These States," 267.

96. Alice Corbin Henderson, "Review: *The Sharing* by Agnes Lee and *The Congo and Other Poems* by Vachel Lindsay," *Poetry* 5, no. 6 (1915): 297, JSTOR.

97. Henderson, "Review: *The Sharing*," 297–98.

98. Tompkins, *Racial Indigestion*, 90, 112.

99. Tompkins, *Racial Indigestion*, 92.

100. Tompkins, *Racial Indigestion*, 112.

101. Vachel Lindsay, "Mr. Lindsay Protests Against Jazz," *Poetry* 21, no. 5 (1923): 286, JSTOR.

102. Roberts, "African American Diversity," 160–61.

103. Churchill and Jaffee, "New Poetry," 309–10.

104. Rusert, "Plantation Ecologies," 344; Jackson, *Becoming Human*, 11.

105. Clukey, "Dreaming of Palestine," 176.

106. See the "Poems by Children" sections in the issues from July 1916, July 1917, and July 1918. *Poetry* also published many reviews of poetry books written for children that highlighted the importance of training future generations of poets. I am proposing that we can understand this emphasis on white children through Alys Weinbaum's reading of Etienne Balibar's account of nationalism. Weinbaum notes that, "as Etienne Balibar helps explain, 'the symbolic kernel of the idea of race' within the context of the modern nation is 'the schema of genealogy'—a schema in which issues of reproduction, maternity, and kinship play starring roles." Weinbaum, *Wayward Reproductions*, 189. Within a racialized nationalist logic, *Poetry*'s emphasis on Anglo-Saxon poetic genealogies thus fits neatly with its simultaneous emphasis on white child poets and readers.

Chapter Three

1. Alfred Kreymborg, "Red Chant," *Crisis* 17, no. 1, (1918): 31, https://modjourn.org/issue/bdr511548/.

2. Ron Silliman, for instance, credits Johnson with writing "the first instance in English of a prose poem which calls attention to a discursive or poetic effect." Silliman, *New Sentence*, 83.

3. The most thorough accounts of Johnson as a modernist poet are found in Smethurst, *African American Roots*; and in Thomas, *Extraordinary Measures*. Rather remarkably, Johnson does not figure prominently in scholarship on modernist periodicals; Churchill, *Little Magazine "Others,"* for instance, contains no discussion of Johnson's work, in spite of Kreymborg's excitement about Johnson.

4. Hutchinson quoted in Thomas, *Extraordinary Measures*, 12.

5. Thomas, *Extraordinary Measures*, 12.

6. Thomas, *Extraordinary Measures*, 26.

7. Smethurst, *African American Roots*, 153.

8. Smethurst, *African American Roots*, 141, 153.

9. Lisa Woolley, for instance, reads Johnson's early work as engaging with modern themes if not with modernist forms, arguing, "although the form of much of Johnson's early poetry recalled the nineteenth century, its spirit often belonged to the twentieth." Woolley, "From Chicago Renaissance," 39. Other critics have positioned Johnson as anticipating later elements of Harlem Renaissance writing by focusing on his reworkings of Black folk music into literary forms; see Long and Collier, *Afro-American Writing*; Bell, "Fenton Johnson"; and Thomas, *Extraordinary Measures*.

10. Thomas does recognize in Johnson's most famous poem, "Tired," "durable Romantic convention" and the "lessons and ideas" of "Victorian poets." Thomas, *Extraordinary Measures*, 34. But aside from briefly tracing the influence of Edgar Allan Poe's essay "The Philosophy of Composition" and Arthur Symons's "In the Wood of Finvarra" on Johnson's view of poetry, Thomas does not explore why these authors and essays appealed to Johnson.

11. Hack, *Reaping Something New*, 74.

12. Hack, *Reaping Something New*, 7.

13. Sandler, *Black Romantic Revolution*, 187.

14. McGill, "Poetry of Slavery," 130.

15. Sherman, *Invisible Poets*, vii.

16. Naming Frances Ellen Watkins Harper is a complicated endeavor. She first published and lectured under her maiden name, Frances Ellen Watkins, in the 1850s, before marrying Fenton Harper in 1860. Harper left the lecture circuit between her marriage and her husband's death four years later and then spoke as "Mrs. Harper." As Meredith McGill argues, the scholarly "impulse to collect, sort, and make sense of Frances Ellen Watkins Harper's poetry under the sign of individual authorship has worked to minimize material differences between and among her published texts," even though "the volumes of poetry published by Frances Ellen

Watkins look nothing like the collections Frances Ellen Watkins Harper published toward the end of her career." McGill, "Frances Ellen Watkins Harper," 54–55. Fenton Johnson referred to her both as Frances Harper and as Frances E. Watkins; throughout this chapter, I use Watkins Harper in part to signal the complexities of Harper's publication history.

17. Courage and Hall, "Fenton Johnson," 11.

18. Fenton Johnson, "The Editor's Blue Pencil," *Champion Magazine* 1, no. 1 (1916): 5, Internet Archive.

19. Courage and Hall, "Fenton Johnson," 1.

20. Courage and Hall, "Fenton Johnson," 9.

21. Courage and Hall, "Fenton Johnson," 5–6.

22. Fenton Johnson, "The Editor's Blue Pencil," *Champion Magazine* 1, no. 7 (1917): 332, Internet Archive.

23. Fenton Johnson, 42 *WPA Poems*, Fisk University Library Special Collections and Archives, Nashville, TN.

24. See Johnson's correspondence with Monroe, housed in the records of *Poetry* at the University of Chicago Library's Special Collections Research Center. In a letter from April 8, 1918, Johnson describes the poems in the most recent issue of *Poetry* he found striking, including Monroe's own "Carolina Woodcuts." He argued, "You placed the aged colored woman of the South in a romantic light that none of your race give her and few of my race have succeeded in giving her." Fenton Johnson to Harriet Monroe, April 8, 1918, box 13, folder 10, *Poetry: A Magazine of Verse* Records, Hanna Holborn Gray Special Collections Research Center, University of Chicago Library, Chicago, IL. A letter from July 16, 1918, mentions that Johnson visited *Poetry*'s office and notes that he "was highly pleased with the reception [his] work received through the June number" of *Poetry*. Fenton Johnson to Harriet Monroe, July 16, 1918, box 13, folder 10, *Poetry: A Magazine of Verse* Records.

25. Courage and Hall, "Fenton Johnson," 4; George Ellis, "The Outlook of the Negro in Literature," *Champion Magazine* 1, no. 1 (1916): 30, Internet Archive.

26. Ellis, "Outlook of the Negro," 30.

27. William H. Ferris, "The Literary Mirror: Matthew Henson, 'A Negro Explorer at the North Pole,'" *Champion Magazine* 1, no. 4 (1916): 202, Internet Archive.

28. Moses, *Afrotopia*, 16. See also Courage and Hall, "Fenton Johnson," 8–10, 14.

29. Moses, *Afrotopia*, 31, 40.

30. This is not to say that the vindicationist tradition always led to salutary or neatly antiracist accounts of world history, as Moses's account emphasizes. Johnson's political stances were often muddy, and my aim in discussing his use of vindicationism is not to position him as the "good" alternative to *Poetry*'s bad example but to think about how Johnson created a dialogue with *Poetry* to offer alternative accounts of literary and world histories.

31. Goldsby and McGill, "What Is 'Black,'" 170.

32. Goldsby and McGill, "What Is 'Black,'" 170.

33. McHenry, *To Make Negro Literature*, 9, 16.

34. Fenton Johnson, "The Editor's Blue Pencil," *Champion Magazine* 1, no. 2 (1916): 55, Internet Archive.

35. Ellis, "Outlook of the Negro," 34.

36. William H. Ferris, "The Literary Mirror: Phillis Wheatley Once More," *Champion Magazine* 1, no. 6 (1917): 314, Internet Archive.

37. Ferris, "Phillis Wheatley," 315.

38. Georgia Douglas Johnson, "Pilgrims," *Champion Magazine* 1, no. 6 (1917): 315, Internet Archive.

39. G. Johnson, *Bronze*, 35.

40. Fielder, "Literary Genealogies," 789.

41. "Prominent Chicago Negroes of Early Days," *Champion Magazine* 1, no. 7 (1917): 339, Internet Archive; Fon Holly, "The First Settler of Chicago (illustration)," *Champion Magazine* 1, no. 7 (1917): 332, Internet Archive.

42. In this view, Johnson was in step with larger trends in Black historiography. As Wilson Jeremiah Moses argues, "Black American historical consciousness," particularly in the nineteenth and early twentieth centuries, was "based not only on an African-centered construction of the past, but on a variety of attempts to fashion visions of a better future." Moses, *Afrotopia*, 17.

43. Foster, *'Til Death or Distance*, xvii.

44. Burks, "First Black Literary Magazine," 318.

45. Wilson, "Brief Wondrous Life," 27.

46. Wilson, "Brief Wondrous Life," 22.

47. Burks, "First Black Literary Magazine," 319.

48. Burks, "First Black Literary Magazine," 318.

49. Wilson, "Brief Wonderous Life," 35.

50. Eckstrom and Rusert, "Afric-American Picture Gallery." While it is beyond the scope of my chapter, it is significant that *The Champion* shared *The Anglo-African's* concern with Black visual cultures. As Eckstrom and Rusert note, "one of the most surprising, if not vexing aspects of the Picture Gallery is that it circulated without actual pictures," in part because of how cost-prohibitive lithographic reproductions were in 1859 and because of the incredibly "scarc[e] resources with which black editors and printers worked." And yet the "Afric-American Picture Gallery" made "a protected space of black art for black patrons," thus "register[ing] the activity of practicing black artists in the antebellum period" (artists such as Robert Douglass Jr., Mary Edmonia Lewis, Robert S. Duncanson, and Edward Mitchell Bannister), while also thematizing "the institutional politics that frequently frustrated artistic activity among African Americans." Eckstrom and Rusert, "Afric-American Picture Gallery." *The Champion* positioned itself as the heir to *The Anglo-African's* ambitions in many ways, including in its laudatory coverage of Black visual artists and in its regular series of photographs of Black life and in its monthly cartoons. It is also notable that, in the first installment, Ethiop describes "a number of paintings . . . related to the history of African American editorial practices," including portraits of Thomas Hamilton, "who is portrayed surrounded by 'piles of all the journals edited by colored men from the commencement [of African American publishing] up till the present.'" William J. Wilson quoted in Ivy Wilson, "Brief Wondrous Life," 23.

51. Eckstrom and Rusert, "Afric-American Picture Gallery."

52. Fenton Johnson, "The First Negro Magazine," *Champion Magazine* 1, no. 1 (1916): 12, Internet Archive.

53. William J. Wilson, "Afric-American Picture Gallery—Third Paper," *Anglo-African Magazine* 1 (1859): 174, https://jtoaa.americanantiquarian.org/welcome-to-just-teach-one-african-american/afric-american-picture-gallery/.

54. Wilson, "Afric-American Picture Gallery," 174.

55. Wilson, "Afric-American Picture Gallery," 174.

56. Wilson, "Afric-American Picture Gallery," 176–77.

57. Eckstrom and Rusert, "Afric-American Picture Gallery."

58. Sandler, *Black Romantic Revolution*, 3.

59. Sandler, *Black Romantic Revolution*, 3–4.

60. McGill, "Poetry of Slavery," 117.

61. Sandler, *Black Romantic Revolution*, 4.

62. F. Johnson, "First Negro Magazine," 12.

63. Zapędowska, "Hope, Sound, and the Materiality of Print," 337.

64. Sandler, *Black Romantic Revolution*, 140.

65. Sandler, *Black Romantic Revolution*, 46–48.

66. Martin, *Rise and Fall*, 28.

67. Dunbar, *Oak and Ivy*, 6.

68. F. Johnson, *Visions of the Dusk*, 42.

69. Nurhussein, *Black Land*, 6.

70. Whitman, *Not a Man*, 221.

71. Whitman, *Not a Man*, 221–22.

72. Sandler, *Black Romantic Revolution*, 169.

73. Sandler, *Black Romantic Revolution*, 167.

74. Fielder, "Literary Genealogies," 794.

75. F. Johnson, *Visions of the Dusk*, 45.

76. F. Johnson, *Visions of the Dusk*, 45.

77. Sandler, *Black Romantic Revolution*, 26–27.

78. Sandler, *Black Romantic Revolution*, 28.

79. Watkins, *Poems on Miscellaneous Subjects*, 11–12.

80. F. Johnson, *Visions of the Dusk*, 48.

81. Courage and Hall, "Fenton Johnson," 7.

82. McKittrick, *Demonic Grounds*, xii.

83. McKittrick, *Demonic Grounds*, xiii.

84. This strategy echoes and amplifies Dunbar's. As Smethurst notes, in the organization of Dunbar's books of poetry, he "seems consciously to confound any easy linkage of racial categories to divisions of high, folk, and popular literature." Smethurst, "Paul Laurence Dunbar," 380.

85. F. Johnson, *Songs of the Soil*, i.

86. McKittrick, *Demonic Grounds*, xxiii.

87. F. Johnson, *Songs of the Soil*, i.

88. F. Johnson, *Songs of the Soil*, iv.

89. Fenton Johnson, "The Editor's Blue Pencil," *Champion Magazine* 1, no. 8 (1917): 381, Internet Archive.

90. Fenton Johnson, "The Editor's Blue Pencil," *Champion Magazine* 1, no. 8 (1917): 381, Internet Archive.

91. McKittrick, *Demonic Grounds*, xiii.

92. McKittrick, *Demonic Grounds*, xiv.

93. Fenton Johnson, "Aunt Hannah Jackson," "Aunt Jane Allen," "The Drunkard," "The Minister," and "The Scarlet Woman," in Kreymborg, *Others for 1919*, 78–82.

94. Melamed, *Represent and Destroy*, 89.

95. For more on "ballad reading," see Michael Cohen, *Social Lives*.

96. Gelmi, "Speaker, Photographed," 83.

97. Gelmi, "Speaker, Photographed," 81.

98. Gelmi, "Speaker, Photographed," 81.

99. For an account of the longer history of the abstraction of poetic genres into genres of persons in American poetry and poetics, see V. Jackson, *Before Modernism*.

100. Gelmi, "Speaker, Photographed," 74.

101. Gelmi, "Speaker, Photographed," 81.

102. Gelmi, "Speaker, Photographed," 92.

103. Fenton Johnson, "The Banjo Player," in Kreymborg, *Others for 1919*, 80.

104. Gelmi, "Speaker, Photographed," 86.

105. McKittrick, *Demonic Grounds*, xv.

106. Gelmi, "Speaker, Photographed," 88.

107. Fenton Johnson, "The Artist," *Others* 5, no. 5 (1919): 20, https://modjourn.org/issue/bdr523742/.

108. See, for instance, "Beloved," which celebrates a love as "warm/As the honey-bees that swarm/In the June-time, happy time"; "When I Reach Manhood," which includes the lines "And when years have changed my hair to white,/Roses will be sweeter far than now;/Time will never dim the mystery/Of a blossom in its summer glow"; "The Awakening of Poesy," which portrays the birth of poetry as occurring on "a joyous day in June"; and "Of the Rose," which includes the lines "And the heart of the rose is love;—/Love who sleeps at the poet's feet." F. Johnson, *Little Dreaming*, 10, 32, 50, 52.

109. See, for instance, poems in *A Little Dreaming* including "The Lover's Soliloquy," which recalls, "In Ethiop, beneath the rose-dipped sun,/My fathers wooed their dusky paramours,/As you and I, in this, our latter day"; "To an Afro-American Maiden," in which the speaker sees in the titular maiden's face "Rich old Ethiop"; "The Ethiopian's Song." F. Johnson, *Little Dreaming*, 27–28, 54–55, 37. In *Visions of the Dusk*, see "Ethiopia," discussed in detail earlier. F. Johnson, *Visions of the Dusk*, 42–48.

110. Johnson's disappointed poetic hopes can also be connected to material changes in Chicago. As Courage and Hall note, "Fenton Johnson was a product of a nascent petit bourgeois, pre–Great Migration black milieu in Chicago and of a period in which it was not yet clear how de facto segregation would impact the city's human ecology. Even with the solidification of African American communities on the South Side and West Side, the established black middle and working classes still enjoyed some fluidity in housing, employment, and public accommodation and facilities and learned quickly to manipulate Chicago's commercial opportunities and political ward-boss system to their own ends." Courage and Hall, "Fenton Johnson," 2. Johnson's youth coincided with "a

period of unusual optimism that allowed aspirant black families in Chicago to believe that possibly the full fruits of American modernity might be available" and in which Black civic and social institutions in Chicago flourished. Courage and Hall, "Fenton Johnson," 2. Johnson's bitterest free verse poems were written just before the red summer of 1919, and he himself had been the target of FBI anticommunist investigations.

111. V. Jackson, *Before Modernism*, 3.

112. V. Jackson, *Before Modernism*, 3.

113. McKittrick, *Demonic Grounds*, xxiii.

114. Fielder, "Literary Genealogies," 791.

Chapter Four

1. Critics have understood the move to categorize songs and ceremonies as poetry variously, with some praising the anthology for attempting to value Native American cultural practices and others viewing the anthology as a key text in attempts to promote "an oral tradition that whites produce[d], without regard to the conditions of that production." Konkle, *Writing Indian Nations*, 29. Michael Castro argues that *The Path on the Rainbow* "represents the first attempt to anthologize Indian poetry on its own" and that "the total effect of the material collected in *Path on the Rainbow* was to reveal a rich Native American poetic tradition." Castro, *Interpreting the Indian*, 19–20. Kenneth Lincoln notes that *The Path on the Rainbow* was "lead text in Jorge Luis Borges's classes on the American canon," and Lincoln credits the anthology with inspiring A. Grove Day's dissertation, directed by Yvor Winters, later published as *The Sky Clears*, which collected additional examples of unpublished ethnographic texts and which helped to spawn interest in the idea of a "Native American Renaissance." Lincoln, foreword to *American Indian Poetry*, xvi, xxvi. Jeremy Braddock has read the anthology as marking a shift in the way anthologists sought to institutionalize modernism, away from the "school-defining mode of the coterie anthology" toward representing modernism "as a set of aesthetic and cultural practices," and he notes that the anthology can be read as an early instance of what Walter Benn Michaels named "nativist modernism." Braddock, *Collecting as Modernist Practice*, 160–61. Elizabeth Barnett has identified *The Path on the Rainbow* as "the first anthology to follow the little magazine trend [inaugurated by *Poetry*] of presenting Native American songs and ceremonies as poetry." Barnett, "Destroyed by *Poetry*," 668. Robert Dale Parker's *The Invention of Native American Literature* historicizes the phenomenon of ethnographic texts getting anthologized as poetry and traces its eventuation in the ethnopoetics of Jerome Rothenberg, Dennis Tedlock, and Dell Hymes. Maureen Konkle notes the continuation of the practice of presenting ethnographic texts as "authentic" Native literature in undergraduate survey classes, explaining that "college textbook editors habitually put translated Native narratives at the beginning of American literature anthologies as a means of representing, one suspects, the essentially American or the first American. . . . The fact that there is seldom information on how or why or when or under what circumstances these narratives were written down is secondary to the more fundamental requirement of incorporating Indians—somehow—into the United States." Konkle, *Writing Indian Nations*, 298n53. For an account of the

question of orality and literacy more broadly, see Teuton, "Theorizing American Indian Literature," which provides an overview of twentieth- and twenty-first-century critical trends in Native American and Indigenous studies surrounding questions of the oral and literary traditions of Native nations. See also Spry, *Our War Paint*, which provides a useful case study of Gerald Vizenor's reworkings of Frances Densmore's ethnographic translations as a "recasting [of] the songs as the ephemera of colonization rather than as artifacts of an authentic tribal culture." Spry, *Our War Paint*, 25.

2. Louis Untermeyer, "The Indian as Poet," *Dial* 8 (1919): 241, Internet Archive.

3. Untermeyer, "Indian as Poet," 241.

4. Fee, "Publication, Performances, and Politics," 51.

5. Simpson, *Mohawk Interruptus*, 149.

6. Simpson, *Mohawk Interruptus*, 21 (italics in original).

7. Simpson, *Mohawk Interruptus*, 127.

8. The imbrication of anti-Blackness and settler colonialism in culturally appropriative literary practices can be seen in a historical episode related by Jodi Byrd in *The Transit of Empire*. Byrd notes that Charles Peabody, while on an archaeological expedition for the Harvard Peabody Museum "to grave rob Southeastern mounds, most likely Chickasaw and Choctaw," outside of Clarksdale, Mississippi, hired Black workers to do the physical work of digging up the burial mounds. Byrd, *Transit of Empire*, 119. Peabody became interested in the songs the workers sang and published an account of those songs in the *Journal of American Folk-Lore* in 1903. Peabody's language is telling: "Busy archaeologically, we had not very much time left for folk-lore, in itself of not easy excavation, but willy-nilly our ears were beset with an abundance of ethnological material in song, —words and music." Peabody quoted in Byrd, *Transit of Empire*, 148.

9. For a thorough overview of scholarship that reads modernist primitivism as primarily about cultural appropriation and Anglo-American fantasies of the purity of primitive cultures, as well as an alternative account that attempts to recuperate the political force of some primitivist projects, see Etherington, *Literary Primitivism*. Etherington tracks a broad critical consensus, emerging in the 1990s, that all works of literary primitivism were politically suspect and points to the diminished reputation of D. H. Lawrence as one highly visible effect of such a reading of literary primitivism.

10. Taylor, "Not Primitive Enough," 53–54.

11. Strong-Boag and Gerson, *Paddling Her Own Canoe*, 149.

12. Socarides, *In Plain Sight*, 4, 30.

13. Austin's work for the *Cambridge History* highlights the still blurry line between professional academics and amateur scholars in the early twentieth century, discussed in more detail in chapter 2. As Claudia Stokes notes, literary history became a genre especially associated with this middle ground between professionalism and amateur enthusiasm, as it did not require generalist scholars to "learn medieval languages or embark on lengthy graduate training" like their more professionalized (meaning philologically trained) peers. Stokes, *Writers in Retrospect*, 107–8.

14. Goodman and Dawson, *Mary Austin and the American West*, 221.

15. As Margaret Bruchac argues, such posturing was typical of the salvage ethnography era in all fields in which "Indigenous cultural material[s] . . . were collected and

sorted," leading to a situation in which "speculative theories and opinions," uninformed by "Indigenous knowledge-bearers and without consideration for Indigenous philosophies and sensitivities," could be "routinely accepted as fact . . . if voiced by a prominent enough researcher." Bruchac, *Savage Kin*, 13.

16. For more on Austin's interactions with and knowledge of Indigenous communities, see especially Hoyer, *Dancing Ghosts*; and Metcalfe, "Singing Like the Indians Do."

17. My reading of Austin's poetics diverges sharply from existing scholarship. Austin's poetics are generally read as having supported the salutary effort to create more "organic" forms of poetry and as having promoted the intrinsic value of Native American poetry and literature. Take, for instance, Michael Castro's influential reading, which posits that Austin helpfully "dissociat[ed] poetic rhythm from predetermined forms imposed . . . by convention" and that in the process she also positioned Native American poetry as the fountainhead of all modern poetry. Castro, *Interpreting the Indian*, 40, 43. In Castro's telling, which has influenced much of the scholarship on Austin's poetics to this point, Austin's advocacy for free verse forms dovetailed with her advocacy for Native American cultural expressions, and both forms of advocacy were progressive. But when we look more closely at Austin's theories of poetic rhythm, a much more complicated picture emerges.

18. Austin, *American Rhythm*, 36. Austin's papers, housed at the Huntington Library, include copious notes on Gummere's writings, indicating that her idea of the "poetic orgy" is derived from Gummere's theorization of the primal throng. See the Mary Hunter Austin Papers, 1845–1950, Huntington Library, San Marino, CA.

19. On the misrepresentation and fetishization of oral traditions, see Brooks, *Common Pot*; Konkle, *Writing Indian Nations*; Teuton, "Theorizing American Indian Literature"; and Womack, *Red on Red*.

20. See Lowell, "Some Musical Analogies"; Lowell, "Vers Libre"; Patterson, "New Verse and New Prose"; Patterson, *Rhythm of Prose*. Though Lowell and Patterson understood their insight to be unprecedented, Coventry Patmore's theory of isochronous intervals, and the many theories that grew outward from Patmore's, beat them to the punch by half a century. See Prins, "Patmore's Law."

21. Braddock, *Collecting as Modernist Practice*, 162.

22. Austin, *American Rhythm*, 20–21. For more on the idea of "degraded" and "genuine" ballads, see Michael Cohen, *Social Life of Poems*, especially chapter 4.

23. Austin, *American Rhythm*, 23 (italics in original).

24. Braddock, *Collecting as Modernist Practice*, 161.

25. Rifkin, *Beyond Settler Time*, 26.

26. Rifkin, *Beyond Settler Time*, 22.

27. Austin, *American Rhythm*, 64.

28. Glen Sean Coulthard argues that, in discussions of "Indigenous–state relations," there is "a perceived relationship between the affirmative recognition and institutional accommodation of societal cultural differences" and an erroneous assumption that a move away from assimilationist state policies toward "mutual recognition" automatically results in better conditions for Indigenous communities. Coulthard, *Red Skin, White Masks*, 2–3. Though Coulthard's analysis focuses specifically on "the colonial

relationship between Indigenous peoples and the Canadian state," it has broad applications for understanding colonial relationships as they are constituted by legal, political, cultural, and literary systems, among others. Coulthard calls for analysis of how settler colonial relationships "continue to facilitate the dispossession of Indigenous peoples of their lands and self-determining authority." Coulthard, *Red Skin, White Masks*, 3, 7. Here I am suggesting the ways in which Austin and other white literary tastemakers dispossessed Indigenous peoples of their self-determining authority within the realm of literary production.

29. Austin, *American Rhythm*, 33, 29. This positing of an absolute rhythmic difference was a common move in folklore studies and allied disciplines; as Andrea Brady notes, a similar logic structured white theorists' and song collectors' approaches to Black speech. Folklorists and song collectors "represented the 'easy and careless speech' of African American informants . . . as fugitive from transcription." Brady, *Poetry and Bondage*, 234.

30. Austin, *American Rhythm*, 63, 61.

31. Austin, *American Rhythm*, 32, 54, 9.

32. Austin, *American Rhythm*, 11, 64.

33. Austin, *American Rhythm*, 56.

34. Labeling these works as "songs" may seem to indicate an awareness that "poetry" and "verse" are non-Native categories, but the anthology works to fit these transcribed and translated oral expressions into a stadial theory of generic evolution, in which the earliest poetry was a communally authored oral expression that included ritual dance as a necessary component and in which the end goal of generic evolution is individually authored printed poems. In the table of contents, the translators of the collected "songs" are named, but they are not named in the text of the anthology itself, reinforcing the idea that the songs were anonymously or communally authored or that they emerged from the geographical areas named in the section headings.

35. Simpson, *Mohawk Interruptus*, 21.

36. Austin, introduction to *The Path on the Rainbow*, xxxi–xxxii.

37. Denetdale, "Return to 'The Uprising,'" 75.

38. Denetdale, "Return to 'The Uprising,'" 73.

39. Denetdale, "Return to 'The Uprising,'" 74.

40. Cronyn, *Path on the Rainbow*, 3.

41. Cronyn, *Path on the Rainbow*, 4.

42. Cronyn, *Path on the Rainbow*, 193–94.

43. Cronyn, *Path on the Rainbow*, 197–98.

44. Cronyn, *Path on the Rainbow*, 222.

45. Barker, "Introduction," 3.

46. Cronyn, *Path on the Rainbow*, 202.

47. Cronyn, *Path on the Rainbow*, 202–3.

48. Cronyn, *Path on the Rainbow*, 203–4.

49. Barker, "Introduction," 2.

50. Goeman, *Mark My Words*, 44.

51. Simpson, *Mohawk Interruptus*, 148.

52. Simpson, *Mohawk Interruptus*, 192.

53. Funnily enough, in the framing of Johnson's verse, the anthology appears to invent a new Native nation, as it includes Johnson's Indigenous pen name (spelled incorrectly) in parentheses after her name, in the same position as Indigenous national markers in other entries in the table of contents.

54. Cronyn, "Indian Melodists," *Dial* 67, no. 797 (1919): 162, Internet Archive.

55. Eliot, "War-Paint and Feathers," 122.

56. Eliot, "War-Paint and Feathers," 121.

57. Untermeyer, "Indian as Poet," 241.

58. On the sexualization of Johnson's performances, see Carpenter, *Seeing Red*, 58–70. On the conflicts between Johnson and First Nations political leaders and thinkers, see Monture, *We Share Our Matters*, 83–84.

59. Strong-Boag and Gerson, *Paddling Her Own Canoe*, 181.

60. Strong-Boag and Gerson, *Paddling Her Own Canoe*, 175.

61. Monture, *We Share Our Matters*, 68.

62. Strong-Boag and Gerson, *Paddling Her Own Canoe*, 116.

63. Strong-Boag and Gerson, *Paddling Her Own Canoe*, 101.

64. Hale quoted in Strong-Boag and Gerson, *Paddling Her Own Canoe*, 145.

65. Strong-Boag and Gerson, *Paddling Her Own Canoe*, 145.

66. Strong-Boag and Gerson, *Paddling Her Own Canoe*, 105.

67. Simpson, *Mohawk Interruptus*, 70–71.

68. Simpson, *Mohawk Interruptus*, 182.

69. Kristen Brown, "Queering the Waters"; Revie, "Pauline Johnson's Sapphic Wampum"; Strong-Boag and Gerson, *Paddling Her Own Canoe*. The canoe was a heavily burdened symbol in turn-of-the-century Canada. Canoes are of course an Indigenous technology, and they were also quickly appropriated as a symbol of Canadian nationalism. They were also linked to the New Woman and especially to movements for clothing reform and athletic recreation, as well as to sexual license. As Strong-Boag and Gerson note, the "sexual explicitness" of Johnson's canoe poems "enhance[d] the bohemian identity she also claims in her articles about her canoe and camping trips." Strong-Boag and Gerson, *Paddling Her Own Canoe*, 140. Indeed, Johnson's first book publisher was John Lane at Bodley Head, who "specialized in 'New Woman' fiction, naturalistic short stories, and 'decadent' poetry and art," including that of Aubrey Beardsley and Oscar Wilde. Lane and Johnson were thus associated with "inappropriate sexual knowledge" and with a bohemian literary avant-garde. Strong-Boag and Gerson, *Paddling Her Own Canoe*, 144. Kristen Brown notes that canoes were conventional "erotic symbol[s]" at the turn into the twentieth century, though such erotic symbolism was generally used to describe heterosexual sex. By contrast, in Johnson's sexy canoe poems, "a lack of identifying referents . . . leaves gender ambiguous," inviting queer readings of these supposedly staid nineteenth-century verses. Brown, "Queering the Waters," 143.

70. Simpson, *Mohawk Interruptus*, 148.

71. E. Johnson, *Flint and Feather*, 41–44.

72. Brown, "Queering the Waters," 160.

73. E. Johnson, *Flint and Feather*, 41–42.

74. Strong-Boag and Gerson, *Paddling Her Own Canoe*, 95.

75. Gerson, "Rereading Pauline Johnson," 54.

76. E. Johnson, *Flint and Feather*, 45.

77. E. Johnson, *Flint and Feather*, 44 (italics added).

78. Dickinson, "To 'Hear the Call,'" 7. (Dickinson's scholarship was produced for Margaret Linley's Making Nineteenth-Century Environments course at Simon Fraser University and published in the class's student-reviewed online journal. I want to credit both Dickinson's exceptional work and Linley's efforts to make public the scholarship students have produced in this course.) As Strong-Boag and Gerson note, Capilano was "characterized by [the Canadian press] as an activist and agitator . . . [who] was regularly blamed for inciting a series of conflicts and rebellions, most notably those in the Nass and Skeena Valleys in Northern British Columbia." Strong-Boag and Gerson also point out that "Johnson's versions of Su-á-pu-luck's stories appeared in the weekend magazine of a newspaper that was distinctly hostile to the Aboriginal cause" and argue that we can see this publication history either as Johnson "participating in the colonial project of appropriation—of using the Squamish stories to create a usable past for the White community"—or as "Johnson countering the dominant discourse." The latter reading is supported by the fact that Johnson intended to call the book of stories collected from Su-á-pu-luck and Líxwelut "Legends of the Capilano." In this view, Johnson "immortalize[d] her friend and fellow advocate . . . in the very pages that had tried so hard to discredit him." Strong-Boag and Gerson, *Paddling Her Own Canoe*, 177.

79. Dickinson, "To 'Hear the Call,'" 18.

80. Dickinson, "To 'Hear the Call,'" 18.

81. Dickinson, "To 'Hear the Call,'" 2.

82. Daniher, "Looking at Pauline Johnson," 13; Strong-Boag and Gerson, *Paddling Her Own Canoe*, 158.

83. Monture, *We Share Our Matters*, 101–2.

84. Monture, *We Share Our Matters*, 102.

85. Monture, *We Share Our Matters*, 104.

86. Monture, *We Share Our Matters*, 102.

87. B. Johnson, "Apostrophe, Animation, and Abortion," 31.

88. B. Johnson, "Apostrophe, Animation, and Abortion," 38.

89. Gerson, "Rereading Pauline Johnson," 54.

90. Notably, Johnson parodied "The Song My Paddle Sings" in a poem titled "His Majesty, the West Wind," published in *The Week* in 1895. Strong-Boag and Gerson, *Paddling Her Own Canoe*, 109. The parody pokes fun at the idea of metaphor by noting its distance from the (literally) gritty reality of being in the physical world. Whereas the speaker of "The Song My Paddle Sings" unsuccessfully tries to woo the west wind and then has a thrilling canoe journey, the speaker of "His Majesty, the West Wind" winkingly laments the limits of the metaphor employed in other poems, adding another layer to Johnson's rejection of Romantic poetic devices in "The Song My Paddle Sings."

91. E. Johnson, *Flint and Feather*, 28.

92. E. Johnson, *Flint and Feather*, 28.

93. E. Johnson, *Flint and Feather*, 29.

94. Strong-Boag and Gerson, *Paddling Her Own Canoe*, 153.

95. Melamed, *Represent and Destroy*, 199.

96. E. Pauline Johnson, "The Song My Paddle Sings," *Detroit Free Press*, June 15, 1893, https://cwrc.ca/islandora/object/tpatt%3A66e1d242-56e5-4ab7-aec4-f74f516c930e#page/1/mode/1up.

97. E. Johnson, "Song My Paddle Sings."

98. To be sure, Johnson goes on to endorse a vanishing Natives narrative in her article, explaining that "in the midst of this territory the little Dutch village has sprung up; its citizens, stolid, prosaic, unromantic, are as great a contrast to the erstwhile legend-loving Indians, who lived and hunted and died here, as two nations of continents could well be." E. Johnson, "Song My Paddle Sings." In contrast to the present-tense declarations about the Six Nations in the preceding paragraph, here Johnson relegates them to the past, as a people who lived and hunted and died in the time of legend. We see a pattern in her political thought that Monture has analyzed, in which Johnson "served as an advocate for the benefits of Native assimilation" but "punctuated this overarching view with the occasional harsh criticism of Canadian society's treatment of the Indigenous population." Monture, *We Share Our Matters*, 84. As Monture notes, Johnson's assimilationist arguments "placed her at odds with a large majority of Six Nations people . . . who were opposed to a Canadian identity and sought to maintain Haudenosaunee autonomy and nationhood." Monture, *We Share Our Matters*, 83. There were pragmatic reasons for Johnson's assimilationist stance, including "her financial needs" and the general tenor of public discourse about First Nations sovereignty. Monture also points to Johnson's "incomplete understanding of Haudenosaunee political thought" as a reason for her frequent endorsements of assimilationist, colonial policies. Monture, *We Share Our Matters*, 91.

99. Barker, "Introduction," 11.

100. Byrd, *Transit of Empire*, 222.

101. Spry, *Our Warpaint*, 19–20.

102. Cronyn, *Path on the Rainbow*, 344–45.

Conclusion

1. Jackson, *Before Modernism*, 32. See McGill, "The Poetry of Slavery"; McGill, "Frances Ellen Watkins Harper and the Circuits of Abolitionist Poetry"; Goldsby and McGill, "What is 'Black' about Black Bibliography?"; Cavitch, "The Poetry of Phillis Wheatley in Slavery's Recollective Economies, 1773 to the Present"; Cavitch, "Slavery and Its Metrics"; Lootens, *The Political Poetess*; Cohen, "Paul Laurence Dunbar"; Cohen, *The Social Lives of Poems*; Prins, "Metrical Translation"; Prins, "Victorian Meters"; Rudy, "Manifest Prosody."

2. Posmentier, "Lyric Reading," 78 (italics in original).

3. Zora Neale Hurston, "Proposed Recording Expedition into the Floridas," May 1939, American Folklife Center, Digital Collections, Library of Congress, Washington, DC, https://www.loc.gov/item/flwpa000213.

4. Posmentier, "Lyric Reading," 57 (italics in original).

5. Hurston, "Proposed Recording Expedition," 1.

6. Posmentier, "Lyric Reading," 57.

7. Posmentier, "Lyric Reading," 57 (italics in original).

8. Posmentier, "Lyric Reading," 77 (italics added).

9. Hurston, "Proposed Recording Expedition," 1–7.

10. Posmentier, "Lyric Reading," 77.

11. Posmentier, "Lyric Reading," 57, 77.

12. Prins, "Historical Poetics," 229.

13. Posmentier, "Lyric Reading," 77.

14. Gelmi, "Speaker, Photographed," 81.

15. Posmentier, "Lyric Reading," 57.

16. Posmentier, "Lyric Reading," 76.

17. Posmentier, "Lyric Reading," 57.

18. Hurston, "Proposed Recording Expedition," 1–7.

19. To say that abstractions of poetic terms have produced racialized reading practices is not to say that all abstractions produce racialized readings; abstractions of course do not have a singular ideological function. But understanding that critical abstractions of poetic terms have, at different points in history, produced modes of racialized reading can help us as modern critics to think about when and why we are participating in the abstraction of specific poetic terms into broader categories and when and why we may not want to perform such abstractions if our goal is to better understand the literary and political aims of poets and readers located at different historical moments. I have shown how the specific abstractions of genre into form and meter into rhythm in the modernist era created modes of anti-Black and dispossessive reading on the part of white critics and poets and how some marginalized authors turned to specific generic and formal conventions to evade or counter those racializing abstractions. Of course, for many poets of many different backgrounds, poetic abstractions were enabling rather than limiting. For an alternative account of the role of abstraction in the works of Black artists and authors, see Harper, *Abstractionist Aesthetics*.

20. Fielder, "Literary Genealogies," 791.

21. Scott, *Gender of Modernism*, 10.

22. Spires, "Genealogies of Black Modernities," 614.

23. Sharpe, *In the Wake*, 21.

24. Reed, *Freedom Time*, 7.

25. Kirby Brown, "American Indian Modernities."

26. Brown, Ross, and Sayers, *Routledge Handbook*.

27. Kirby Brown, "Introduction."

28. Kirby Brown, "Introduction."

29. Parker, "Modernist Literary Studies."

30. Radocay, "Winnemem Wintu Geographies."

31. Radocay, "Winnemem Wintu Geographies."

32. Radocay, "Winnemem Wintu Geographies."

33. Reed, *Freedom Time*, 3.

Bibliography

Archives

American Folklife Center, Digital Collections, Washington, DC
Fisk University Library Special Collections and Archives, Nashville, TN
Hanna Holborn Gray Special Collections Research Center, University of Chicago
  Library, Chicago, IL
Huntington Library Manuscript Collections, San Marino, CA
Library of Congress, Washington, DC

Periodicals

Anglo-African Magazine   *Dial*
Atlantic Monthly   *New York Sun*
Champion Magazine   *Poet Lore*
Crisis   *Poetry*
Detroit Free Press

Books and Articles

Alden, Raymond Macdonald. *English Verse: Specimens Illustrating Its Principles and
  History*. Henry Holt and Company, 1903. Princeton Prosody Archive.
Amos, Ashley Crandell. *Linguistic Means of Determining the Dates of Old English
  Literary Texts*. Medieval Academy of America, 1980.
Andrews, Richard. *A Prosody of Free Verse: Explorations in Rhythm*. Routledge, 2017.
Austin, Mary. *The American Rhythm*. Harcourt, Brace, 1923. HathiTrust.
Austin, Mary. Introduction to *The Path on the Rainbow: An Anthology of Songs and
  Chants from the Indians of North America*, edited by George W. Cronyn. Boni and
  Liveright, 1918. Internet Archive.
Badaracco, Claire. "Writers and Their Public Appeal: Harriet Monroe's Publicity
  Techniques." *American Literary Realism, 1870-1910* 23, no. 2 (1991): 35–51.
Baker, Houston A. *Modernism and the Harlem Renaissance*. University of Chicago
  Press, 1987.
Barker, Joanne. "Introduction: Critically Sovereign." In *Critically Sovereign:
  Indigenous Gender, Sexuality, and Feminist Studies*, edited by Joanne Barker. Duke
  University Press, 2017.
Barnett, Elizabeth. "Destroyed by *Poetry*: Alice Corbin and the Little Magazine
  Effect." *Modernism/modernity* 24, no. 4 (2017): 667–93.

Beissinger, M. H. "Oral Poetry." In *The Princeton Encyclopedia of Poetry and Poetics*, edited by Roland Green, Stephen Cushman, Clare Cavanagh, et al., 4th ed. Princeton University Press, 2012. Credo Reference.

Bell, Bernard W. "Fenton Johnson." In *Dictionary of American Negro Biography*, edited by Rayford Logan and Michael R. Winston. Norton, 1982.

Bell, Michael. *Primitivism*. Methuen, 1972.

Bendix, Regina. *In Search of Authenticity: The Formation of Folklore Studies*. University of Wisconsin Press, 1997.

Beyers, Chris. *A History of Free Verse*. University of Arkansas Press, 2001.

Braddock, Jeremy. *Collecting as Modernist Practice*. Johns Hopkins University Press, 2012.

Bradley, Sculley. "The Fundamental Metrical Principle in Whitman's Poetry." *American Literature* 10, no. 4 (1939): 437–59. JSTOR.

Brady, Andrea. *Poetry and Bondage: A History and Theory of Lyric Constraint*. Cambridge University Press, 2021.

Brinton, Daniel. *Aboriginal American Authors and Their Productions*. Brinton, 1883.

Brinton, Daniel. *The Basis of Social Relations: A Study in Ethnic Psychology*. G. P. Putnam's Sons, 1902.

Brogan, T. V. F. "Foot." In *The New Princeton Encyclopedia of Poetry and Poetics*, edited by Alex Preminger, T. V. F. Brogan, Frank J. Warnke, et al., 3rd ed. Princeton University Press, 1993. Literature Online Reference Works.

Brogan, T. V. F. "Meter." In *The New Princeton Encyclopedia of Poetry and Poetics*, edited by Alex Preminger, T. V. F. Brogan, Frank J. Warnke, et al., 3rd ed. Princeton University Press, 1993. Literature Online Reference Works.

Brooks, Lisa Tanya. *The Common Pot: The Recovery of Native Space in the Northeast*. University of Minnesota Press, 2008.

Brown, Kirby. "American Indian Modernities and New Modernist Studies' 'Indian Problem.'" *Texas Studies in Literature and Language* 59, no. 3 (2017): 287–318.

Brown, Kirby. "Introduction: Developing Thoughts on Indigenous Modernities and Modernisms." *Modernism/modernity Print Plus* 5, no. 4 (2021). https://doi.org/10.26597/mod.0188.

Brown, Kirby, Stephen Ross, and Alana Sayers, eds. *The Routledge Handbook of North American Indigenous Modernisms*. Routledge, 2022.

Brown, Kristen. "Queering the Waters: The Subversive Potential in E. Pauline Johnson's Canoe." *Western American Literature* 55, no. 2 (2020). 137–65.

Bruchac, Margaret M. *Savage Kin: Indigenous Informants and American Anthropologists*. University of Arizona Press, 2018.

Burks, Mary Fair. "The First Black Literary Magazine in American Letters." *CLA Journal* 19, no. 3 (1976): 318–21.

Byrd, Jodi A. *The Transit of Empire: Indigenous Critiques of Colonialism*. University of Minnesota Press, 2011.

Carpenter, Cari M. *Seeing Red: Anger, Sentimentality, and American Indians*. Ohio State University Press, 2008.

Carr, Helen. "*Poetry: A Magazine of Verse* (1912–36), 'Biggest of Little Magazines.'" In *The Oxford Critical and Cultural History of Modernist Magazines*, vol. 2, *North*

America 1894–1960, edited by Peter Brooker and Andrew Thacker. Oxford University Press, 2012.

Castro, Michael. *Interpreting the Indian: Twentieth-Century Poets and the Native American*. University of New Mexico Press, 1983.

Cavitch, Max. "The Poetry of Phillis Wheatley in Slavery's Recollective Economies, 1773 to the Present." In *Race, Ethnicity, and Publishing in America*, edited by Cécile Cottenet. Palgrave Macmillan, 2014.

Cavitch, Max. "Slavery and Its Metrics." In *The Cambridge Companion to Nineteenth-Century American Poetry*, edited by Kerry Larson. Cambridge University Press, 2011.

Cavitch, Max. "Stephen Crane's Refrain." *ESQ* 54, nos. 1–4 (2008): 33–54.

Cecire, Natalia. *Experimental: American Literature and the Aesthetics of Knowledge*. Johns Hopkins University Press, 2019.

Chatterjee, Ronjaunee, Alicia Mireles Christoff, and Amy R. Wong. "Introduction: Undisciplining Victorian Studies." *Victorian Studies* 62, no. 3 (2020): 369–91.

Churchill, Suzanne. *The Little Magazine "Others" and the Renovation of Modern American Poetry*. Ashgate, 2006.

Churchill, Suzanne, and Ethan Jaffee. "The New Poetry: *The Glebe* (1913–14); *Others* (1915–19); and *Poetry Review of America* (1916–17)." In *The Oxford Critical and Cultural History of Modernist Magazines*, vol. 2, *North America 1894–1960*, edited by Peter Brooker and Andrew Thacker. Oxford University Press, 2012.

Churchill, Suzanne, and Adam McKible, eds. *Little Magazines and Modernism: New Approaches*. Ashgate, 2007.

Clark, Donald Lemen. *Rhetoric and Poetry in the Renaissance: A Study of Rhetorical Terms in English Renaissance Literary Criticism*. Columbia University Press, 1922. Princeton Prosody Archive.

Clukey, Amy. "Dreaming of Palestine: James Joyce's *Ulysses* and Plantation Modernism." *Modernism/modernity* 26, no. 1 (2019): 167–84.

Cohen, Matt. *Whitman's Drift: Imagining Literary Distribution*. University of Iowa Press, 2017.

Cohen, Michael. "Paul Laurence Dunbar and the Genres of Dialect." *African American Review* 41, no. 2 (2007): 247–57.

Cohen, Michael. *The Social Lives of Poems in Nineteenth-Century America*. University of Pennsylvania Press, 2015.

Coulthard, Glen Sean. *Red Skin, White Masks: Rejecting the Colonial Politics of Recognition*. University of Minnesota Press, 2014.

Courage, Richard A., and James C. Hall. "Fenton Johnson, Literary Entrepreneurship, and the Dynamics of Class and Family." In *Roots of the Black Chicago Renaissance: New Negro Writers, Artists, and Intellectuals, 1893–1930*, edited by Richard A. Courage and Christopher Robert Reed. University of Illinois Press, 2020.

Cronyn, George W., ed. *The Path on the Rainbow: An Anthology of Songs and Chants from the Indians of North America*. Boni and Liveright, 1918.

Csicsila, Joseph. *Canons by Consensus: Critical Trends and American Literature Anthologies*. University of Alabama Press, 2004.

Cushman, Stephen. *Fictions of Form in American Poetry*. Princeton University Press, 1993.

Daniher, Colleen Kim. "Looking at Pauline Johnson: Gender, Race, and Delsartism's Legible Body." *Theatre Journal* 72, no. 1 (2020): 1–20.

Denetdale, Jennifer Nez. "Return to 'The Uprising at Beautiful Mountain in 1913': Marriage and Sexuality in the Making of the Modern Navajo Nation." In *Critically Sovereign: Indigenous Gender, Sexuality, and Feminist Studies*, edited by Joanne Barker. Duke University Press, 2017.

Dickinson, Steve. "To 'Hear the Call of the Singing Firs': (Re)Reading E. Pauline Johnson's 'Lost Lagoon' as Eco-Elegy." In *Making Nineteenth-Century Literary Environments*. Simon Fraser University, 2017. https://course-journals.lib.sfu.ca/index.php/eng435/article/view/2.

Dunbar, Paul Laurence. *Oak and Ivy*. Press of United Brethren Publishing House, 1893. Internet Archive.

Eckstrom, Leif, and Brit Rusert. "Afric-American Picture Gallery (1859)." *Common-Place: The Journal of Early American Life*, no. 2 (Fall 2015). http://jtoaa.common -place.org/welcome-to-just-teach-one-african-american/introduction-afric -american-picture-gallery/.

Edelman, Lee. *No Future: Queer Theory and the Death Drive*. Duke University Press, 2004.

Ehlers, Sarah. *Left of Poetry: Depression America and the Formation of Modern Poetics*. University of North Carolina Press, 2019.

Ehlers, Sarah. "Making It Old: The Victorian/Modern Divide in Twentieth-Century American Poetry." *MLQ* 73, no. 1 (2012): 38–67.

Eliot, T. S. "War-Paint and Feathers." In *Primitivism and Twentieth-Century Art: A Documentary History*, edited by Jack Flam and Miriam Deutch. University of California Press, 2003.

Erskine, John. "A Note on Whitman's Prosody." *Studies in Philology* 20, no. 3 (1923): 336–44. JSTOR.

Etherington, Ben. *Literary Primitivism*. Stanford University Press, 2018.

Fee, Margery. "Publication, Performances, and Politics: The 'Indian Poems' of E. Pauline Johnson/Tekahionwake (1861–1913) and Duncan Campbell Scott (1862–1947)." In *Anthologizing Canadian Literature: Theoretical and Cultural Perspectives*, edited by Robert Lecker. Wilfrid Laurier University Press, 2015.

Fielder, Brigitte. "Literary Genealogies and the Kinship of Black Modernity." *American Literary History* 32, no. 4 (2020): 789–96.

Fielder, Brigitte. "Recovery." *American Periodicals: A Journal of History & Criticism* 30, no. 1 (2020): 18–21.

Finch, Annie. *The Ghost of Meter: Culture and Prosody in American Free Verse*. University of Michigan Press, 1993.

Foster, Frances Smith. *'Til Death or Distance Do Us Part: Love and Marriage in African America*. Oxford University Press, 2010.

Frantzen, Allen. *Desire for Origins: New Language, Old English, and Teaching the Tradition*. Rutgers University Press, 1990.

Furey, Hester. "*Poetry* and the Rhetoric of Dissent in Turn-of-the-Century Chicago." *Modern Fiction Studies* 38, no. 3 (1992): 671–86.

Gayley, Charles Mills, and Fred Newton Scott. *An Introduction to the Methods and Materials of Literary Criticism: The Bases in Aesthetics and Poetics*. Ginn, 1899. Internet Archive.

Gelmi, Caroline. "The Speaker, Photographed: Paul Laurence Dunbar's *Poems of Cabin and Field*." *J19: The Journal of Nineteenth-Century Americanists* 8, no. 1 (2020): 67–95.

Genette, Gérard. *The Architext: An Introduction*. University of California Press, 1992.

Gerson, Carole. "Rereading Pauline Johnson." *Journal of Canadian Studies/Revue d'études Canadiennes* 46, no. 2 (2012): 45–61.

Glaser, Ben. *Modernism's Metronome: Meter and Twentieth-Century Poetics*. Johns Hopkins University Press, 2020.

Glazener, Nancy. *Literature in the Making: A History of U.S. Literary Culture in the Long Nineteenth Century*. Oxford University Press, 2016.

Goeman, Mishuana. *Mark My Words: Native Women Mapping Our Nations*. University of Minnesota Press, 2013.

Goldsby, Jacqueline, and Meredith L. McGill. "What Is 'Black' about Black Bibliography?" *Papers of the Bibliographic Society of America* 116, no. 2 (2022): 161–89.

Goldstone, Andrew. "Modernist Studies without Modernism." Open Science Framework, 2018. https://osf.io/frcys.

Gollancz, Sir Israel. *The Middle Ages in the Lineage of English Poetry*. George G. Harrap, 1921. Princeton Prosody Archive.

Goodman, Susan, and Carl Dawson. *Mary Austin and the American West*. University of California Press, 2008.

Graff, Gerald. *Professing Literature: An Institutional History*. University of Chicago Press, 1987.

Guillory, John. "Literary Study and the Modern System of the Disciplines." In *Disciplinarity at the Fin de Siècle*, edited by Amanda Anderson and Joseph Valente. Princeton University Press, 2002.

Gummere, Francis Barton. *The Beginnings of Poetry*. Macmillan, 1901. Internet Archive.

Gummere, Francis Barton. *Democracy and Poetry*. Houghton Mifflin, 1911. Internet Archive.

Gummere, Francis Barton. "English in Secondary Schools." *School and College* 1, no. 2 (1892): 84–88. JSTOR.

Gummere, Francis Barton. *Germanic Origins: A Study in Primitive Culture*. D. Nutt, 1892. Internet Archive.

Gummere, Francis Barton. *A Handbook of Poetics for Students of English Verse*. Ginn, 1885. HathiTrust.

Gummere, Francis Barton. "Old English Ballads in the School." *English Journal* 1, no. 4 (1912): 203–7. JSTOR.

Gummere, Francis Barton. "Primitive Poetry and the Ballad I." *Modern Philology* 1, no. 1 (1903): 193–202. JSTOR.

Gummere, Francis Barton. "What Place Has Old English Philology in Our Elementary Schools?" *Transactions of the Modern Language Association of America* 1 (1884–85): 170–78. JSTOR.

Hack, Daniel. *Reaping Something New: African American Transformations of Victorian Literature.* Princeton University Press, 2017.

Hall, Jason David, ed. *Meter Matters: Verse Cultures of the Long Nineteenth Century.* Ohio University Press 2011.

Harper, Phillip Brian. *Abstractionist Aesthetics: Artistic Form and Social Critique in African American Culture.* New York University Press, 2015.

Hart, Matthew. *Nations of Nothing But Poetry: Modernism, Transnationalism, and Synthetic Vernacular Writing.* Oxford University Press, 2010.

Hartman, Charles O. *Free Verse: An Essay on Prosody.* Princeton University Press, 1980.

Hill, John M. *The Anglo-Saxon Warrior Ethic: Reconstructing Lordship in Early English Literature.* University Press of Florida, 2000.

Hills, Catherine. "Overview: Anglo-Saxon Identity." In *The Oxford Handbook of Anglo-Saxon Archaeology,* edited by David A. Hinton, Sally Crawford, and Helena Hamerow. Oxford University Press, 2011.

Hines, Andy. *Outside Literary Studies: Black Criticism and the University.* University of Chicago Press, 2022.

Horsman, Reginald. *Race and Manifest Destiny: The Origins of American Racial Anglo-Saxonism.* Harvard University Press, 1981.

Hoskins, John Preston. "Biological Analogy in Literary Criticism I: Variation and Personality." *Modern Philology* 6, no. 4 (1909): 407–34. JSTOR.

Hoskins, John Preston. "The Place and Function of a Standard in a Genetic Theory of Literary Development." *PMLA* 25, no. 3 (1910): 379–402. JSTOR.

Hoyer, Mark. *Dancing Ghosts: Native American and Christian Syncretism in Mary Austin's Work.* University of Nevada Press, 1998.

Jackson, Virginia. *Before Modernism: Inventing American Lyric.* Princeton University Press, 2023.

Jackson, Virginia. "The Cadence of Consent: Francis Barton Gummere, Lyric Rhythm, and White Poetics." In *Critical Rhythm: The Poetics of a Literary Life Form,* edited by Ben Glaser and Jonathan Culler. Fordham University Press, 2019.

Jackson, Virginia. *Dickinson's Misery: A Theory of Lyric Reading.* Princeton University Press, 2005.

Jackson, Virginia. "Specters of the Ballad." *Nineteenth-Century Literature* 70, no. 2 (2016): 176–96.

Jackson, Zakiyyah Iman. *Becoming Human: Matter and Meaning in an Antiblack World.* New York University Press, 2020.

Johnson, Barbara. "Apostrophe, Animation, and Abortion." *Diacritics* 16, no. 1 (1986): 28–47.

Johnson, E. Pauline. *Flint and Feather.* Musson, 1912. Project Gutenberg.

Johnson, Fenton. *A Little Dreaming*. Peterson Linotyping, 1913. Google Books.

Johnson, Fenton. *Songs of the Soil*. Trachtenberg, 1916. Internet Archive.

Johnson, Fenton. *Visions of the Dusk*. Trachtenberg, 1915. HathiTrust.

Johnson, Georgia Douglas. *Bronze: A Book of Verse*. B. J. Brimmer, 1922. Internet Archive.

Kabir, Ananya Jahanara. "Anglo-Saxon Textual Attitudes." In *The Cambridge History of Literary Criticism*, vol. 2, *The Middle Ages*, edited by Alastair Minnis and Ian Johnson. Cambridge University Press, 2008.

Kappeler, Erin. "Constructing Walt Whitman: Literary History and the Histories of Rhythm." In *Critical Rhythm*, edited by Jonathan Culler and Ben Glaser. Fordham University Press, 2019.

Kelley, Robin D. G. *Freedom Dreams: The Black Radical Imagination*. Beacon, 2002.

Kirby, D. P. *The Earliest English Kings*. Routledge, 2000.

Kirby-Smith, H. T. *The Origins of Free Verse*. University of Michigan Press, 1996.

Konkle, Maureen. *Writing Indian Nations: Native Intellectuals and the Politics of Historiography, 1827-1863*. University of North Carolina Press, 2004.

Kreymborg, Alfred, ed. *Others for 1919: An Anthology of the New Verse*. Nicholas L. Brown, 1920. Internet Archive.

Kuper, Adam. *The Invention of Primitive Society: Transformations of an Illusion*. Routledge, 1988.

Lincoln, Kenneth. Foreword to *American Indian Poetry: An Anthology of Songs and Chants*, edited by George W. Cronyn. Fawcett Columbine, 1991.

Lloyd, David. *Under Representation: The Racial Regime of Aesthetics*. Fordham University Press, 2019.

Long, Richard, and Eugenia W. Collier, eds. *Afro-American Writing: An Anthology of Prose and Poetry*. 2 vols. New York University Press, 1972.

Lootens, Tricia. *The Political Poetess: Victorian Femininity, Race, and the Legacy of Separate Spheres*. Princeton University Press, 2017.

Lowell, Amy. "Some Musical Analogies in Modern Poetry." *Musical Quarterly* 6, no. 1 (1920): 127-57. JSTOR.

Lowell, Amy. "Vers Libre and Metrical Prose." *Poetry* 3, no. 6 (1914): 213-20. JSTOR.

Lowes, John Livingston. *Convention and Revolt in Poetry*. Houghton Mifflin, 1919. Internet Archive.

MacDougall, Hugh A. *Racial Myth in English History: Trojans, Teutons, and Anglo-Saxons*. Harvest House, 1982.

Manly, John Matthews. "Francis Barton Gummere, 1855-1919." *Modern Philology* 17, no. 5 (1919): 57-62. JSTOR.

Manly, John Matthews. "Literary Forms and the New Theory of the Origin of Species." *Modern Philology* 4, no. 4 (1907): 577-95. JSTOR.

Marek, Jane. *Women Editing Modernism: "Little" Magazines and Literary History*. University Press of Kentucky, 1995.

Martin, Meredith. "Imperfectly Civilized: Ballads, Nations, and Histories of Form." *ELH* 82, no. 2 (2015): 345-63.

Martin, Meredith. *The Rise and Fall of Meter: Poetry and English National Culture, 1860-1930*. Princeton University Press, 2012.

Massa, Ann. "'The Columbian Ode' and *Poetry, A Magazine of Verse*: Harriet Monroe's Entrepreneurial Triumphs." *Journal of American Studies* 20, no. 1 (1986): 51–69.

Matthiessen, F. O. *American Renaissance: Art and Expression in the Age of Emerson and Whitman*. Oxford University Press, 1941.

McGill, Meredith. "Frances Ellen Watkins Harper and the Circuits of Abolitionist Poetry." In *Early African American Print Culture*, edited by Lara Langer Cohen and Jordan Alexander Stein. University of Pennsylvania Press, 2012.

McGill, Meredith. "The Poetry of Slavery." In *Cambridge Companion to Slavery in American Literature*, edited by Ezra Tawil. Cambridge University Press, 2016.

McGill, Meredith. "What Is a Ballad? Reading for Genre, Format, and Medium." *Nineteenth-Century Literature* 70, no. 2 (2016): 156–75.

McHenry, Elizabeth. *To Make Negro Literature: Writing, Literary Practice, and African American Authorship*. Duke University Press, 2021.

McKittrick, Katherine. *Demonic Grounds: Black Women and the Cartographies of Struggle*. University of Minnesota Press, 2006.

Melamed, Jodi. *Represent and Destroy: Rationalizing Violence in the New Racial Capitalism*. University of Minnesota Press, 2011.

Metcalfe, Dale. "Singing Like the Indians Do: Mary Austin's Poetry." In *Exploring Lost Borders: Critical Essays on Mary Austin*, edited by Melody Graulich and Elizabeth Klimasmith. University of Nevada Press, 1999.

Monroe, Harriet, and Alice Corbin Henderson. Introduction to *The New Poetry: An Anthology*, edited by Harriet Monroe and Alice Corbin Henderson. Macmillan, 1917. Internet Archive.

Monture, Rick. *We Share Our Matters: Two Centuries of Writing and Resistance at Six Nations of the Grand River*. University of Manitoba Press, 2014.

Moses, Wilson Jeremiah. *Afrotopia: The Roots of African American Popular History*. Cambridge University Press, 1998.

Moulton, Richard. *The Modern Study of Literature: An Introduction to Literary Theory and Interpretation*. University of Chicago Press, 1915. Google Books.

Mufti, Aamir. *Forget English! Orientalisms and World Literatures*. Harvard University Press, 2016.

Nelson, Cary. *Repression and Recovery: Modern American Poetry and the Politics of Cultural Memory, 1910–1945*. University of Wisconsin Press, 1989.

Newcomb, John Timberman. *How Did Poetry Survive? The Making of Modern American Verse*. University of Illinois Press, 2012.

Newman, Steve. *Ballad Collection, Lyric, and the Canon: The Call of the Popular from the Restoration to the New Criticism*. University of Pennsylvania Press, 2007.

North, Michael. *The Dialect of Modernism: Race, Language, and Twentieth-Century Literature*. Oxford University Press, 1994.

Nurhussein, Nadia. *Black Land: Imperial Ethiopianism and African America*. Princeton University Press, 2019.

Nurhussein, Nadia. *Rhetorics of Literacy: The Cultivation of American Dialect Poetry*. Ohio State University Press, 2013.

Parker, Robert Dale. *The Invention of Native American Literature*. Cornell University Press, 2003.

Parker, Robert Dale. "Modernist Literary Studies and the Aesthetics of American Indian Literatures." *Modernism/modernity Print Plus* 5, no. 4 (2021). https://doi .org/10.26597/mod.0189.

Patterson, William Morrison. "New Verse and New Prose." *North American Review* 207, no. 747 (1918): 257–67. JSTOR.

Patterson, William Morrison. *The Rhythm of Prose: An Experimental Investigation of Individual Difference in the Sense of Rhythm*. Columbia University Press, 1916. Internet Archive.

Perloff, Marjorie. *21st-Century Modernism: The "New" Poetics*. Wiley, 2002.

Posmentier, Sonya. "Lyric Reading in the Black Ethnographic Archive." *American Literary History* 30, no. 1 (2018): 55–84.

Pound, Ezra. *Lustra*. Elkin Mathews, 1916. Internet Archive.

Pound, Louise. "The Ballad and the Dance." *PMLA* 34, no. 3 (1919): 360–400. JSTOR.

Pound, Louise. "High-School Ballad Composition." *English Journal* 18, no.6 (1929): 495–97. JSTOR.

Prins, Yopie. "Historical Poetics, Dysprosody, and *The Science of English Verse*." *PMLA* 123, no. 1 (2008): 229–34.

Prins, Yopie. "Metrical Translation: Nineteenth-Century Homers and the Hexameter Mania." In *Nation, Language, and the Ethics of Translation*, edited by Sandra Bermann and Michael Wood. Princeton University Press, 2005.

Prins, Yopie. "Patmore's Law, Meynell's Rhythm." In *The Fin-de-Siècle Poem*, edited by Joseph Bristow. Ohio State University Press, 2005.

Prins, Yopie. "Victorian Meters." In *The Cambridge Companion to Victorian Poetry*, edited by Joseph Bristow. Cambridge University Press, 2000.

Radocay, Jonathan. "Winnemem Wintu Geographies and Lyric Modernity." *Modernism/modernity Print Plus* 5, no. 4 (2021). https://doi.org/10.26597/mod .0192.

Rambaran-Olm, Mary. "Misnaming the Medieval: Rejecting 'Anglo-Saxon' Studies." *History Workshop*, 2019. www.historyworkshop.org.uk/misnaming-the-medieval -rejecting-anglo-saxon-studies.

Reed, Anthony. *Freedom Time: The Poetics and Politics of Black Experimental Writing*. Johns Hopkins University Press, 2014.

Renker, Elizabeth. *The Origins of American Literature Studies: An Institutional History*. Cambridge University Press, 2007.

Revie, Linda. "Pauline Johnson's Sapphic Wampum." *torquere: Journal of the Canadian Lesbian and Gay Studies Association* 4–5 (2002–3): 38–62.

Rifkin, Mark. *Beyond Settler Time: Temporal Sovereignty and Indigenous Self-Determination*. Duke University Press, 2017.

Roberts, John W. "African American Diversity and the Study of Folklore." *Western Folklore* 52, no. 2/4 (1993): 157–71.

Robinson, Cedric. *Black Marxism*. Rev. and updated 3rd ed. University of North Carolina Press, 2020.

Rudy, Jason. "Manifest Prosody." *Victorian Poetry* 49, no. 2 (2011): 253–66.

Rusert, Britt, "Plantation Ecologies: The Experimental Plantation in and Against James Grainger's *The Sugar-Cane*." *Early American Studies* 13, no. 2 (2015): 341–73.

Saintsbury, George. *A History of Prosody from the Twelfth Century to the Present Day*. Vol. 1, *From the Origins to Spenser*. Macmillan, 1923. Internet Archive.

Sandler, Matt. *The Black Romantic Revolution: Abolitionist Poets at the End of Slavery*. Verso, 2020.

Schuller, Kyla. *The Biopolitics of Feeling: Race, Sex, and Science in the Nineteenth Century*. Duke University Press, 2017.

Schuller, Kyla, and Jules Gill-Peterson. "Introduction: Race, the State, and the Malleable Body." *Social Text* 38, no. 2 (2020): 1–17.

Schulze, Robin G. *The Degenerate Muse: American Nature, Modernist Poetry, and the Problem of Cultural Hygiene*. Oxford University Press, 2013.

Schulze, Robin G. "Harriet Monroe's Pioneer Modernism: Nature, National Identity, and *Poetry, a Magazine of Verse*." *Legacy* 21, no. 1 (2004): 50–67.

Scott, Bonnie Kime, ed. *The Gender of Modernism: A Critical Anthology*. Indiana University Press, 1990.

Scott, Fred Newton. "The Most Fundamental Differentia of Poetry and Prose." *PMLA* 19, no. 2 (1904): 250–69. JSTOR.

Scott, Fred Newton. "A Note on Walt Whitman's Prosody." *Journal of English and Germanic Philology* 7, no. 2 (1908): 134–53. JSTOR.

Sharpe, Christina. *In the Wake: On Blackness and Being*. Duke University Press, 2016.

Sherman, Joan R. *Invisible Poets: Afro-Americans of the Nineteenth Century*. University of Illinois Press, 1974.

Silliman, Ron. *The New Sentence*. Roof Books, 1987.

Simpson, Audra. *Mohawk Interruptus: Political Life Across the Borders of Settler States*. Duke University Press, 2014.

Smethurst, James. *The African American Roots of Modernism: From Reconstruction to the Harlem Renaissance*. University of North Carolina Press, 2011.

Smethurst, James. "Paul Laurence Dunbar and Turn-into-the-20th-Century African American Dualism." *African American Review* 41, no. 2 (2007): 377–86.

Smith, Egerton. *The Principles of English Metre*. Oxford University Press, 1923. Princeton Prosody Archive.

Snorton, C. Riley. *Black on Both Sides: A Racial History of Trans Identity*. University of Minnesota Press, 2017.

Socarides, Alexandra. *In Plain Sight: Nineteenth-Century American Women's Poetry and the Problem of Literary History*. Oxford University Press, 2020.

Socarides, Alexandra. "What Happens When We Don't Read Ballads Closely Enough: The Cautionary Tale of the American Woman Poet and the Ballad." *Nineteenth-Century Literature* 71, no. 2 (2016): 215–26.

Sorby, Angela. *Schoolroom Poets: Childhood, Performance, and the Place of American Poetry, 1865–1917*. University of New Hampshire Press, 2005.

Spillers, Hortense. "Mama's Baby, Papa's Maybe: An American Grammar Book." *Diacritics* 17, no. 2 (1987): 65–81.

Spires, Derrick R. "Genealogies of Black Modernities." *American Literary History* 32, no. 4 (2020): 611–22.

Spry, Adam. *Our War Paint Is Writers' Ink: Anishinaabe Literary Transnationalism*. SUNY University Press, 2018.

Stedman, Edmund Clarence. *Poets of America*. Houghton Mifflin, 1885. Internet Archive.

Steele, Timothy. *Missing Measures: Modern Poetry and the Revolt Against Meter*. University of Arkansas Press, 1990.

Stewart, Susan. *Crimes of Writing: Problems in the Containment of Representation*. Duke University Press, 1994.

Stokes, Claudia. *Writers in Retrospect: The Rise of American Literary History, 1875–1910*. University of North Carolina Press, 2006.

Strong-Boag, Veronica, and Carole Gerson. *Paddling Her Own Canoe: The Times and Texts of E. Pauline Johnson (Tekahionwake)*. University of Toronto Press, 2000.

Sutton, Walter. *American Free Verse: The Modern Revolution in Poetry*. New Directions, 1973.

Taylor, Michael. "Not Primitive Enough to Be Considered Modern: Ethnographers, Editors, and the Indigenous Poets of the American Indian Magazine." *Studies in American Indian Literatures* 28, no. 1 (2016): 45–72.

Teuton, Christopher B. "Theorizing American Indian Literature: Applying Oral Concepts to Written Traditions." In *Reasoning Together: The Native Critics Collective*, edited by Craig S. Womack, Daniel Heath Justice, and Christopher B. Teuton. University of Oklahoma Press, 2008.

Thacker, Andrew. "Poetry in Perspective: The Melange of the 1920s: *The Measure* (1921–6); *Rhythmus* (1923–4); and *Palms* 1923–30)." In *The Oxford Critical and Cultural History of Modernist Magazines*, vol. 2, *North America 1894-1960*, edited by Peter Brooker and Andrew Thacker. Oxford University Press, 2012.

Thomas, Lorenzo. *Extraordinary Measures: Afrocentric Modernism and Twentieth-Century American Poetry*. University of Alabama Press, 2000.

Tompkins, Kyla Wazana. *Racial Indigestion: Eating Bodies in the 19th Century*. New York University Press, 2012.

Torgovnick, Marianna. *Gone Primitive: Savage Intellects, Modern Lives*. University of Chicago Press, 1990.

Wang, Dorothy. *Thinking Its Presence: Form, Race, and Subjectivity in Contemporary Asian American Poetry*. Stanford University Press, 2014.

Ware, Lois. "Poetic Convention in *Leaves of Grass*." *Studies in Philology* 26, no. 1 (1929): 47–57. JSTOR.

Warner, Michael. "Professionalization and the Rewards of Literature: 1875–1900." *Criticism* 27 (1985): 1–28.

Watkins, Frances Ellen. *Poems on Miscellaneous Subjects*. Merrihew and Thompson, 1857. Internet Archive.

Weeks, Ruth Mary. "Phrasal Prosody." *English Journal* 10, no. 1 (1921): 11–19. JSTOR.

Weinbaum, Alys Eve. *Wayward Reproductions: Genealogies of Race and Nation in Transatlantic Modern Thought*. Duke University Press, 2004.

Whitman, Albery Allson. *Not a Man, and Yet a Man*. Republic, 1877. https://quod.lib.umich.edu/a/amverse/BAQ6224.0001.001?view=toc.

Wilson, Ivy G. "The Brief Wondrous Life of the *Anglo-African Magazine*, or, Antebellum African American Editorial Practice and Its Afterlives." In *Publishing*

Blackness, edited by John K. Young and George Hutchinson. University of Michigan Press, 2013.

Wilton, David. "What Do We Mean by *Anglo-Saxon*? Pre-Conquest to the Present." *Journal of English and Germanic Philology* 119, no. 4 (2020): 425–56.

Womack, Craig S. *Red on Red: Native American Literary Separatism*. University of Minnesota Press, 1999.

Woolley, Lisa. "From Chicago Renaissance to Chicago Renaissance: The Poetry of Fenton Johnson." *Langston Hughes Review* 14, nos. 1–2 (1996): 36–48.

Wynter, Sylvia. "The Ceremony Must Be Found: After Humanism." *Boundary 2* 12/13, no. 3 (1984): 19–70.

Yorke, Barbara. *Kings and Kingdoms of Early Anglo-Saxon England*. Routledge, 1997.

Yu, Timothy. *Race and the Avant-Garde: Experimental and Asian American Poetry Since 1965*. Stanford University Press, 2009.

Zapędowska, Magdalena. "Hope, Sound, and the Materiality of Print in Frances Ellen Watkins Harper's Periodical Poems." *ESQ* 68, no. 3 (2022): 333–82.

Index

abolitionist poetry, US nineteenth-century, 17, 81–83, 92, 95–98, 147

abstraction, 25, 35, 115, 117, 141–42; of genre into form, 17, 82, 109, 139, 177n19; of meter into rhythm, 19–20, 43, 115, 177n19; as racializing, 8, 15, 104, 108–9, 139–40, 143–44, 177n19

accent, poetic, 37–38, 49, 61, 118–19, 161n33

aesthetics, 145–47; modernist, 5–9, 113, 137–38; racialized hierarchies of, 5–9, 15, 17–19, 21, 24, 71, 82, 150n20

African American literature, 16, 79, 81–83, 86, 95–96, 105

Allen, Hervey, 74

Amos, Ashley Crandell, 30, 52

Anderson, Benedict, 30

Anglo-Saxons, 10, 13, 23, 26, 52; culture, imagined continuity of, 11–12, 45–46, 56, 60–62, 67, 84, 149n8; culture, as masculine, 14, 46, 56; as exonym, 11, 51, 157n122; plasticity of, perceived, 13, 28, 153–54n29; poetic rhythms, 12, 33, 35, 37–39, 43, 60–61, 67; prosody, 23, 30, 61, 98; as racial group, 10–11, 23, 30, 35–40, 51–52, 62; society as democratic, 12–13, 23, 30–31, 35–36, 38–40, 45–46, 61–63, 155n75

Anglo-Saxonism, 11–12, 24–25, 29, 35, 38–40, 52–53, 60–62, 65–66

Aryan race, imagined, 28, 39–40, 60–61, 65–66, 85–86, 151–52n7

Austin, Mary, 19–20, 111, 119, 123, 136, 171n13, 172nn17–18; free verse, theory of, 112, 114–15, 117–18, 173n29; "Song for the Passing of Beautiful Women (from the Paiute)," 121

authenticity, cultural, 70, 122, 126, 146; of folk poetry, 100, 104–7, 163n74; racial, 19–20, 70, 73–74, 76, 120, 123, 125–26, 170–71n1

avant-garde, poetic, 8, 15, 79–81, 150n19

Badaracco, Claire, 158n3

Baker, Houston, 7–8

ballads, 31–32, 61, 69–70, 104–8, 115, 143–44, 156n85

Barker, Joanne, 121–22, 136

Barnett, Elizabeth, 158–59n4, 170–71n1

Bendix, Regina, 70

Bergson, Henri, 116–17

Black Romanticism, 81–83, 92–93, 96–100, 109

blank verse, 3, 12, 28, 93–94, 98, 156–57n100

Braddock, Jeremy, 18, 115, 170–71n1

Bradley, Sculley, 48–49

Brady, Andrea, 173n29

Brinton, Daniel, 32–33, 154n47

Brooks, Cleanth, 24, 41

Brown, Kirby, 145–46

Brown, Kristen, 126, 128, 174n69

Brown, Sterling, 72–73

Brownell, Baker, 64

Bruchac, Margaret, 171–72n15

Burks, Mary Fair, 89

Byrd, Jodi, 136, 171n8

Byron, George Gordon, Lord, 82, 93, 97–98

Carr, Helen, 54–55, 59

Castro, Michael, 170n1, 172n17

Cavitch, Max, 2, 139

Cecire, Natalia, 8, 150n30

Chatterjee, Ronjaunee, 8

Finch, Lucine, 73

folk poetry, 22; African American, 56, 68–71, 73–77, 100, 102, 104–9, 113, 140–44; European, 23, 32, 61, 69, 85, 104–6, 161n27, 162n66

form, poetic, 1, 21; conventional, 1–2, 5, 8, 15–17, 113, 138, 151n33; creation of new, 10, 27, 29–30, 41, 56, 71, 73–76, 78; experimental, 1–17; *passim*, 52–56, 59, 71, 75, 78, 113, 138, 150n20, 150n30; hierarchy of, 4, 82, 113–14, 124, 138; as opposed to content, 17–18, 113; racialization of, 4, 14, 24–25, 53, 55, 77, 111, 139

Foster, Frances Smith, 89

Frantzen, Allen, 30, 51–52, 154n40

free verse, 8, 25, 73–74, 77, 117; as Anglo-Saxon, 10–12, 50, 56, 60–68, 70, 76–78, 84, 87–88, 97–98, 161–62n43; as evolution of poetic form, 7, 9, 47–50, 97, 119, 147; Native American poetry as earliest form of, 114, 118, 122–24; racialization of, 1, 8, 10, 14–15, 21–24, 53, 78, 144, 147; scholarship about, 1, 4, 7, 9–10, 14, 149n18, 161–62n43

Frost, Robert, 17

Furey, Hester, 158–59n4

Garvey, Marcus, 83

Gelmi, Caroline, 104–6

Genette, Gérard, 50

Gerson, Carole, 113, 125–26, 129, 134, 174n69, 175n78

Gill-Peterson, Jules, 11, 28

Glazener, Nancy, 27, 57, 157n100

Goeman, Mishuana, 122

Goldsby, Jacqueline, 86

Goldstone, Andrew, 6, 149n11

Gollancz, Israel, Sir, 28, 156–57n100

Graff, Gerald, 24, 152n12, 153n23

Guillory, John, 152n12

Gummere, Francis Barton, 14, 22–23, 27, 29, 32–34, 104; Anglo-Saxonist beliefs of, 12, 30, 39–40; and communal origins theory, 12, 24–26, 30–40,

59–60, 63, 69, 85, 114–15, 162n66; *Democracy and Poetry*, 36, 38, 154n56; *A Handbook of Poetics for Students of English Verse*, 26, 36–38; influence of, 24–26, 30, 40–42, 49–50, 153n15, 157n116

Hack, Daniel, 81

Hale, Horatio, 125

Hall, James C., 83, 99, 169–70n110

Hamilton, Thomas, 89–90, 167n50; *Anglo-African Magazine*, 89–92

Harlem Renaissance, 7–8, 16, 72, 78, 81, 145

Harper, Frances Ellen Watkins, 82, 88–89, 92–94, 98–99, 144–45, 165–66n16; "Ethiopia," 98–99; "Our Greatest Want," 89

Harris, Joel Chandler, 72–73

Henderson, Alice Corbin, 14, 54, 56, 58, 63–64, 93; anti-Blackness of, 68–72, 74–76, 77–78, 84, 113, 159n5

Heyward, DuBose, 74

Hines, Andy, 9

historiography, Black, 82, 84–85, 89–95, 97, 102, 106, 109, 167n42

hooks, bell, 76

Hopkins, Gerard Manley, 49, 163n70

Horsman, Reginald, 39, 65, 155n75

Hoskins, John Preston, 29

Hoyt, Helen, 72

Hughes, Langston, 73

Hurston, Zora Neale, 140–45

Hutchinson, James P., 80

Imagism, 13, 59

inclusion and recognition, liberal, 6, 13, 16, 53–55, 116–17, 172–73n28

Indian Act, Canada, 112, 122, 128

Jackson, Virginia, 31, 139

Jackson, Zakiyyah Iman, 55

Jaffee, Ethan, 77, 161–62n43

Johnson, Barbara, 132–33

Johnson, E. Pauline, 15–16, 18–20, 125, 145–46; "A Cry From an Indian Wife," 125; "The Idlers," 127–29; "The Indian Death Cry," 125; "The Lost Lagoon," 125, 127–31; mastery of poetic convention of, 112, 114, 124, 136–37; in *The Path on the Rainbow*, 111–12, 123–27, 130–31, 137; queer canoe poetry of, 123, 126–28, 130, 135, 174n69; "Re-Voyage," 127–30; "The Song My Paddle Sings" (article), 134–36; "The Song My Paddle Sings," (poem), 126, 131–34, 136, 175n90; and Su-á-pu-luck (Chief Joe Capilano), 131, 175n78; "Wave-Won," 127, 129; *The White Wampum*, 125

Johnson, Fenton, 15, 17; "African Nights," 103–8; "The Artist," 108; "Aunt Hannah Jackson," 103; "Aunt Jane Allen," 103; as avant-garde poet, 79–81, 165n3, 165n9; "The Banjo Player," 105–8, 143; *Champion* magazine, as editor of, 17, 83–92, 101, 167n50; and Harriet Monroe, 84, 166n24; dialogic poetics of, 94–96, 99–100, 109, 144; "The Drunkard," 103; "Ethiopia," 93–99; free verse poems of, 83, 99, 102–10; *A Little Dreaming*, 80, 100–101, 108, 169nn108–9; "The Minister," 103–4; "Rosemary for Chicago Poets," 84; "The Scarlet Woman," 104; *Songs of the Soil*, 71, 80, 100–102; "Tired," 103; *Visions of the Dusk*, 80, 93, 100–101, 108, 169n109

Johnson, Georgia Douglas, 87–88
Johnson, James Weldon, 72–73
Johnson, John "Smoke," 125
Jones, Mrs. Orrie, 141–43

Kelley, Robin D. G., 8
Kittredge, George Lyman, 26
Klopstock, Friedrich, 98
Konkle, Maureen, 155–56n82, 170–71n1
Kreymborg, Alfred, 79, 105

Langland, William, 62–64, 67
Lindsay, Vachel, 75–76, 118
Longfellow, Henry Wadsworth, 3, 37, 49, 156n85
Lootens, Tricia, 139
Lowell, Amy, 115
Lowes, John Livingston, 3, 52
lyric poetry, 31, 60, 73, 96, 138–44

Manly, John Matthews, 29–30, 153n15
Marek, Jayne, 54, 158n3, 159n5
Martin, Meredith, 2, 23, 61, 69, 152n10, 160n25
Massa, Ann, 158n3
Matthews, Brander, 29–30
Matthiessen, F. O., 12–13, 49
McGill, Meredith, 82, 86, 92, 139, 165–66n16
McHenry, Elizabeth, 16, 86
McKittrick, Katherine, 100–101
Melamed, Jodi, 6, 17, 104, 134
meter, English, 1–3, 25; as abstraction, 5, 38, 43, 114; accentual-syllabic, 2–3, 37–38, 61, 98; Anglo-Saxonist histories of, 65, 75, 93, 98; as classical inheritance, 38, 43, 48–49, 60–61; as disciplinary technology, 23, 28, 30–31, 35–37, 59–60, 75–77, 108; as French import, 64–65; iambic, 65, 94–96; and Indigenous survivance, 137; pre-Norman Conquest, 23, 28, 48, 61–64; quantitative, 37, 149n8; and queerness, 129–30; tetrameter, 18, 20, 61, 88, 98, 113, 123, 137; traditional, idea of, 7, 9, 15, 138, 146
Mill, John Stuart, 31–32, 42–43
modernism, 1, 4–7, 15–17, 21, 78–82, 137, 145–47
Modern Language Association, 10, 25–26, 42, 52
Monroe, Harriet, 13–14, 53–60, 62–78, 113, 158n3, 159n5; Anglo-Saxonism of, 63, 66–68, 86, 93, 160n14; and communal origins theory, 59–60, 63, 69, 162n66; and Fenton Johnson, 84,

166n24; pedagogical ambitions of,
56–59, 160n15

Monture, Rick, 125, 132, 176n98

Moses, Wilson Jeremiah, 85, 166n30

Moten, Fred, 142

Moulton, Richard, 25, 27

Mufti, Aamir, 23, 51, 151–52n7

Murray, Lindley, 61

Neihardt, John, 65–66

Nelson, Cary, 150–51n33

Newcomb, John Timberman, 54–55,
158n3, 160n15

New Critics, 9, 24, 140

Newman, Steve, 26, 41

Norman Conquest, 11–12, 23, 43, 48,
51, 61–62, 157–58n122

oral poetry, 22, 31–34, 48–52, 64, 67,
104, 115, 118–19, 173n34; ethnographic collection of Native American, 16, 18–19, 32–34, 111–12, 118,
120, 122, 124, 170–71n1

Others (magazine), 1, 15, 57, 79–80,
102–3, 108–9

Page, Thomas Nelson, 72

Parker, Robert Dale, 146, 170–71n1

The Path on the Rainbow (anthology),
15–16, 18–20, 111–12, 114, 116,
118–23, 126–27, 130, 137, 170–71n1

Patterson, William Morrison, 64,
115

Perloff, Marjorie, 150n19

Peterkin, Julia, 57, 73–74

plasticity, 10–14, 28–29, 41, 56, 70, 75,
153–54n29, 156–57n100, 160n14

poetry: dialect, 71–74, 80, 100–101,
104–5, 108, 163n74; lyric, 31, 60, 73,
96, 138–44. *See also* abolitionist
poetry; folk poetry; oral poetry

Poetry (magazine), 1, 13, 53–57;
Anglo-Saxonist ideology of, 59–69;
anti-Blackness of, 14, 53, 55–56,
71–78, 87; as cosmopolitan, 13,

53–54, 57, 59, 66; gender parity of, 13,
55, 78

Posmentier, Sonya, 140–45

Pound, Ezra, 11, 13, 46, 158n3

Pound, Louise, 40–41

primitivism, 19, 70, 113, 121, 155n66,
163n73, 171n9

*Princeton Encyclopedia of Poetry and
Poetics*, 22, 50

Prins, Yopie, 2, 139, 142

prosody, 1–5, 8–9, 25, 138, 144, 160n25;
evolutionary narratives of, 7, 41–43,
47–50, 61, 119, 152n10, 161n27,
173n34; and national identity, 2, 23,
45–46, 48, 69, 117, 152n10; temporal
approaches to, 43, 115, 117, 172n20

racialized reading, 9, 14–15, 24,
100, 104–10, 112, 139–40, 143,
157n100, 177n19. *See also* dispossessive reading

Radocay, Jonathan, 147

Rambaran-Olm, Mary, 52

Ravenel, Beatrice, 73

reading: dispossessive, 19, 111–13, 119,
172–73n28, 177n19; racialized, 9,
14–15, 24, 100, 104–10, 112, 139–40,
143, 157n100, 177n19

Reed, Anthony, 145, 150n20

Renker, Elizabeth, 24, 46

rhyme, 18, 48, 62, 65, 95, 113, 123–24,
127, 129, 137

rhythm, 2–3; as communal, 22, 36–37,
63, 114–15; loss of in modernity, 34,
42, 47–48; of Native American
poetries, 19, 117–18, 123, 137; as
nonmetrical, 2, 7, 44, 48, 77, 114–15;
of poetry versus prose, 42–43, 46, 115;
racialized, 19–20, 34, 39–40, 75–76; as
unifying force, 12, 36, 48–49, 59–60,
114–15, 118; as universal, 3, 36, 43,
49, 59, 77, 114, 160n25, 161n27

Rifkin, Mark, 116–17

Roberts, John W., 76

Robinson, Cedric, 51

www.ingramcontent.com/pod-product-compliance
Lightning Source LLC
Chambersburg PA
CBHW031133270326
41929CB00011B/1608